James Phelps is an award-winning senior reporter for Sydney's *The Daily Telegraph* and *The Sunday Telegraph*. He began as an overnight police-rounds reporter before moving into sport, where he became one of Australia's best news-breaking rugby league journalists. James was then appointed News Corp Australia's Chief National Motorsports Writer and travelled the world chasing Formula 1 stories, as well as covering Australia's V8 Supercar races. Following the publication of his bestselling autobiography of Dick Johnson, James quickly established himself as Australia's number-one true crime writer with his bestselling prison series, including *Australia's Hardest Prison*, *Australia's Most Murderous Prison*, and *Australia's Toughest Prisons*. His most recent book, *Australian Heist*, was a dramatic retelling of the true story behind Australia's largest gold robbery.

AUSTRALIAN CODE BREAKERS

JAMES PHELPS

HarperCollinsPublishers

HarperCollins*Publishers*

First published in Australia in 2020
by HarperCollins*Publishers* Australia Pty Limited
ABN 36 009 913 517
harpercollins.com.au

HarperCollins*Publishers*
Level 13, 201 Elizabeth Street, Sydney NSW 2000, Australia
Unit D1, 63 Apollo Drive, Rosedale, Auckland 0632, New Zealand
A 53, Sector 57, Noida, UP, India
1 London Bridge Street, London SE1 9GF, United Kingdom
Bay Adelaide Centre, East Tower, 22 Adelaide Street West, 41st floor, Toronto, Ontario M5H 4E3, Canada
195 Broadway, New York NY 10007, USA

A catalogue record for this book is available from the National Library of Australia

ISBN 978 1 4607 5622 5 (paperback)
ISBN 978 1 4607 1022 7 (ebook)
ISBN 978 1 4607 8155 5 (audiobook)

Cover design by Darren Holt, HarperCollins Design Studio
Front cover images: (top, left to right) Captain Walter Hugh Charles Samuel Thring, courtesy of Royal Australian Navy; Dr Frederick William Wheatley, courtesy of Royal Australian Navy; Sir George Edwin Patey © National Portrait Gallery, London; Sir William Rooke Creswell, courtesy State Library of South Australia (B 11220); (bottom) The Royal Navy battlecruiser HMS *Inflexible* standing by to pick up survivors from the German cruiser SMS *Gneisenau* after the Battle of the Falkland Islands, 1914, taken by Paymaster Sub. Lieutenant A. D. Duckworth, courtesy Wikimedia Commons
Back cover image: German warships en route to the Battle of the Falkland Islands, by Sueddeutsche Zeitung Photo/Alamy Stock Photo
Typeset in Bembo Std by Kirby Jones
Printed and bound in Australia by McPherson's Printing Group
The papers used by HarperCollins in the manufacture of this book are a natural, recyclable product made from wood grown in sustainable plantation forests. The fibre source and manufacturing processes meet recognised international environmental standards, and carry certification.

Author's note

Codes, cyphers, keys and cryptologists – it can all be quite confusing. So, to spare you headaches and trips to textbooks, I have simplified both the codes and the code-cracking process where the technicalities stopped the story. The original coded messages have been used if suitable, but where they were too complex or confusing, they have also been simplified. All the original codes and messages can be found in the National Archives of Australia, and some of the documents are reproduced in this book's appendix.

Most of the letters, telegrams and reports included in the story are presented exactly as they appear in the original documents. The dialogue, on the other hand, though often taken directly from letters, texts and reports, has occasionally been adapted to help this adventure flow. While I've done my best to keep the period detail authentic, a few present-day words and phrases have been introduced to give the story a modern spin.

While some of the dialogue has been modified or re-imagined, the story hasn't. This is the true, remarkable and, until now, untold tale of what could be Australia's greatest unknown contribution to World War I.

Welcome to *Australian Code Breakers* …

Measurements

All measurements are given in the units commonly used in the World War I era. Readers unfamiliar with imperial measurements may find the following conversion chart helpful:

1 inch	2.5 centimetres
1 foot	30 centimetres
1 yard	0.9 metres
1 mile	1.6 kilometres
1 ton	1,016 kilograms

Contents

Prologue

Potts Point, Sydney, 2 July 1934

In fading light, he struggled to see the number six. 'There it is,' he mumbled, pushing his frail finger, arthritic and spotted with age, into the metal hole. He dialled the last digit.

'Yes,' he said. 'My name is Dr Frederick Wheatley … Yes, Wheatley. That's right. Can you put me through to the editor, please?'

He pushed the receiver hard against his ear. 'Sorry, can you speak up, love?' he asked. 'My hearing is not what it used to be.' He squinted, as if it would help, as she repeated herself.

'A story?' he said. 'Oh yes. I have a hell of a story indeed.' He looked at the book on his lap, the title in German, the leather cover worn thin, as the receptionist patched him through to the editor.

'Is that Mr Hadfield?' Wheatley asked. 'The editor of the RSL magazine *Reveille*?' He listened hard for the response.

'Good,' he replied. 'I have a story I would like you to print. It's the most remarkable untold tale. A story of spies, codes and battleships. Of how Australia was behind the greatest naval victory of World War I.'

The old man took a deep breath. 'Shall I start?' he asked.

Chapter 1

THE FIRST SHOT

Victoria Dock, Melbourne, 4 August 1914, 7 am

Captain Montgomery Robinson walked over to the German ship's commander. 'What's going on?' he asked. 'We are supposed to be launching. We are going to miss our window. Get your men into gear.'

Captain Wilhelm Kuhlken shook his head. '*Nein*,' he huffed. 'We depart tomorrow.'

'What do you mean?' Robinson demanded. 'You will never get out.'

The Australian sea pilot was scheduled to guide Captain Kuhlken and his 6,500-ton merchant ship, SS *Pfalz*, to the safety of open water at 8 am, from Port Victoria to the Pacific Ocean. He knew every inch of the often treacherous Port Phillip Bay – the rips, the reefs and the fast-rising tides. He also knew Australia was on the verge of declaring war on Germany.

'Your funeral,' Robinson shrugged.

The grisly German turned his back and marched towards his crew. 'Hurry!' he shouted as he gestured at his men. 'Work faster!'

Robinson was stunned. *What's he thinking? Doesn't he know that we could be at war tomorrow? That he could be taken, become a prisoner of war?*

That was exactly what Kuhlken was trying to avoid. 'We can't go to Sydney as scheduled,' he'd told his chief mate the night before. 'War will be upon us by the time we arrive and we will be detained. We are sailing straight to prison. We must set a new course.'

'But we only have enough fuel to make it to Sydney,' said the chief mate.

And that was why SS *Pfalz* was still berthed at the number-two dock in Melbourne. Why the veteran seaman was barking at his men to hurry up as they shovelled coal. And why he wouldn't sleep a wink that night.

Observatory Point, Victoria, 5 August 1914, 5 am

'It's happening,' shouted the navy reserve. 'Blimey, it's really happening. Take a look at this!'

Stanley Veale snatched the telegram from his mate. 'Here, give me a look,' he said, scanning the typed words.

SECRET
5 August 1914

Director of Naval Reserves,
I am directed by the Naval Board to inform you that you are

to take immediate steps for putting in force the Examination Service at all defended ports.

Such of the Naval Reserve Forces as may be required for this purpose are to be ready for duty pending issue of proclamation.

By direction of the Naval Board.
W.R.S.
For Naval Secretary

'Pfft,' Veale scoffed as he handed back the telegram. 'Business as usual. That's just another alert. We're not at war.'

But the volunteer feared it was only a matter of time, and he wasn't sure he was ready for war. Now part of a Royal Australian Naval Reserve Examination Service fleet – a crew of part-timers given the job of inspecting incoming and outgoing vessels during war – the twenty-year-old thought back to his one and only 'test' run in December 1913. To the time he'd spewed on the deck and shot his captain in the foot.

'Oh, my boy,' one of the sailors had said when he found Veale curled up in a corner as the examination vessel *Alvina* cruised towards its target, *Countess of Hopetoun*, a Royal Australian Navy torpedo gunboat playing the part of enemy runaway. They had orders to stop the pretend enemy ship.

'Are you sick?'

'Not just sick,' Veale had replied. 'I think I am going to die.'

The crewmate had laughed. 'Yeah, it's a bit rough out here,' he said. 'She is kicking up a fuss, isn't she? But I've got just the thing to fix you up.'

The burly veteran grabbed a rope with a bucket attached to the end. He heaved it into the rolling deep and scooped up a bucket of blue.

'Here, get a gulp of this,' he said after bringing the bucket back onto the ship. 'It will taste like shit, but it will get you back on your feet.'

Veale had summoned all his strength to shake his head. 'Nah,' he said. 'Might as well drink poison.'

'Trust me, lad,' the crewmate replied. 'Go on. Just pinch your nose and get it down.'

'Ah, blimey,' Veale said. 'It couldn't make me feel any worse.'

He had placed both hands around the bucket and lifted it to his face, pale white with a tinge of green, holding his breath as he skolled a mouthful.

Bleuh! He'd gagged and coughed. *Baaaaaaggghhhhh!* Then he'd spewed. Veale became Vesuvius, a volcanic force shooting the slush from his stomach into the air. The vile mess splattered the freshly polished deck.

The rookie had cursed the veteran. 'Arsehole' he said. 'Thought this was supposed to make me feel better!'

But he was soon thanking him. 'You know what?' he'd said as he climbed to his feet. 'I think that worked.'

And it had: twenty minutes later he was well enough to shoot his captain in the leg.

Alvina had been fast closing in on the 'enemy' ship they had been ordered to stop.

'Rig up the rocket tube,' ordered Captain John Tracy Richardson. 'We need to fire a warning shot.'

Without a real gun on board, the flare would be the fleeing *Countess of Hopetoun*'s signal to stop.

Veale had rigged the rocket, wincing as he fired.

'Bloody hell!' Richardson said, jumping first and then stamping to put out the fire at his feet. The rocket had backfired, sending the explosive into the captain's foot. After jumping around like a tap-dancer on the deck, Richardson had fallen flat on his arse.

The crew had laughed. And, thankfully for Veale, so had the captain.

'Remind me to never let you near a rocket again,' Richardson had said.

But today there would be no jokes. This wasn't a drill.

Victoria Dock, 5 August 1914, 7.16 am

The sun edged its way over the horizon, the first rays of winter light meeting Captain Robinson as he stepped onto the dock. SS *Pfalz* glittered, all straight lines and sharp edges. Built by Bremer Vulkan and launched in Bremen, Germany, on 8 November 1913, the Norddeutscher Lloyd steamer was partway through her maiden voyage, having docked in Cape Town before conquering the Pacific. And now she was destined for Sydney.

Or was she? Robinson had watched the Germans shovel two hundred tons of coal into the ship's cargo hold, and he also wondered whether the ship was packing more than just coal and crew. Capable of carrying 70,000 tons, the 470-foot ship was looking heavy, the propeller sunk deep below the water line.

The extra weight could have been ammunition. Maybe guns? Robinson had been warned that the Germans may convert merchant vessels into warships called cruisers. But it wasn't his job to search for weapons. He would board the ship, guide it through the rips and waves and get off, to be picked up by an eighteen-foot work boat before *Pfalz* steamed through the heads. Job done.

'All in order?' Robinson asked. 'Ready to depart?'

Captain Kuhlken nodded before picking up the telephone that connected the bridge to the engine room. 'Half steam ahead,' he said, issuing the order to the engine room.

SS *Pfalz* departed the dock at 7.45 am, destination unknown.

Observatory Point, 5 August 1914, 8 am

Navy Reserve Officer Stanley Veale soon had another order, this one delivered in person, not by way of telegram.

'Men,' said the chief examining officer and commander of *Alvina*, Captain Alexander McWilliam. 'I have received a signal from the Navy Office. We, the Examination Service, have been advised to delay the departure of the German steamer SS *Pfalz* from Port Phillip.

'As you are aware, the ultimatum given to Germany will expire at 9 am our time. Our job is to try to stall her from departing Port Melbourne for as long as possible, in the expectation that war against Germany will be declared and *Pfalz* will therefore become an enemy vessel.'

The men from the Examination Service stood still. Suddenly the war was real.

Veale made his way along the dock towards *Alvina*, a 27-year-old steam yacht that had been bought by the Port Phillip Pilot Service and passed on to the Examination Service. The midshipman was second-in-command to the chief examining officer. He boarded the yacht with another eight Naval Reserve signalmen.

'What does delay her actually mean?' Veale asked Captain McWilliam. 'And for how long? What if war isn't declared? Do we just delay her forever? And how will we even know if war has been declared?'

After German troops had begun advancing on Belgium, all previous attempts to broker peace having failed, Britain had warned the German Empire, or Kaiser's Reich, that it would be war if it did not withdraw. Germany had been given until 11 pm Greenwich Mean Time.

The clock was ticking fast.

Rope in hand, ready to push off, McWilliam raised an eyebrow. 'Guess we will have to improvise,' he said. 'We will give her the most thorough search in the history of the Examination Service and see where we are at when we finish.' McWilliam, rope now pulled onto the deck of *Alvina*, stopped and put a hand on Veale's shoulder. 'But don't go hoping for this declaration,' McWilliam said. 'Best if it never comes. A lot of good Australians never came back from South Africa. And a lot that did, well, after the Boer they were never the same. We don't want this war, son. No good will come of it.'

Churned water pushed the yacht forward after McWilliam yanked a stainless-steel lever. 'Anyway,' he said, 'we've gotta find them first.'

Veale stared back at the port as they crept away from the dock, water calm, swell small. He wouldn't need the bucket today.

Veale had been dreaming of becoming a war hero since 1899 when, as a five-year-old, he'd watched thousands of Australians board SS *Medic* at Port Melbourne, bound for South Africa to fight in the Boer War. Sitting on his father's oversized shoulders, Veale had cheered and waved as the departing soldiers climbed up the rigging to better see their mums and dads. Their brothers and sisters. Their wives and kids. A high-calibre shot fired from Port Melbourne beach to salute the departing ship sealed it for Veale: he wanted to be just like them. And he still did ten years later, even though he knew many of the men he farewelled that day never made it home. The three-year conflict that ended in 1902 had claimed the lives of a thousand Australian men.

Veale had joined the Australian Naval Cadet Corps the day after he'd turned fifteen. He'd made his own way to the Williamstown Depot and signed up to become one of 120 boys who would spend their evenings, weekends and whenever else they could cruising Port Phillip Bay in an old Victorian second-class torpedo boat called *Lonsdale*.

Sometimes they got to train aboard a real navy ship, HMAS *Cerberus*. They would fake shoot the .45 four-barrel Nordenfelt guns. They even got to sit in the turret and aim the ten-inch muzzle-loading guns.

Veale had volunteered for the Royal Australian Naval Reserves on 5 September 1911. It was the day he turned eighteen. He'd continued his training in a new brick-built drill-room at the bottom of Bay Street in Port Melbourne. When asked, Veale had jumped at the chance of joining the Examination Service, which was front line and in the action.

'Vessel approaching,' Captain McWilliam shouted, bringing Veale back to 1914. Bringing him back to the brink of war. 'Starboard side. South Channel.'

Pfalz was just a speck of white on blue.

'Is that it?' Veale asked.

'We will soon find out,' replied McWilliam. The captain lowered his binoculars. 'All hands,' he ordered. 'Man your stations. This is not a drill.'

Slowly but surely, the distant speck became a ship. A big ship. SS *Pfalz*, new and shiny and moving half steam ahead, dwarfed *Alvina*, a patina-coated relic.

'What will we do if she won't stop?' Veale asked.

He was met with silence.

Port Phillip Bay, 5 August 1914, 10 am

The edge of Australia was soon in sight. Captain Kuhlken could now see Point Nepean. He and his crew would soon be out of the South Channel and heading into The Rip, the corridor of water between the Port Phillip heads, then Bass Strait.

Freedom beckoned.

A butterfly was released from the captain's stomach every time the bow of *Pfalz* conquered a swell. Spray was sent into the air, ten feet high and brilliant, and he was another inch closer to escape with every wave the ship swallowed.

Still, there was the nosy Australian sea pilot with all the questions.

'Should we increase the speed?' Kuhlken asked Robinson. 'Conditions are favourable.'

Robinson, in charge of *Pfalz* until they reached Bass Strait, shook his head. 'Nah, mate,' he said. 'We will soon be heading into The Rip. Might look like plain sailing but there is plenty going on down below. Half speed is safe and sound.' Robinson looked at the German. 'You in a hurry or something?'

Robinson winked and with that the butterflies were back. Was the sea pilot a plant? An Australian navy officer in disguise? Did he have a gun hidden away in that oversized coat? Kuhlken reasoned he wasn't and that he didn't. The sea pilot had kept *Pfalz* at half speed since departing the dock. The Australian could have reduced the speed on several occasions but he hadn't, ploughing through the larger swells the same as the small. And as far as Kuhlken could tell, the Australian had taken a direct route.

Kuhlken looked back out towards Point Nepean. So close yet so far. SS *Pfalz* was in a race against the clock. Kuhlken knew that war would be declared; he'd been told as much two nights before when a German consular official had come knocking on his door.

'The Kaiser will not respond to Britain's ultimatum,' the official had said. 'We expect to be at war with Britain and her colonies by the day after next.'

The official had handed the captain a document. He'd read the following:

HIGHLY CONFIDENTIAL AND TOP SECRET

War with Holland, Belgium, Spain and Portugal may be considered out of the question. The ports of these countries and their colonies are therefore especially worth consideration when neutral ports are in question.

In the Mediterranean (leaving out of account the Suez Canal) endeavours should be made to reach ports belonging to Turkey, Greece and possibly Italy.

In the Atlantic Ocean, the Canaries, the Cape Verde group and the Azores would be worth considering. In the South Atlantic: Brazil or Portuguese South-West Africa, especially the port of St Paul de Loanda.

Vessels that should happen to be in or near South African ports should run for Delanga if on the outward journey, or for Cape Verde Islands when on the journey home.

Vessels in Australian waters should try to reach the Dutch Indies. If they have coal enough, they should avoid the Torres Strait route and go south about, outside Tasmania, if possible. If they have not enough coal, they are recommended to stay quietly in port, or run to the port where the best and most economical shelter is to be had – Sydney – and stay there. If the authorities insist on leaving the port, it may then be possible to get coal enough to reach a neutral port without being immediately chased and caught by the enemy.

Vessels making for home via the Suez Canal should try to reach Marmagoa Harbour in Portuguese Goa.

Vessels with all or most of their cargo on board and can carry enough coal to take them home via South America should take that route. To enter the Strait of Magellan a pilot should be taken as far as Punta Arenas, and another from there on. Charts for the onward voyage could presumably be procured at Punta Arenas.

A vessel that happens to be off the Western Australian coast that has enough coal to reach Cape Verde Island via the Cape of Good Hope should take that route.

In these deviations from the regular course special care must be taken to a) avoid the usual steamer tracks as much as possible b) keep well away from enemy coasts c) where possible to enter by night the port one is making for – further, to make the port as nearly as possible at right angles to the coast line.

In selecting the neutral port to be made for, care must be taken to choose (if possible) one in which at the end of the war coal can be got without its having to be brought there by sea first.

With reference to speeds, it is recommended to proceed at normal full speed in waters not safe from enemy attacks – if circumstances demand it, at even greater speed – but, in areas where no enemy attack is expected, to proceed at economic speed, since at the conclusion of peace coal will be scarce everywhere.

Kuhlken was no longer going to Sydney. Nor was he leaving the following day. He was to load an extra two hundred tons of coal onto *Pfalz* and set steam for the Dutch East Indies. There he would await further instruction.

'You will also be taking some extra passengers,' the official had said. 'Some Germans who need to get out of Australia, mostly officials. The consul general will provide me with a list of names tomorrow. And burn that letter.'

Coal and human cargo now safely on board, note turned into ash, *Pfalz* was about to enter The Rip. Bass Strait loomed.

Robinson picked up the handset. 'Slow ahead,' the sea pilot said, his order sent to the engine room.

Kuhlken, fists clenched and shaking, stormed towards the Australian. 'What is the meaning of this?' he asked. 'Give me that.' Kuhlken pushed past his second mate and went for the phone. He wanted to issue an order of his own.

'Settle down, mate,' Robinson said. 'It's just the Examination Service. Look!' Robinson pointed towards the fast-approaching steam yacht, a solitary smokestack spewing black. A flag sporting two yellow squares and two black was being raised, the sailor doing the hoisting momentarily losing his balance as the 200-foot vessel hit *Pfalz*'s wake.

'It's just a routine check,' Robinson said. 'They have been boarding ships all week.'

'Check?' Kuhlken said. 'Check what? We have nothing to hide. We have done nothing wrong.'

'They'll just look at your papers,' Robinson said. 'See that everything is in order and then we'll be on our merry way.'

Kuhlken started to sweat. *Has war been declared? Are we too late?*

The Examination Service vessel was now alongside *Pfalz*. 'Stop,' came an amplified shout from the vessel sporting the Blue Ensign of the Australian Navy. 'We are coming aboard.'

Kuhlken took a deep breath. He hoped the Australian sea pilot was right. Reaching down to a brass lever, with a jerk of his wrist he rang for the engine to stop.

'Drop the ladder,' Kuhlken ordered in German. 'Let them board. No concern. Just a routine check.'

An officer and two seamen climbed over the rail onto SS *Pfalz*. All in full white Australian naval uniform, the trio approached the captain on the bridge.

'I am Chief Examining Officer Captain Alexander McWilliam from the Royal Australian Naval Reserves,' said the one with the highest rank. 'You have been stopped by the Examination Service steamer *Alvina*, part of the Royal Australian Naval Reserve Examination Service that was enacted on Monday by orders of the Governor-General of Australia. May we search the ship?'

The sea pilot had been right. This was no seizure. Kuhlken, his crew and his ship were not to be interned. These men were only naval reserves.

The German gave the intruders the nod. 'Of course,' Kuhlken said.

The chief examining officer turned to the Australian sailor standing on his left. 'Lieutenant,' he said. 'Stand fast on deck with the captain. We will examine the ship. Ensure he does not interfere.'

Seconds turned into minutes.

'So where ya from, mate?' the lieutenant asked. 'Germany, right?'

Kuhlken replied with a raised brow.

More seconds. More minutes.

'What is taking so long?' Kuhlken demanded, breaking his silence. 'We are on a tight schedule.'

The lieutenant gave the German a wry smile and shrugged.

More minutes passed.

'This is ridiculous,' Kuhlken said. 'They will find nothing that is not supposed to be here. You are violating my rights under the Geneva Convention.'

And they were, but the lieutenant shrugged again. 'Speak to the captain when he gets back,' he suggested mildly.

Kuhlken was sweating.

'Righto,' said McWilliam, suddenly back on the bridge. 'All seems in order. Sorry for the trouble, old chap, you can be on your way.'

'What about the logs?' asked the lieutenant. 'We haven't checked the paperwork.'

'Oh, right you are,' McWilliam said before turning his attention to Kuhlken. 'Sorry, mate. Do you mind if we have a peek at your logs?'

Kuhlken held back a snarl and forced himself to nod. 'I'll retrieve them,' he said.

The navy officers pored over the paperwork for what seemed an eternity to Kuhlken, the German pacing back and forth from one end of the bridge to the other, hands behind his back, eyes glued to the ground.

'Yep,' said the chief examining officer. 'We are all good here too. You have permission to proceed.'

Kuhlken didn't smile until the three officers had left his ship. Not until they were down the rope, back on their yacht and pulling astern.

'Full speed ahead,' Robinson ordered.

Now the German wasn't just smiling – he was beaming.

Port Phillip Bay, 5 August 1914, 11.35 am

'I thought old Fritz was going to knock ya block off when you told him you needed to check the log,' Veale grinned as *Alvina* pulled away from *Pfalz*.

'Yep,' McWilliam replied. 'He was an angry old bastard. But Christ, we did everything we could to piss him off. That was the longest examination in naval history.'

'Too right,' Veale laughed. 'You should have seen the look I got when I asked him if he was a German! So what now?'

'We head back and wait for orders,' McWilliam said. 'But I'm not sure if any are going to come. That was the last German ship. We could be done.'

Veale didn't reply. There were no more quips about the Kraut. Instead he walked towards the aft and silently studied *Pfalz*, the ship still stationary but soon to set steam.

Veale suddenly felt flat. He was done without having done anything. The prospect of action had put him on edge, knots in his stomach and jelly in his legs. But now the excitement was gone, McWilliam stealing all that adrenaline with a solitary word.

Done.

Then a series of bright flashes hit him like a thousand volts to the heart.

'You see that?' Veale shouted. 'Did you *see* that?'

Captain McWilliam came rushing to the aft. 'Where?' he demanded.

'There,' Veale pointed. 'Fort Queenscliff. There it is again. That's a dash. Now a dot. A dash. Another dot. That's a 'C'. They're signalling us.'

Veale shoved his hand into his shirt pocket, his fingers emerging with a notepad. The knots, the jelly and the adrenaline were back. Once again, his heart was racing. Normal was gone.

McWilliam handed him a pen and he started scribbling: first the letter C and then, after another four flashes – a dot, a dash, a dot and a dot – he wrote the letter 'L'.

'It's a heliograph,' Veale said. 'They're reflecting the sun.'

Another thirteen flashes came.

'Is that it?' Veale asked.

He looked at his notepad.

'What does it say?' McWilliam asked.

'C, L, A, R, E, D,' Veale said. 'Clared. That's all I got.'

McWilliam stood silently.

'Well?' Veale said. 'What are we going to do?'

'Nothing,' McWilliam said. 'Clared? What does that mean? Nothing. So we do nothing.'

Veale turned and began to argue with his commanding officer. 'It's not nothing,' he insisted. 'We only caught the end of the message. Clared – that's the end of "declared". The message was "war is declared". We are at war, captain. They are ordering us to stop *Pfalz*. We have to stop that ship.'

McWilliam turned back towards the metal behemoth. She was not yet under full steam but *Alvina* had now travelled almost a mile in the opposite direction.

'We'll never get to her,' McWilliam said. 'She'll being doing eleven knots before we even get this old junk pointing the right way.'

Veale was unrelenting. 'Then we need to order fire,' he said. 'We have to order Fort Nepean to stop *Pfalz*. We need to order a shot.'

McWilliam shook his head. 'We only have half a message,' he said. 'And even if we had a full message, we wouldn't be bound to act. We are only required to act on orders from the Examination Service. Fort Queenscliff is not part of the Examination Service. Son, even if I am wrong then we are right.'

They were now stationary in The Rip. Veale pointed left towards Fort Queenscliff. 'They can't get a message to Fort Nepean,' he said, before pointing to his right. 'There is no line of sight. We can't let an enemy ship escape. We just can't.'

Pfalz was building steam. It was now the men on *Alvina* who were racing the clock.

'I understand what you are saying,' McWilliam said. 'But what if you fire a shot and war hasn't been declared? You will start this war all on your own. It's too big a call to make.'

Veale continued his argument. 'What else would the message have been?' he asked. 'Why else would they be sending us an emergency signal? We were told the declaration was coming. We were told that we had to stop the German ship. Now the declaration has been made and now we have to stop that ship. This is what we have trained for. This is our duty.'

'Dorgan!' McWilliam shouted. 'Chief Petty Officer Dorgan! Over here.'

Chief Yeoman of Signals John Dorgan joined McWilliam and Veale on the bridge.

'We received a partial message from Fort Queenscliff,' McWilliam said. 'We only got six letters: C, L, A, R, E, D. I am inclined to dismiss the part message, but Veale is adamant that we take action. He believes we got the end of the word "declared" and the full message was "war is declared". He thinks we should order Port Nepean to fire on *Pfalz*. What is your opinion?'

The signals expert took a moment before replying. 'I agree with Veale. Given we have been expecting war to be declared all morning, I don't see what else the message could have been. I suggest we hoist the signal flag "R" and give the order to fire.'

'Alright,' the captain said. 'But let it be on the record that I was against this. If this ends up going south then it will be on your heads. You will be answering for this. I won't take the blame.'

Dorgan wasted no time, the officer riffling through a pile of flags before pulling out the piece of fabric that could make or break his career. He handed it to Veale.

'You do the honours,' he said. Veale hoisted the flag and looked towards the battery on the top of Point Nepean, part of a network of fortifications built around the headlands that separated Port Phillip Bay from Bass Strait.

Flag waving in the stiffening breeze, Veale could see four of the eight gun emplacements that were in operation at Fort Nepean. He wondered which gun he was signalling, which gun he was ordering to shoot. Which gun would possibly go down in history as having fired the first shot of the war.

Fort Nepean, Victoria, 5 August 1914, 11.40 am

Assistant Fire Commander Captain Charles Morris addressed the man standing beside the twenty-five-ton gun that filled the belly of Fort Nepean's number six gun emplacement.

'Something is happening out there,' Morris said. 'Stand by.'

The captain returned his full attention to the sea. Back to *Pfalz*. Back to *Alvina*.

Standing in a concrete bunker on a cliff, part of the series of fortifications known as Victoria's 'Gibraltar', the Royal Australian Garrison Artillery officer did as he had done all morning: watched and waited.

'Man the gun,' shouted Morris. 'They are hoisting a flag. Prepare for the signal.'

Bombardier John Purdue positioned himself back behind the barrel of his gun, seven yards of metal that had been named 'F1'. The army gunner had been within a yard of the BL six-inch Mark VII since sunrise. Like his commander, he had spent the morning watching and waiting. But despite Battery Commander Moreton Williams breaking the news about half an hour before that war had been declared between Great Britain and Germany, he hadn't expected to be shooting.

'What's going on, sir?' Purdue asked.

'It's the navy Examination Service,' Morris said. 'They are signalling.'

From his vantage point, a concrete bunker on the top of Point Nepean, Morris had a prime view of The Rip, whose waters were right now rushing out with the tide into Bass Strait. On a clear day, to the west he could see all the way to Torquay, sometimes even to Anglesea. And to the south, well, once he even swore he saw Tasmania.

Now he was looking at a flag. 'That's it,' he said after making out the red flag with the yellow cross. 'They want us to stop *Pfalz*.'

Purdue's fingers hovered over the fire button. He was just an inch away from exploding a 110-pound charge of cordite. Just a push away from initiating the blast that would see a 100-pound shell – packed tight with shrapnel – launched into the sky. First built in 1899, the Mark VII naval gun had replaced the inferior BL 9.2-inch Mark VI gun at Fort Nepean in 1911. The state-of-the-art weapon had a range of 17,250 yards and could fire off eight rounds in a minute. The gun could bring down a building. Right now, it was pointed firmly at a ship.

'What are my orders, sir?' Purdue asked the battery commander as he stood next to Morris, observing the flag.

'Stand fast and man your gun,' Williams replied. 'Let's give them the stop signal first.'

In the blink of an eye a series of flags were hoisted high into the sky. They were several flags but they contained just one message: stop or sink.

Tick tock.

'She is still steaming ahead,' said Morris after a minute had passed. 'She is ignoring the order.'

Tick tock.

'Time's up,' said Battery Commander Williams finally. 'Fire a shot across her bow.'

'Yes, sir,' Purdue said. 'Order received and acknowledged.'

Hands shaking, heart racing, Purdue leaned forward until his left eye was looking down the barrel of the gun's telescopic sight.

He had *Pfalz* slap-bang in the middle of the crosshair.

A little to the left.

He steadied his hands before reaching down and turning a metal wheel.

Just a little.

He was looking at water a quarter turn later.

That's it.

He pressed the trigger.

* * *

Purdue's hands were cuffing his ears a moment after he fired the gun, but neither his palms nor his earplugs dulled the near-deafening blast to a bearable volume.

Boom!

The entire bunker shook and concrete dust fell from the ceiling as the recoil from the weapon rattled the room.

Hands over ears, heart in mouth, Purdue watched as the 100-pound projectile screamed towards the target. He fretted about the possibility of a miscalculation.

Had he accounted for the wind? The early morning whisper now a steady breeze.

Had he taken into account the recoil? The 110-pound explosion of cordite turned the gun-barrel into a prodigious death-dealing piston.

And how about riffling, the spiral on a shell caused by grooves in the barrel that can send the projectile slightly to the right?

He assured himself that his aim was true. He assured himself that he would hit water and not ship.

But what if?

He was sickened by the possibility of actually hitting SS *Pfalz*. Of sinking the ship and killing its crew. Purdue thought he might vomit as the shell made its final descent.

Kaapooooom!

The sea suddenly split.

Vzzzzzzzzzzttttt!

Then the spray, a wall of white water rushing into the sky as a crater formed in the sea.

Purdue took a deep breath. He was dead centre on his mark, the shell hitting the ocean about fifty yards past the *Pfalz* after crossing her bow. He took a moment to wonder what he would do if he was ever asked to fire on a target. Not a warning – a kill shot.

Port Phillip Bay, 5 August 1914, 11.45 am

First came the thunder.

On board *Pfalz* Robinson screamed 'Fuuuck!' as a deafening blast shattered the mid-morning silence. 'What the …!'

Then came the splash, the brilliant blue sea erupting into a rushing wall of white.

'Take cover!' ordered the sea pilot as he threw himself on the deck.

Robinson covered his head with his hands as he was peppered with sea spray, the dislodged water leaving him drenched.

'Someone took a shot!' Robinson shouted as the boat was hit by another wave. 'They're shooting at us. Stop the ship.'

Robinson steeled himself and jumped to his feet. He looked towards Captain Kuhlken, the German now standing with the telephone receiver in hand. He remained silent.

'I said stop the ship,' Robinson repeated. 'Full speed astern.'

Kuhlken pushed the receiver into the side of his face. 'Full speed ahead,' he ordered.

'No!' shouted Robinson. 'What do you think you are doing? You will kill us all.'

Kuhlken stood tall. 'I won't let them take this ship,' he said. 'I won't let them take my crew. I won't let them take me. We are making a run for it.'

'Like hell you are,' snarled Robinson. The Australian gritted his teeth before beginning his charge. Arms raised, fists clenched, he exploded from a standing start and rushed towards the captain.

Fort Nepean, 5 August 1914, 11.47 am

'She hasn't come to,' said Captain Morris. 'She is still under steam.'

Purdue moved his finger back over the trigger, hand shaking.

'She stops,' said Battery Commander Williams, 'or she sinks.'

Purdue pressed his left eye back against the sight.

'Prepare to fire on target,' Williams said.

Purdue turned the wheel, a half turn this time. He was now looking directly at *Pfalz*, the ship in the centre of his scope. He steeled himself for a life-changing order.

'Wait,' said Morris, observing *Pfalz* through his high-powered scope. 'There is movement on the bridge. Wait. It looks like ... It looks like a fight.'

Purdue rolled his wheel, the gunner forced to make another quarter turn to keep the ship in the centre of the crosshair.

'She's stopping,' Morris said. 'She's stopping!'

'Stand down,' Williams said.

Purdue pulled his finger away from the trigger. He looked at his hand – the hand that would still be shaking the next day – and sighed.

Port Phillip Bay, 5 August 1914, 12 pm

'This is the Royal Australian Navy,' came the cry. 'We are coming aboard. Deploy the accommodation ladder. I repeat, deploy the accommodation ladder, we are boarding this vessel.'

Kuhlken looked at his first mate and nodded. He was out of fight.

The German captain knew there was no escape. He'd known he was not leaving Australia even before the sea pilot had crash-tackled him. For a moment he'd even thought he would rather die than become a prisoner of war. But as he lay on the deck after being taken down by the broad-shouldered Australian, he decided he wanted to live.

Kuhlken could have got up. Could have sprung to his feet and gone toe-to-toe with the sea pilot. But he thought of his crew. Of their families. So instead of punching the Australian, he'd raised his hands.

'Do as you wish,' he'd said, sitting up against the cold steel wall of the bridge.

'Full steam astern,' the Australian had ordered. Suddenly gears screamed and the engine roared. Kuhlken's head rocked to the right and then to the left. And then had come the calm. The quiet.

But pandemonium now returned, the ship awash with Royal Australian Navy men.

'Are you the captain?' one of the uniformed intruders asked.

'*Ja*,' Kuhlken replied. 'I am the captain of SS *Pfalz*.'

The officer – a captain too, Kuhlken presumed – was flanked by armed men.

'Inform your crew that the Royal Australian Navy is now in command of this ship,' the officer said. 'Under the Articles of War, this ship has been seized as a prize.'

Kuhlken already knew the answer, but he asked the question all the same. 'And what about us?' he asked. 'What about me and my crew?'

'You are now in the custody of the Royal Australian Navy,' the officer said. 'You will be taken back to Williamstown and placed under guard.'

So there it was: Kuhlken, his crew and the German officials had been arrested, the first fifty-seven prisoners of this freshly declared war.

Observatory Point, 5 August 1914, 12.15 pm

Veale still didn't know if he had done the right thing in ordering the shot. Whether he was a hero – the man responsible for the Allies' first win against Germany – or the villain who had started a world war.

'You'd better hope you were right,' said Captain McWilliam as *Alvina* pulled anchor and set for home. 'This is on you. Either way.'

Veale stood in silence, head spinning and heart racing. He still didn't know if war had definitely been declared, whether he had ordered fire on an enemy attempting to flee or an innocent merchant carting his cargo.

Neither did McWilliam. 'You too,' he said, turning his rage on Dorgan, the signalman who had backed Veale.

Veale switched his attention to *Pfalz*, the source of his angst soon to disappear behind the headland as *Alvina* puttered home. He replayed the moment in his mind when he saw the shot fired from Fort Nepean, fireworks of red, yellow and orange at first, then the smoke, a rush of white that billowed and bloated into a ball, soon just another cloud in the sky. Next came the noise, an earthquake in his ear. Last came the shell and the vapour trail that sliced the sky.

He'd thought he was about to become a murderer of men.

Time had slowed as he watched the shell tear towards its target. He'd prayed that they had only fired a warning shot, but the projectile seemed certain to hit steel and metal, flesh and bone. Impact imminent, Veale had held his breath.

'Just water,' Veale had murmured with relief. 'Hit nothing but water.'

Pfalz was now out of view, but Veale could still make out the Royal Australian Navy ship that had stormed the German ship after the warning shot. Dorgan joined Veale at the rail.

'We should have gone too,' Veale said. 'Helped them search the ship.'

'Nah,' Dorgan said. 'We were too far away by the time she stopped. This is exactly what they are paid to do.'

Dorgan was right: the Royal Australian Navy were armed and ready for war.

'Let's go and see what shit we are in,' Veale said.

Dorgan smiled. 'Don't worry, I am with you,' he said. 'I won't let you take the blame on your own.'

As the pair joined the captain back on the bridge, they hoped he was in a better mood. He wasn't.

'I should have you court-martialled for disobeying me, Veale,' McWilliam threatened. 'The hide of you to question a superior. I am not going down for this.'

A horn blast stopped the tirade.

'Here is Richardson now,' McWilliam said. 'I wonder what he will make of all this.'

McWilliam rang the engine to stop as *Countess of Hopetoun* – the torpedo gunboat Veale had chased during his sea-sickening training drill – drew alongside *Alvina*. A dinghy was ordered to fetch Captain Richardson, the district naval officer Veale had shot in the foot during the very same drill. The man who would decide his fate.

A sip of seawater wouldn't save Veale this time.

'Well, bloody good on you for showing initiative, Veale,' Richardson said after McWilliam had given his superior a blow-by-blow account. 'We are indeed at war with Germany. Your actions stopped an enemy ship. And you just might have ordered the first shot of this whole damn thing.'

Turned out he had. The first shot of what would soon be known as the Great War hadn't been fired in Manchester or Munich but Melbourne.

'You are a hero, son,' the captain continued.

Chapter 2

WAR AND ORDER

Melbourne, Victoria, 29 June 1914

It had all begun two months earlier, when two shots that slayed an archduke and his wife in Europe triggered a political tsunami that reached Australia as a ripple.

Captain Walter Hugh Charles Samuel Thring, second-in-command of the Royal Australian Navy, was at his kitchen table, bacon and eggs half eaten, when he read about it on a grease-stained page of newspaper:

> *As the royal carriage was passing through the dense crowd a student in the front of the line fired a Browning automatic pistol at close quarters. The Archduke was shot in the face and fell back into his carriage with blood pouring from his wound. Endeavouring to shield her husband, the Duchess was wounded in the abdomen by a second shot fired by a student. Both the wounded Royals were taken to Government House where they died in a few minutes.*

Morning sun streaming through the kitchen window, Captain Thring was half a world away from the assassination. He sipped his tea – English Breakfast with a dash of milk – without taking his eyes away from the article, which continued:

> *The assassination of the Archduke will be viewed with especial concern by the Chancelleries of Europe. Owing to the uncertain future of the Hungarian Empire, it has long been considered doubtful whether the empire would be held together after the death of the Emperor Francis Joseph, who is now in his 84th year. The Archduke's death is likely to greatly aid the forces of disruption in Europe.*

The story had been buried in the broadsheet. The front page of *The Herald* had once again been devoted to federal politics, an election looming after Prime Minister Joseph Cook plunged the parliament into an unprecedented double dissolution. So were pages two and three. Thring had then read about farmers rejoicing – rain in Ballarat sparking a celebration and a dream that the drought could end – before moving on to a story about smallpox in Sydney. Next there had been a report on a pickpocket who had been spotted at an election meeting at Moonee Ponds town hall. It wasn't until he'd got to page seven that he'd read about bombs and bullets. Of the archduke and the assassin.

'This might just kick it all off,' Thring muttered.

'What was that, dear?' asked Lydia as she sat rocking their newborn. 'What's happened?'

Glancing up at his wife of only a year, Thring gave her the grisly news. That the Austro-Hungarian Archduke Franz Ferdinand and his wife, Sophie, the Duchess of Hohenberg, had been shot by a nineteen-year-old assassin in Sarajevo the day before. That with blood gushing from his neck, the archduke had pleaded with his wounded wife. 'Don't die. Live for our children.' But the duchess was dead before the motorcade even stopped. The archduke died but moments later.

Thring swiped his cup from the table and skolled what was left. 'I'd best be off,' he said. 'Could be a busy day.'

It wasn't. Australia paid little notice to the pistol shots that went off in Sarajevo on 28 June. The young nation was without a parliament after Cook's stunning double-dissolution decision. Politicians were campaigning and the people were complaining. There was also the drought. A bone-dry winter was crippling the economy: crops dead, farmers fleeing spent land to search the cities for work. Few paid any attention to the regional rumblings in the Balkans.

'Have you seen the papers?' Thring asked, slapping his bacon-stained copy of *The Herald* on his commander's desk. 'Heard the news coming out of Sarajevo?'

Vice Admiral William Creswell nodded. 'The assassinations?' he replied. 'Yes. And what do you make of it, Walter? Cause for concern?'

'Concern?' Thring pondered. 'Probably. You know as well as I do how one thing can lead to another. What do you think?'

Creswell shrugged. 'Let's leave that to the Admiralty. We will wait to hear what they have to say.'

Thring shook his head at the mention of the organisation that had brushed him aside. Born in Bradford, England, in 1873, Thring had given twenty-five years of his life to the Royal Navy. He had served loyally, capably, even brilliantly. But they had thrown it all in his face.

Thring's rise and fall had been spectacular. Graduating from HMS *Britannia* as a midshipman in 1886, he had served as a gunnery lieutenant in the Channel, Pacific and China squadrons. Tall, broad and bearded, Thring had the brains to match his brawn. Despite being the son of a reverend with no pedigree or power in his lineage, Thring had been earmarked for bigger things early on and described by his seniors as clever, zealous and full of promise.

Thring had officially caught the eye of the Admiralty in 1900 when he'd put his life on the line to stop an explosion. Serving as a lieutenant on HMS *Revenge*, he'd rushed into a fume-filled compartment to put out a cordite charge that had caught fire. The charge was sitting next to a pile of live ammunition.

Thring got his big break in 1903 when he was promoted to captain. He spent the next five years earning praise as the second-in-command of HMS *Vengeance*. He was then appointed to Admiral Lord Charles Beresford's staff.

And that's when it had all fallen apart. Thring had found himself on the wrong side of a dispute between Lord Beresford and First Sea Lord Admiral John Fisher. Seven officers were promoted over his head in 1910 as a punishment for the company he kept.

So he quit. He was done and dusted, finished with the navy. Or so he'd thought.

The offer of six hundred pounds a year and the second most senior position in the newly formed Royal Australian Navy had been too good to refuse.

So here he was, standing in the Navy Office in Melbourne, Australia, second-in-command of a fledgling fleet and once again waiting on orders from the Admiralty.

The telegraph remained silent.

Truk, Caroline Islands, Micronesia, 7 July 1914

Vice Admiral Maximilian von Spee snatched the decryption. 'Back to your station,' he ordered.

The cryptologist saluted and then scurried away.

Von Spee groaned as he shuffled his way towards a bench on the bridge. Having just celebrated his fifty-third birthday, the German admiral moved liked he was a hundred.

'Rheumatism,' he blasted whenever anyone looked concerned. 'Caused by a fever I got in Kamerun. I almost died. It's nothing.'

Von Spee was now suffering a particularly bad bout, muscles and joints screaming and feeling as if they could break. He put it down to the tropical heat.

'So what do we have here?' he murmured, placing the freshly decoded message on the bridge bench as he also leaned his weary frame against it.

As commander of the German East Asia Squadron, von Spee had just begun what was scheduled to be a long and demanding tour of duty. Departing Nagasaki on 28 June aboard SMS *Scharnhorst* – a 13,000-ton battleship with thirty-six guns, all death and destruction – he had just arrived north of New Guinea. He was making plans for the seven ships that formed his fleet.

Chief backup to the *Scharnhorst*, and in every way her equal, was the *Gneisenau*. The sister ship also came packing thirty-six guns: eight 8.2-inch, six 5.9-inch, eighteen 3.5-inch and four torpedo tubes. More death. More destruction.

And then there were the light cruisers – *Leipzig*, *Nürnberg* and *Emden* were all armed with ten 4.1-inch guns and two torpedo tubes, and sported 3.1-inch armoured decks.

Two unarmoured cruisers, the *Cormoran* and the *Geier* – both fitted with eight 4.1-inch guns – completed the fleet.

'*Nein*,' von Spee groaned as he read. The captain's worst fears had just been realised: his carefully laid plans to set steam for Samoa, then Fiji and back to New Guinea for a quick stop before finishing at Tsingtao in China were now tossed into the tropical ocean.

'What is it, captain?' enquired von Spee's right-hand man, Captain Felix Schultz. 'A problem?'

'Yes,' von Spee said. 'The Japanese. Our China base has been compromised.' He read out the decoded message informing him that the British had instructed the Japanese into action under the terms of an alliance signed in 1902. 'This changes everything,' he sighed.

Unlike most of Australia, consumed with politics and the economy, von Spee knew what was coming.

Melbourne, 27 July 1914

Thring was back at his kitchen table, bacon and eggs untouched, tea freshly poured. He couldn't miss this story; it was on page one.

> *THE EUROPEAN CRISIS. GREAT CONFLICT FEARED. THE ARMIES. COMPARED. TEUTONIC-SLAV HATRED.*
>
> *Melbourne, Thursday.*
>
> *Synchronous with Austria's declaration of war on Serbia is the fear of a great conflict that will involve the great nations of the world. Sir Edward Grey, the British Foreign Minister, is striving to limit the dispute to the two nations directly concerned. However, extreme difficulties are ahead. Russia has declared that war on Serbia means war on that Empire. Consequently, it will require the greatest diplomatic ability, tact, and patience to save Europe from the threatening calamity.*
>
> *France has expressed her willingness to cooperate with Great Britain, and it is understood that Italy desires peace. Russia's attitude has been so well defined that the outlook is extremely gloomy. Germany is uncertain. That nation's influence at Vienna is so marked that it is realised that her efforts on one side and Great Britain's on the other could save Europe from the impending disaster. The situation is made all the more serious by the fact that Austria knew, when she declared war, what Russia's attitude was. Then the question arises, has Austria been promised support from Germany in the event of Russian intervention?*

If diplomacy fails a great struggle is inevitable. Millions of men will be thrown against each other in a bloody conflict with all its horrors and reprisals. The sole cause of such a war would be racial hatred.

War? Hatred? Strong stuff, Thring thought. He bit off a chunk of toast without taking his eyes from the paper.

The extent of bitterness between the heterogeneous races of Eastern Europe has no limitations. Teutons and Slavs are diametrically opposed to each other. The atrocities committed by the Slavs from time immemorial have astounded the civilised powers of the world.

There has always been bickering between the two races, and the hatred culminated in the assassination of the Archduke of Austria and his consort.

The incidents, which led to the declaration of war, are not well known.

Recently a native of Bavaria, now residing in Victoria, gave vent to his feelings against the Slavs.

'They are treacherous,' he said. 'And will not scruple to commit the most heartrending atrocities, and in fact are nothing less than cut-throats.'

Such expressions of opinion would naturally bring retorts of similar bitterness from the Slavs. And so the hatred must grow.

Again the talk of war, hatred. *Serious stuff,* Thring thought. This time he scooped his egg, shoving it into his mouth without missing a word.

Correspondence received from the Southern States of Germany from private individuals who have relatives there show that for months the tension has become greater and greater.

'We are in pins and needles,' said a resident of Saxony.

'Don't be surprised to hear of a great conflict in Europe.'

But there is still hope that the great powers will be able to use conciliatory means to maintain peace. At this time statistics regarding the armies of Europe are interesting. The armies of the Triple Entente (Great Britain, France and Russia) number 11 million men.

Now Thring put down his forkful of untouched bacon. This was getting intriguing.

The grand total of the British military establishment for 1914 is 803,037. France has an active army of 609,685. Accounting for the reserves, the total first line effective of the French Army on war footing is estimated at 2,500,000 men. Russia has the greatest army of any European individual. The war strength of the Russian force is about 5,000,000 men. In addition, there are about 3,000,000 reserves. After the Japanese war the army underwent complete retraining. The training of the army was improved and modernised.

Approximately, the Triple Alliance (Germany, Austria, and Italy) possesses 14,000,000 trained men. Germany has about 4,353,000. The army has been materially strengthened of late. Italy has a total war strength of 3,380,202 men, which includes a reserve force of 2,275,631. The peace army of the Austro-Hungarian Empire consists of 431,194 men, while the total war strength is 3,710,000 men. In considering the state of the armies of the six great powers in connection with the present dispute Serbia must be considered. Although comparatively a small nation, Serbia can put 200,000 officers and men into the field.

The Triple Entente has great advantage as regards the naval forces.

They have a total of 1,243 ships and 313,000 men, made up as follows: Great Britain, 624 ships, 146,000 men; France, 361 ships, 114,000 men; Russia, 258 ships, 53,000 men.

What about us? How about Australia? Thring picked up the bacon again and shoved it in his mouth.

The Triple Alliance has 598 ships and 131,000 men, made up as follows: Germany, 305 ships, 73,000 men; Austria, 106 ships, 18,000 men; Italy, 187 ships, 40,000 men. While the Triple Entente would have the advantage on water, they have approximately 3,000,000 soldiers less than their rivals. Figures regarding the serial services of the war powers are not definite, but it is certain that the Entente has an enormous advantage in this aspect of modern warfare. There are no figures available for Russia, but Great Britain and France possess 528 aeroplanes and 203 dirigibles. Austria has a small naval air service of hydroaeroplanes, while Germany has 24 military dirigibles and a few aeroplanes. The figures, however, are not definite.

Thring snatched up his cup from the table and downed the rest of his tea, slamming it back onto the table in his haste as his wife looked up in alarm. 'Love, I have to run,' he said. 'I could be a while. Don't expect me home tonight.'

The captain rushed back to Admiral Creswell's office, paper in hand, but this time there was no reason to slap it down. Creswell was on leave, the First Naval Member in Brisbane, enjoying a rare break. The news of the inevitable war had caught the Royal Australian Navy by surprise.

They had been expecting to hear from the Admiralty following the assassination of the archduke and the duchess, and again after Austro-Hungary declared it wanted revenge.

They hadn't.

They had expected to hear from the Admiralty when Germany promised to back Austro-Hungary or when Russia issued a warning to the nation.

They hadn't.

In fact, everything the Royal Australian Navy knew about the escalating situation in Europe had come from the press. As far as Australia knew, Britain was intent on peace.

Thring and everyone else in Australia had read about Britain's attempts to distance itself from the conflict. There had been a joint naval exercise with the Germans in Kiev on 30 June, then the declaration that Britain had no plans to back either France or Russia on 9 July – after all, the German Kaiser Wilhelm II was King George V's cousin. And then, just the day before, British Foreign Secretary Sir Edward Grey had put forward a proposal for a peace conference.

So the Royal Australian Navy had continued as normal. The squadron had gone on its annual winter cruise and was now off the coast of Queensland. Of the fledgling seven-ship fleet, only two had stayed behind, *Gayundah* in Sydney Harbour and *Pioneer* in Port Phillip. Creswell had taken leave and the minister for defence, Edward Millen, was in Sydney campaigning ahead of the election.

'Have you heard?' Thring asked when the captain finally got through to Creswell on the phone. He listened hard through the crackling connection. 'You have? Good. And we have just received notice that the British Admiralty has countermanded the dispersal of the First Fleet and retained the Second Fleet at home ports. This can only mean they have enacted naval precautions in anticipation of war.'

He nodded as Creswell spoke.

'Right then,' Thring said. 'I'll see you soon.'

Sydney, New South Wales, 29 July 1914

Senator Edward Millen would not budge. The former journalist who had become a Federation-opposing politician was all by the book.

'No,' he said down the phone line. 'Not without instruction from the Admiralty. We have not received a war warning.'

Thring pleaded his case. 'We need to move the fleet,' he said. 'And we need to do it now. We all know what is coming. It is bleeding obvious. And we all know what needs to be done. The First and Second Fleets have been moved into position. We need to do the same.'

Thring wanted to bring the Australian Squadron back from its winter cruise and send it to Sydney for coal and supplies. He wanted to get ready for war.

'I think I have made myself quite clear,' Senator Millen said. 'We don't act until we have the official warning of war.'

Click!

Thring refused to take no – or an abruptly ended phone call – for an answer. With Creswell still making his way back to Melbourne, he sent a telegram to Rear Admiral Sir George Edwin Patey, commander of the Royal Australian Navy fleet.

'Captain Thring here again, sir,' Thring said when Senator Millen picked up the phone a couple of hours later. 'I've had word from Admiral Patey and he also is of the opinion that we should begin making preparations for the inevitable warning.' Thring pulled the receiver away as the senator barked. 'Yes, sir,' Thring replied. 'One is better than none.'

Click!

Thring breathed out a sigh of relief. He had permission for one light cruiser to leave the squadron to obtain provisions and coal.

Melbourne, 30 July 1914

Chest puffed out and a smile on his face, Thring picked up the phone knowing there would be no pleading or arguments this time. Or so he thought.

'Connect me to Senator Millen,' Thring said. 'Yes. In Sydney.' He was already issuing orders in his head when the senator picked up the phone.

'We have received the official war warning, senator,' Thring said. 'Do we have your permission to make preparations for war?'

'What?' Millen asked. 'I haven't received notice of anything.'

Thring exhaled, the smile on his face fading with his spent breath. 'Sir, I have just received notification from Admiral Patey,' he said. 'He has been informed that the war warning has been issued.'

'Informed by whom?' Millen demanded. 'The Admiralty? Surely not. I would have received the order had it been issued. There is a protocol for this kind of thing.'

'Senator, the admiral received two messages,' Thring explained. 'One from the commander of the China Station and another from New Zealand. We have also intercepted a message from the East Indies Station. Patey contacted Melbourne ten minutes ago, the notification coming in at 5 pm. He is seeking permission to set steam. All he requires is your assent. Can we move the squadron south?'

The senator still wasn't convinced. 'I'll get back to you,' he said. 'Don't go anywhere.'

Click!

'Damn it!' Thring shouted, a rare outburst from the famously calm captain. He slammed the phone down. 'No one is leaving,' he ordered as he burst into a room full of typewriters and telegraphs. 'We are all going to be working through the night.'

Thring pulled a file before returning to the office and was soon at his desk reviewing the war orders the Admiralty had drafted for the Australian fleet, each ship having been given a very specific set of instructions. He examined the orders for the squadron's flagship, HMAS *Australia*.

> *WAR ORDER FOR HMAS* AUSTRALIA, *1914*
> *1. On the outbreak of war, provided that the government of the Commonwealth shall have placed the naval services of the Commonwealth under the control of the British Admiralty, HMAS* Australia *will be placed under the British Commander-in-Chief on the China Station without further orders, and will remain at their disposal until the termination of hostilities, or until receiving instruction to the contrary.*
> *2. Being in respect ready for service therefore she will first proceed with all dispatch to Thursday Island to complete coaling and await such orders as to her further movements as she may receive by telegraph from the Commander-in-Chief, China Station.*
> *3. Her reserve ammunition and spare stores will be sent to Hong Kong to the custody of the Commodore in Charge by specially chartered steamer, proceeding by such a route as is decided after consultation with the Commodore by cable.*
> *4. The intended movements are based upon the supposition that the outbreak of war finds the ships of the enemy in eastern seas as usually disposed in time of peace. Should it prove to be otherwise in so far that a hostile armoured ship happens to be in Australia waters it will be the duty of the* Australia *to bring her to action before she proceeds on any other service.*

Thring began drafting a new set of orders. *Australia*, now off the coast of southern Queensland, would be brought back to Sydney for resupply.

Sydney was closer than Thursday Island, that is what Thring would officially say. But the captain's true reason for amending the order was that he didn't want to leave both Sydney and Melbourne undefended. Not yet.

The new orders were typed and ready for issue when the call he had been waiting for finally came. It was 9 pm when he was summoned to the telephone.

'Very well,' said Millen, his meeting with Cabinet finally over. 'Proceed.'

Click!

The Australian Squadron was ordered to prepare for war.

Melbourne, 31 July 1914

Vice Admiral Creswell arrived back in Melbourne as the official war warning came in from the Admiralty.

'Good job twisting the senator's arm last night,' Creswell said to Thring. 'The squadron should just about be in Sydney by now. Millen give you a bit of trouble, did he?'

Thring nodded.

'Oh well,' Creswell said. 'No need to worry about him now. I am activating the war room.'

Thring smiled widely. 'Yes, sir,' he said. 'Thank you, sir.'

Creswell had just made Thring arguably the most important person in Australia. Under a plan agreed upon by the Naval Board and the Admiralty in 1913, Thring would become the director of war plans and head the Royal Australian Navy war room, the War Organisation. To be activated by the First Naval Member following a warning or on the outbreak of war, the organisation would be responsible for all Australian naval activities.

And Thring was now in charge of it.

He fast assembled his staff, consisting of a captain, a lieutenant commander and two lieutenants.

'Our first order of business is to find out where the German squadron is,' Thring said in his first address to the war staff later that day. 'We need to know where they are before we do anything with our fleet. I won't leave this country open to attack.'

Thring had been the first person to declare Australia needed to be responsible for her own defence, in his 'War Book', which he'd written after observing Australia's lack of naval strategy and preparedness for war. Thring's War Book was the first account of Australia's naval capabilities that included a road map to make the fleet ready for war.

Outraging the establishment, Thring had sensationally claimed Australia could not rely on Britain anymore. 'The [British Royal Navy] squadron stationed in Australian waters has always been a holiday squadron,' he wrote. 'There is now a possibility that an enemy can strike a deadly blow before help can come. Geographically, the position of Australia with respect to Asia and the Pacific may be compared to that of England to the north of Europe. The danger of a descent by the Japanese, in their own good time, is a very real danger, almost amounting to a certainty unless adequate steps are taken for defence against it. British ships in the case of a European war would be largely occupied with matters other than the defence of Australia.'

Creswell had supported Thring both privately and publicly from the outset. 'Immediately on his appointment Captain Thring prepared the War Book,' Creswell wrote in a letter to a superior. 'He comprehended all that would be necessary to be done in the event of war.'

Creswell and Thring had a lot in common, their histories helping create current respect. Just like Thring, William Rooke Creswell was a Royal Navy runaway. Born in Gibraltar in 1852, the son of a postmaster, Creswell had entered the navy as a cadet on the training ship *Britannia* in December 1865. He was promoted to midshipman in 1867 and spent the next four years cruising the world on HMS *Phoebe*.

Promoted to sublieutenant in 1873, Creswell was shot in a skirmish with pirates while serving on HMS *Midge* off the Malay coast. He stayed at his post despite being inflicted with severe wounds. His gallantry was noted and he was soon promoted to lieutenant. He would go on to serve in East Africa and become fluent in Swahili.

Creswell abruptly retired from the Royal Navy in 1878. He migrated to Australia with his brother Charles and bought a farm in the Northern Territory. Living off the land proved tough. There was no glamour in the dirt and heat, and little money in his crop. Seven years after moving to Australia, a chance meeting in Adelaide with John Walcot, the commander of the South Australian Naval Forces, who had served with Creswell in the Royal Navy, had given him an out.

'I have an appointment for you right now if you are interested,' said Walcot. 'How would you like to be a lieutenant commander?'

Creswell accepted at once. He sold his share of the farm to his brother and returned to the sea. Fast forward twenty-nine years and Creswell was not only a rear admiral but also the founding father of the Royal Australian Navy. He had campaigned tirelessly for Australia to acquire naval forces to supplement the Royal Navy and then, following Federation, for the new nation to have its own force. It was Creswell who in 1909, convinced both the Australian government and the Admiralty of Australia's need for its own fleet.

Creswell was the reason Thring was now directing that fleet.

'Find out where von Spee is,' Thring said, looking squarely at his second-in-command, Captain Arthur Jose. 'And what he is up to. I want all ears turned to him. Tell Balsillie I want to know if he so much as farts.' Thring had already ordered John Graeme Balsillie, Engineer for Radiotelegraphy for the Postmaster-General's department, to begin a radio hunt for von Spee. Balsillie had established the nation's first coastal radio service based on a wireless telegraphy system he had patented himself. His ears stretched to the other side of the world.

Ponape, Caroline Islands, Micronesia, 2 August 1914

The machine beeped.

'*Scheisse*,' swore the wireless operator as he jumped.

The high-pitched shrill from the telegraph had stunned him from his daydream. As he'd sat solitary in a metal box since sunrise, *Scharnhorst* had rocked him into a lullaby. The swell had made him sick when he'd started his shift – a washing machine, up and down, side to side – but subsequently the sound of waves crashing into the hull had become hypnotic.

When the machine burst into life he'd been in the Swiss Alps, arm around the girl he'd promised to never leave, a log on the open fire spitting as he leaned in for a kiss.

'Shit,' he said again, this time more matter of fact. The next noise from the machine snapped him from his romantic reverie. Pencil in hand, he began recording every piece of nonsense the machine spat out. Whatever he was writing wasn't German. It wasn't any language spoken by man. He looked down at the message when the machine finally stopped: 'XCHDR AUSTRALIA, ASDEY RIGOE, FKSDP CNDLO ...'

Like most messages of late, it meant nothing to him.

'More code,' he said as he handed his transcription to the cryptologist, before heading back to the Swiss Alps.

In a metal box of his own, the cryptologist grabbed the gibberish and placed it on his desk. He looked down at the message, ten-letter groups except for a solitary legible word, Australia.

'Fool,' he said. 'Lazy buffoon. All code except for this.' He ran a finger down a stack of books and then up again. 'Here it is,' he said, tapping on a leather spine. He pulled the hulking book from the pile and peeled open the cover. 'Yes,' he said as he examined the title page, 'this one.'

He flicked through the book first, thumb and index finger sending a sandwich-sized stack of pages on a right-to-left race.

Then, when he was nearing the right spot, he slowed and studied each page in turn.

Bingo!

His finger stabbed the page. 'Got it!' he said, then grabbed his pen and wrote. He repeated the process – flicking, thumbing, studying and then writing – three times.

'Done,' he said. He ripped the page from his notepad and marched from his metal box.

'Admiral,' said the cryptologist. 'An urgent message from the consul in Sydney.'

Von Spee snatched the paper. 'Back to your station,' the admiral ordered.

The cryptologist saluted and turned.

Von Spee hobbled to the bridge's bench and turned on his lamp. 'Kiliani,' he said, noting the author. 'Good.'

The message had been sent by the German consul general in Sydney, Richard Kiliani, a man who was fast proving himself as the valuable and fearless head of an extensive German spy network in Australia. Established in 1902 to gather naval intelligence through the so-called War Intelligence System used 'reporters' and 'confidants' to collect information about the Royal Australian Navy and the merchant shipping trade. The reporters and confidants – almost exclusively German nationals working in Australia – were each responsible to a chief reporter, who in turn gave information to the consul general and the senior German naval officer of the Australian Station.

Kiliani kept a 'blue book' in his safe which contained a list of his reporters, each with a location, name, function, code name, address and allocated number. His safe also contained reams of reports from his agents – men including Oscar Plate (Agent 640), manager of the Norddeutscher Lloyd shipping agency, Sydney businessman Otto Bauer (Agent 6401) and commercial attaché Walter de Haas (Agent 602).

The ultimate goal of these activities was to strike a deadly blow to Australian trade. The Germans were aware that the Australians considered the Allied naval forces in their waters insufficient to protect them. If the German Navy could plan and implement a penetrating attack, it would likely cause immense disruption. Germany had begun planning for this as early as 1900, when consuls had been sent a top-secret document entitled 'Implementation Instruction for the Australian Station'. They were advised to keep the document locked in a safe, and to burn it if they suspected a raid.

There were orders in the document for confidants on the Australian Station to gain control of one steamer for every warship in the German squadron. In the event of war, the steamers were to be sent to the Bismarck Archipelago to join the German fleet. Some would be converted into cruisers – guns placed on the decks – and join the attack, others would be used for support and supply. They would then be given orders, told which enemy ships to destroy, which trade routes to wipe out.

Another document sent out in 1903, 'Attack by the Cruiser Squadron on English Wool Imports from Australasia', went into more detail and listed targets. 'The greatest volume of shipping in Australasian waters is in the region from Sydney to Adelaide,' the document read. 'Around fifty British steamers a month pass through the Bass Strait. There are three major harbours from Sydney to Adelaide and they are the locations for the most valuable British lines. With the advantage of surprise and a superior fleet, control of local waters, or at least a blockade, should be easily achieved.'

The document even suggested a hypothetical timeframe for an attack with suggestions for what could be achieved and when. Beginning with a departure from the cruiser squadron's home base in Tsingtao in northern China on 1 January, the report predicted:

> *24 January: The squadron would stand before Melbourne with the following possibilities:*
>
> *a) Australian warships engaged. The extent of success will depend on the degree of control over the Bass Strait and speed of progression to Sydney.*
> *b) If Australia declines battle in the expectation of arrival of reinforcements from the China Squadron, Melbourne should be blockaded. Australia's foremost trading and second wool export port would be isolated. If the blockade included warships in port, the light cruisers could be ordered to blockade Sydney. If Australian heavy cruisers stood outside Melbourne, circumstances would determine how many ships could be spared for Sydney.*
> *c) If the bulk of the Australian force stands before Sydney, it should be blockaded there by the main body of the German Squadron.*

d) If Australian warships are in Adelaide or Brisbane – considered unlikely to be a formidable force because flagships will be defending the vital Southern ports – they should be drawn away and attacked in one undertaking.

Von Spee, Kiliani and Germany's network of spies had several other reports secreted away in safes and hiding holes, including 'Implementation of Operational Orders on the Australian Station'. It read:

With some accuracy, it can be predicted that the superior ships of the Australian Fleet Unit would be sent immediately on the outbreak of war to New Guinea and Samoa in order to capture our cruisers and neutralise coaling stations. Trade routes from New Guinea south should be cut and coastal harbours harassed as far as Tasmania. Coal can be forcibly obtained without difficulty from coastal towns, particularly along the Queensland coast. The poor defence of Australia makes the accessing of harbours there for replenishing of supplies appear quite possible. For example, Gladstone is recommended as a coaling harbour.

Von Spee's heart was now racing. He knew this message must be of the utmost importance if Kiliani was risking his cover to send whatever it was he was about to read. He traced his finger along each handwritten word: 'In the event of war, *Australia* and three cruisers will patrol the China Stations. They will be under orders to engage and destroy.'

Von Spee already knew war was coming – he had been issued orders to implement cruiser warfare on 31 July. He'd prepared his fleet for battle the next day, ordering all non-essential equipment to be shipped ashore. Wood panelling and tapestries were stripped from wardrobe walls. Sofas and armchairs were carried off the ship. Formal jackets and brocaded coats were packed into trunks alongside gold-striped breeches, sports clothes and equipment. All the souvenirs were ordered off too: vases, lanterns, ivory carvings, silks, bows and arrows were left behind, the men reluctantly parting with their foreign treasures.

The officers weren't spared, with silverware, chairs and carpets ordered out. Even a piano left the ship. All they were permitted to keep was a writing table, a chair and a picture of the Kaiser.

They all knew war was coming. Now von Spee knew HMAS *Australia* was coming too.

And while he didn't fear war itself, he was rightly fearful of facing the 22-gun ship they had named *Australia*. None of the reports, documents and plans held in his safe accounted for the warship, with most authored before she was delivered to the Royal Australian Navy in 1911 and those penned after adamant HMAS *Australia* would be sent to Europe to join the Royal Navy.

'The British Australian squadron has a flagship, HMAS *Australia*,' he had written to Berlin in a previous report. 'This ship alone for our squadron is such a superior opponent that it must be avoided. *Australia* is likely to be accompanied by torpedo boats which makes the situation even more difficult.'

He had hoped everyone in Berlin was right, that *Australia* would be commandeered by the Royal Navy and sent to the North Sea. But according to Kiliani, they were wrong. HMAS *Australia* was coming.

Von Spee shook his head and limped from the bridge.

'What is it, sir?' asked a lieutenant. 'Do you have an order?'

He ignored the question and made for the quiet of his quarters. It was only there he dared speak the truth, not out loud but in letters to his daughter and wife. He released his fears with paper and pen.

'This is all unmentionably saddening,' he wrote. 'My thoughts are quite mixed. All here and there. I have to prepare myself for the most serious eventuality. We all rest in God's hands. Whatever will come will come regardless and we have to come to terms with it. If we fail, then it is in the service of a good cause.'

Melbourne, 3 August 1914

Thring closed the door behind him as he entered Australia's very first intelligence room, a concrete bunker buried in the basement of the Navy Office in Lonsdale Street.

'Have we found von Spee?' he demanded. 'Do we know where he is?'

The room came to a standstill as twelve officers, three officers retired, six pensioner clerks and one active service rating put down their pens and notes and lifted their heads to attention.

'Sir,' said one of the officers, rising from his school-desk-like table, with its well-worn wooden top held up by cast iron, 'here is the signals report from Mr Balsillie.'

'Good,' Thring said as he took the paper pile. 'Back to work.'

The Naval Intelligence Service had been established in September 1911. Stuck on a wall right in front of the twenty-two staff, some now reading, others writing, typing or talking, was the organisation's charter:

INSTRUCTIONS FOR THE ROYAL AUSTRALIAN NAVAL INTELLIGENCE SERVICE

GENERAL

1. The collection and distribution of naval intelligence will be conducted by the same organisation in peace as in war, except that in war there will be certain extensions and modifications to the system.

2. The Navy Office will be the principal centre for Australia in the Admiralty Intelligence System.

3. The Intelligence Branch of the Navy Office will receive information from and report to the Admiralty, and will supply the Australian fleet with information. It will also communicate with neighbouring intelligence centres in the Admiralty system.

4. The primary use of intelligence is:

a) To ensure that on and after the outbreak of hostilities the Admiralty, Navy Office and officers commanding detached squadrons or ships will be kept informed of the distribution and movements of all ships of war and merchant vessels, and other matters likely to affect the operations of the fleet.

b) To give such warning information and advice to the British merchant vessels as will enable them to avoid capture and molestations by the enemy.

5. It should be remembered that the value of most intelligence lies in the rapidity with which it can be communicated to the officers concerned.

6. There are many sources from which intelligence may be obtained, and officers should be able gradually to develop a system by which the most is made of them, e.g. collector of customs, chief of police, postmaster, local press, shipping officials, masters of vessels, persons returning from the islands etc. Should there be a military intelligence officer at the port, the district naval officer should arrange to keep in touch with him, with a view to mutual assistance being afforded.

WAR ORGANISATION

7. The systems in force in peace will continue in time of war, with the following modifications and extensions:

> *a) A different system of communication will be adopted.*
>
> *b) Censorship of radio telegraphy will be established.*
>
> *c) District naval offices will become transmitting stations where HM ships may receive latest intelligences, and British merchant vessels receive information as to the safety of the trade routes.*

8.

> *a) Alteration in system of communication.*
>
> *All reports will be made by telegraph in cipher or code, unless in the case of a lengthy communication it is clear that no delay would be caused by its being forwarded by post. As a general rule, all reports should be made direct to the Navy Office as well as to the district naval officer.*

b) Censorship of radiotelegraphy.

The censors appointed to radiotelegraphy stations will assist as far as possible in the collection of intelligence. They will report direct to the Navy Office, and, in cases where urgent local action may be necessary, to the district naval officer or sub-district naval officer as well. All radio signals received or intercepted which may be of enemy origin, or which might prove of assistance to the navy, should be reported at once to the Navy Office. Special instructions are issued for the censorship of radio stations, [and] a list of Commonwealth stations, the censorship of which in war will be under the authority of the Navy Office.

9. *The following information is required in time of war.*

a) Movements of enemy merchant vessels or other suspicious craft.

b) Aircraft.

c) Sounds of gunfire or other indication of the presence of ships of war.

d) Mines.

e) Intercepted radio messages.

Thring had been made the head of the Naval Intelligence Service when the Governor-General transferred all Commonwealth intelligence duties to the Royal Australian Navy early in 1911. Just like von Spee, Thring had his own spies, from customs officials and shopkeepers to police officers and shipping clerks, and his staff at this very minute were sorting through the stacks of intelligence reports provided by his network. There were reports on the movements of suspected German spies. There were lists of the estimated coal stores of German shipping companies. There was even a report alleging that Richard Kiliani, the German consul general in Sydney, was a spy.

Thring wasn't interested in any of those reports right now, only the signals report he held in his hand, which referred to messages coming from Yap in the Caroline Islands, north of New Guinea:

Sir,
I send to you herewith copies of telegrams which I have received from radiotelegraphy stations, and those messages which I consider are of considerable interest to you I have marked important.

From the particulars received the following is evident:

There is no doubt that Yap is transmitting to Scharnhorst. *The result of intercepted messages places her 300 NE of Papua.*

I think Scharnhorst *is being referred to as IO. If I am correct, the vessel must be in the vicinity of the Solomon Islands – probably near Bougainville.*

The long telegram in my opinion is intended for Scharnhorst.

There is no doubt in my mind as to the positions of Planet *and* Komet. *They are in the vicinity of Rabaul.*

All messages are sent in a code we cannot decipher without a key.

John Graeme Balsillie
Engineer for Radiotelegraphy

'Got you,' Thring said. He flipped over the first page of the report and kept reading:

> *2 August*
> *12.53 am, ASB (Scharnhorst) to KBN (Nauru): ASTYP IACUS, GIEST ACUCU, BUICA FIBUB, GAUSJ GALON.*
> *3.20 am, ASB (Scharnhorst) to KCA (Yap): GERMANIA HAPOX ELAND, HOGOV NATHV, FISSI CETAP, HERMI XDIEN, ATTAX ENCIA, HISOP ATFIG, INODA JGUMI, PIAGG AMMON, EUCAC OZETE.*
>
> *3 August*
> *12 am, ASB (Scharnhorst) to KCA (Yap): ADMIRAL BERLIN ASUIT ONIGH, JOPIN ONADO, AJAAF FOBEL, LOZUV ATAPD, OMIJE XIACU, CUBUI CAFIB.*

Thring turned before even reaching his office and marched back the way he had come. He burst back into the bunker, waving the report.

'Codebooks,' Thring demanded. 'We need to find their codebooks.'

Melbourne, 4 August 1914

Thring, Creswell and naval secretary George Macandie went in all guns blazing. Arriving at Parliament House at 9 am, the posse shot straight.

'The German squadron is not in the China Sea as expected,' Thring told Senator Millen. 'We have picked up several transmissions from the fleet at our wireless stations as recently as this morning, meaning they are no more than 1,500 miles away from the Australian coast. Our intelligence reports, which I have made copies of for you, suggest the flagship *Scharnhorst* is 300 miles northeast of Papua, and German cruisers *Planet* and *Komet* are at the German station of Rabaul.'

'So what do you want to do?' the minister for defence asked.

'Send them to hell,' Creswell returned fiercely. 'Let's bloody go and blow them sky-high.'

The minister laughed. 'That's all very well,' he said, 'but I can't just –'

Thring interrupted, handing him a piece of paper with a paragraph circled. 'This should help,' he said.

Millen examined the text:

> *4. The intended movements are based upon the supposition that the outbreak of war finds the ships of the enemy in eastern seas as usually disposed in time of peace. Should it prove to be otherwise in so far that a hostile armoured ship happens to be in Australian waters it will be the duty of the* Australia *to bring her to action before she proceeds on any other service.*

'I see,' Millen said. 'Very well. But I'll still have to seek approval from the Admiralty.'

Creswell stood, his giant form towering over the still-seated minister. 'Well start hunting,' he said. 'Every moment spent waiting is a moment lost.'

The minister stood and shook Creswell's hand. 'Of course,' he said. 'I'll come back to you as soon as I can.'

The answer came early that afternoon.

'Thank you, minister,' Creswell said. 'Orders will go out at once. We'll find the bastards, don't worry about that.'

HMAS *Australia* steamed out of Port Jackson at 9.45 pm. Her mission: seek and destroy.

Chapter 3

THE CODE CATCHER

Esperance, Western Australia, 7 August 1914

The senior signals officer strode into the bunker to issue an order. 'Listen to everything,' he commanded. 'Even what you think could be nothing. It all needs to be recorded and sent to Melbourne. We are on high alert.'

The signals operator raised a brow. 'For what, sir?' he asked. 'Does Fritz fancy a day at the beach?'

The officer yanked the headset off the operator's head. 'This is no joke,' he snapped. 'I have just received orders from Melbourne. They have intelligence that suggests there are still German vessels off the coast of Australia.'

The operator was stunned. 'Really?' he asked. 'I thought they would have all well and truly cleared out by now.'

The supervisor held up the telegram he had received from the naval secretary. 'Signal station to carry out the following,' the supervisor read. 'Report movements of all enemy and suspicious craft, aircraft, gunfire and other occurrences likely to be of interest. They are to receive signals from HM ships and pass on signals that may be directed to HM ships.' He looked up briefly before continuing to read. 'Method of communication. Signal stations are to report by telegraph or telephone to senior district naval officer at the port, otherwise to the district naval officer of the state. DNOs report valuable information by telegraph to the Navy Office.' The supervisor looked up. 'And I also got a telephone call from a district officer telling me a ship could be coming our way,' he continued. 'So yes, this is real.'

'Did they say what sort of ship, sir?' the operator asked nervously. 'A merchant ship? Or –'

'Just be vigilant,' the superior cut in. 'Report everything.'

Prior to this exchange the operator had been expecting an average day sitting behind the hulking radios and receivers covering his steel-top desk, just the usual chitchat from ships coming and going. He hadn't been contemplating the enemy.

'Yes, sir,' he said. 'I won't miss a thing.'

The operator put his headphones back on and was again plugged into the twenty-five-ton tower that climbed out of the coastal cliff and soared into the sky.

The Esperance signal station was over 400 miles southeast of Perth, bunkered into the Great Australian Bight. The fifty-yard signal mast had been speared into a clifftop a hundred yards above sea level giving the state-of-the-art shack an operational range of 350 miles. It was one of nineteen wireless telegraphy stations that lined the Australian coast, the first erected in Sydney in 1910 and others soon shooting up in Melbourne, Hobart and Brisbane. They formed part of a worldwide wireless network built by the British. With emerging radio technology promising to provide rapid communication with the colonies, the Royal Navy had begun construction of what would become a global cable network in 1893. China got the first station, then Gibraltar, Malta, Colombo, Singapore and Hong Kong followed. Soon most of the globe was covered.

Today Australia listened.

'I've got something,' the operator yelped later that day. The supervisor rushed into the room and sat at his side.

'It sounds like someone is trying to make contact,' the operator continued. He listened hard to the static and squelch then heard a voice.

'This is SS *Hobart*,' the caller declared, voice faint and barely discernible over the symphony of sonic mess.

The operator grabbed his pencil and started to scribble.

'I repeat, this is SS *Hobart*. We are entering Australian waters.'

The static returned.

'This is signal station Esperance,' the operator said. 'Can you state your position?'

Static was the only response.

'SS *Hobart*,' the operator resumed, 'can you state your position?'

Still nothing.

'Can you state your destination port?' the operator tried again.

SS *Hobart* had gone quiet.

'I think she's out of range, boss,' the operator said as the supervisor riffled through a pile of shipping logs. 'We've lost her.'

The boss had found the paper with the name of the ship he was looking for. 'That was a German vessel,' he beamed. 'An enemy ship. They mustn't know that we are at war.'

'But we lost the signal,' the operator said.

The supervisor still smiled. 'Doesn't matter,' he said. 'We know she is heading to port somewhere close. They'll find her.'

The supervisor picked up the telephone.

Melbourne, 8 August 1914

Captain Thring scanned the signals report that had just been delivered to his desk.

> *Sir,*
> *I submit herewith a chart prepared from particulars received by me this day. With reference to* Scharnhorst *I cannot definitely say where she is. I think she is moving a little NE of the position she was in last night but she is certainly moving away from Australia. We also have intercepted messages but are unable to know their meaning as they have been transmitted in code.*

Thring looked up from the report and sighed. It wasn't the news he'd been hoping for on the German flagship. He bowed his head to read more.

> *As to the* Geier *nothing absolutely has been heard about her. Yap was heard sending her traffic but no reply was received. Perhaps she might be communicating through the Dutch stations*

> *in the daytime, but we have not heard her work to the Dutch stations, nor have we heard the Dutch stations working to her.*

Another sigh from Thring. He continued to read.

> *It is evident that the German vessels* Alsace, Essen *and* Sydney *are someplace about 117 degrees east and 4 degrees south. Perhaps* Geier *will be acting as a sort of convoy for these vessels and they may be meeting at some point south of Flores.*

'Speculation,' Thring muttered.

> *The German commercial vessel* Hobart *reported to Esperance station last night. Her position is shown approximately on the map. I think she is making for Melbourne, but she could be making for Adelaide. She has not communicated with any other vessel up to present, so she looks like becoming a prize.*

'That's more like it,' Thring exclaimed, punching the air.

> Planet *and* Komet *are certainly at Rabaul. Nothing has been heard from* Emden.
>
> *J.G. Balsillie*
> *Engineer for Radiotelegraphy*

'We've got an enemy ship in Australian waters,' Thring said after bolting down the corridor to find Creswell. 'A German steamer has just contacted the Esperance station to announce her arrival.' Thring was beaming. 'This could be it,' he told the vice admiral. 'We might finally get these infernal codes.'

The First Naval Member was less excitable. Creswell crossed his arms before leaning forward onto his desk, completely covered with telegrams, reports and soon-to-be issued orders. 'Well don't just stand there,' he said. 'Go out and bloody get them. You know what you have to do.'

Thring ordered a lieutenant to bring him every scrap of information they had on a German steamer named *Hobart*. A file, albeit thin, was soon sitting on his desk.

SS *Hobart* was a merchant vessel operated by a shipping company called the Deutsche-Australische Dampfschiffs Gesellschaft. It travelled between Hamburg and Australia and, most notably to Thring, the steamer was wireless station equipped.

So why was Hobart *oblivious to the war declaration?* Thring mused. *Maybe their station has been left unmanned? Were they out of communication range? Or maybe the captain was just a blubbering fool.* The only thing Thring was certain of was that SS *Hobart* needed to be kept in the dark. He didn't want this vessel learning of the war before she had been seized and searched. Before he had captured the codes. Thring was concerned that a vessel that had escaped Sydney before war was declared would warn the *Hobart* away from Australia.

Despite sending HMAS *Parramatta* out to hunt for the ship, SMS *Seydlitz* had embarrassed the navy by sneaking out without clearance on 4 August. Thring had little clue to the whereabouts of the German cruiser. She could be patrolling Australian waters and signalling German ships to avoid Australian ports. She could be telling them to destroy all their secrets. Thring couldn't afford to lose another prize – especially if the vessel was carrying enemy codes.

He picked up a pen and went about drafting his first order. 'All signals across the Australian Bight are to be jammed,' Thring wrote. 'Enemy vessels operating in the Southern Ocean and Bass Strait must be blocked from receiving transmissions or instruction.' Filling the local airwaves with static would ensure that.

Thring did not go home that night. Eager for news, he dragged his emergency mattress from a closet and positioned it behind his desk. After ordering any telegram to be sent straight in, he left the door open and the phone on the hook.

He was surprised to wake up refreshed following a full night's sleep.

'Good timing,' said the naval secretary walking in. 'Here is the latest signals report.'

Thring pushed himself upright and took the offered page.

Melbourne, 9 August 1914
MEMORANDUM TO: Naval Secretary, Melbourne
SUBJECT: Censorship of radio telegrams

You should have copies of telegrams that show Seydlitz *was endeavouring to communicate with* Hobart *last night. I think we have effectively jammed all communication from* Hobart *to any other vessel. I instructed the Melbourne and Adelaide stations to jam* Hobart *all last night. The Melbourne and Mount Gambier stations are jamming this vessel all today. All stations from Broome to Melbourne on the southern side, including Hobart but excluding Flinders Island, have been instructed to jam all communications they hear passing between German vessels. Reports to hand indicate that the workings of German vessels last night and this morning were effectively jammed. SS* Hobart *seems certain to be heading to Melbourne.*

J.G. Balsillie
Engineer for Radiotelegraphy

'So that bastard was trying to warn her,' Thring said to the secretary. 'Give me a look at the messages.'

The secretary handed him another piece of paper.

7.23 pm: Hobart. *Nine words transmitted. In code. Coordinates: 41°26' 131°50'.*
7.50 pm: Seydlitz *to* Hobart. *What is your reckoning and course.*
8.10 pm: Seydlitz *to* Hobart. *What is your reckoning and course.*

Thanks to the jamming, SS *Hobart* had not answered.

'Put me through to the district naval officer in Melbourne,' Thring said to the operator after grabbing the phone.

'Listen closely,' Thring said when Captain Richardson, the district naval officer, answered. 'We have some intelligence that suggests an enemy vessel will soon attempt to dock in Port Melbourne. You will arrange to meet her.'

Thring briefly told Richardson about the code. 'We need to retrieve it at all costs,' he said. 'They may attempt to destroy it and will certainly at least hide it. You can't give them a chance. You will need the element of surprise.'

Port Phillip Bay, 10 August 1914

Captain Richardson issued an extraordinary order on the eve of the expected arrival of SS *Hobart* in Port Phillip.

'Remove any indications of war,' he instructed.

In an all-out attempt to make sure the enemy ship was seized in Melbourne, Richardson ordered the naval Examination Service to suspend patrols and the Port Phillip Fixed Defences to stand down. The guns would be unmanned and the ships would remain unsearched, Melbourne left wide open.

'Proceed as if a peacetime footing exists,' Richardson instructed both the Examination Service and the gunnery command. 'There is to be no indication of war.'

Port Phillip Bay, 11 August 1914

Stanley Veale arrived at the inner examination anchorage at sun-up. The Examination Service lieutenant was still buzzing from the role he'd played in firing the first shot of the war. His family and friends had greeted him as a hero when they'd learned he had been the one to order the shot that stopped SS

Pfalz. The German ship, the gunnery crew, the sea pilot and the navy reserves had all been front-page news.

Veale finally felt like a man. He'd been tested – and he'd passed. The doubt and guilt he'd felt before his decision to order fire on *Pfalz* was long gone. He was ready for war. In fact, he was already making plans to volunteer for service in Europe.

As the sun finally climbed the cliff that hosted the now world-famous gun, Veale was headed for the dock, hoping for another day of action.

Alvina was fast asleep.

'What's going on?' Veale asked Dorgan, the signalman smoking a cigarette on the dock. 'Where is everyone? Why aren't we set to steam?'

Dorgan dragged on his cigarette, the generous serving of tobacco threatening to tear the tissue-thin paper after its rushed roll. 'Haven't you heard?' he replied, exhaling smoke. 'The war is over.'

'What are you talking about?' Veale asked. 'Don't be ridiculous. I went into town last night and got the volunteer forms. I'm going to Europe.'

Dorgan flicked what was left of his cigarette, the force from his fingers finally setting the glutinous ball of tobacco free. 'Well, it's on hold then,' he said. 'Captain Richardson has put us on a peacetime footing. We were ordered to remove all indications of war. We are going to be sitting here until further notice.'

'What?' Veale asked. 'Did he say why?'

Dorgan walked to the still smouldering tobacco and kicked

it off the edge of the dock. 'Nup,' he replied, pulling out his tobacco pouch.

The signalman sat down on the dock and went back to rolling. It was late afternoon and his pouch was empty when Veale pointed out a vessel on the approach.

The torpedo gunboat *Countess of Hopetoun* was following the rippling path made by the setting sun as it neared the dock.

'Who are they?' Veale asked, pointing to the crew, six men wearing civvies, one of them dropping anchor after the torpedo boat pulled up.

'Look like civilian pilots,' Dorgan said.

'What the hell is going on?'

Anchor thrown, the plain-clothed pilots completed the shutdown and Captain John Richardson walked off the bridge.

'I didn't think celebrities had to work,' Richardson said when he spotted Veale. 'What are you doing sloshing about with the likes of us, Veale?'

The lieutenant's face turned red. 'Well, I thought I was coming to work,' Veale said. 'But I've been sitting on my bum all day.'

Richardson was suddenly serious. He called out five other names before adding, 'And you too, Veale. Get yourself over here.' He turned and marched the six navy reserves and six civilian sea pilots towards *Alvina*. 'Remove your clothes,' he ordered. 'Right down to your underwear.'

The men glanced at each other and laughed.

'Yeah, good one, captain,' said a pilot.

'You're a hoot,' said another.

Richardson wasn't joking. 'Now,' he said. 'That's an order.'

Within a couple of minutes the twelve men were standing on the inner examination dock wearing nothing but their underpants, nervously wondering if the captain had gone mad.

Richardson looked at the six men from the Examination Service as they shivered in the icy wind.

'You're swapping clothes, so grab whatever will fit,' he said, pointing towards the pile of discarded clothes. 'Go on. Before you freeze.'

The men slowly dug through the clothes, looking at each other questioningly.

'As you know, orders were issued overnight for all indications of war to be removed,' Richardson said before turning to Veale. 'And that's why you have spent the day sitting on your bum.' He looked around again as the men slowly put on whatever they could find that fitted. 'Well, the order was issued because we have intelligence that suggests an enemy ship, unaware that war has been declared, will steam into Melbourne today. SS *Hobart*, a German steamer, announced her impending arrival to a station in Western Australia on Friday. We think she is heading here.'

Richardson smiled tightly at his men, some wearing oversized jackets, others being strangled by tight pants.

'And it gets better,' he went on. '*Hobart* is suspected to be carrying codebooks that could prove vital in the war. They will try to destroy them if they suspect anything, so we are going to approach the vessel in disguise. We will announce ourselves as customs officers.'

Richardson stressed the importance of the mission, talking

of duty, King and country. When he finally finished he ordered his motley crew to board *Alvina*.

'Half speed ahead,' the captain ordered.

They dropped anchor before they reached the heads. 'Now we wait,' Richardson said.

They didn't have to wait long: SS *Hobart* steamed into Port Phillip Bay just after sunset.

'All hands on deck!' came the cry. 'She's here. It's SS *Hobart*!'

'Let's get her!' said Veale.

Observatory Point, 11 August 1914

Captain Richardson set course for SS *Hobart*, which had stopped suddenly just inside Port Phillip Bay. An anchor had been thrown out.

Why had they anchored? Why had they stopped? He was answered with a thousand-watt flash to the face.

Fort Nepean was operating a searchlight. With the sun now set, the beam cut a hole through the dark – back and forth, right and left, up and down. SS *Hobart* had anchored just out of range. Like frightened prey, the ship was seemingly motionless, watching and waiting while she considered her next move.

'Flaming fools,' Richardson said of the gunnery crew, operating the light in spite of his order to return to a temporary peacetime footing.

Richardson was a class operator. Commissioned into the Victorian navy as a sublieutenant in 1888, he had shot to the rank of lieutenant just ten months later and became a specialist in gunnery and torpedoes. He was promoted to naval commander of the Victorian navy in 1901 and then captain when he moved north to command the Queensland naval force.

Now back in Victoria, the fifty-two-year-old District Navy Officer gritted his teeth as he powered his steamer into the dark, a man on a mission. The searchlight had made his job more complicated. Sure, the light had stopped the ship and he didn't have to chase it down and order it to stop. But SS *Hobart* might suspect that war had been declared. She might turn and flee. She might even fire upon them.

There was no visible movement on *Hobart* as they approached, the ageing workhorse seemingly a lesser threat than the searchlight.

'This is it,' Richardson said. 'This is our only shot. We have to convince them that nothing is out of the ordinary and we have to do it now. All hands on deck. Everyone into position.'

Richardson produced a .455-calibre Webley Mark IV revolver. With a flick of his wrist he snapped the bullet chamber open and counted the six bullets already loaded. With another flick he was locked and ready.

Still wearing his naval uniform, Richardson took off his military jacket and replaced it with a civilian trench coat, concealing the gun in a holster attached to the back of his belt.

The boat edged closer to *Hobart*.

'What about the brass?' Veale asked, pointing to gold braid on the peak of the captain's navy cap.

'Shit,' Richardson said. 'Thanks.'

He snatched the offending item from his head and replaced the ostentatious navy piece with a slouching cloth cap then rang the steamer to quarter speed. 'This is it, lads,' he said.

The captain grabbed the microphone connected to the steamer's loudspeaker. It was showtime.

'SS *Hobart*,' Richardson said, his voice booming across the bay. 'I am captain of customs and excise ship SS *Alvina*. You are now in the port state jurisdiction of the Melbourne Customs and Excise Office. We are conducting customs controls and would like permission to inspect your cargo prior to docking at Port Melbourne.'

Hobart remained silent and still.

'I repeat,' Richardson continued, 'this is Customs and Excise. Do we have permission to board the ship?' He looked back towards the cliffs, where the spotlight was still searching. He was expecting *Hobart* to reply by way of jamming the engine into gear and steaming towards the rising moon.

'Permission granted,' came a reply, the voice most definitely German.

'Well, I'll be,' Richardson muttered. 'Who would have thought?'

The captain laid out the next part of his plan as he, Veale and the five other disguised Examination Service officers rowed a wooden transport boat towards the side of *Hobart*.

A rope appeared seemingly from nowhere, the thrower above them obscured by glare.

'Don't say a thing,' Richardson said. 'Follow my lead.'

One by one, the men climbed up and rolled over the railing before finding their feet. Richardson did not utter a word until all his men were standing on the deck in front of a ragtag group of German sailors.

'Can you take me to your captain?' Richardson asked.

A short, sun-worn sailor stepped forward. '*Ja*,' he said. 'Follow me.'

The captain of SS *Hobart* met Richardson and his posse at the entrance to the bridge. Young for a steamship captain at around forty, Richardson guessed, the German was freshly shaved and neatly groomed.

'I am the captain of this vessel,' the German said after Richardson asked the man to identify himself. 'My name is Jürgen Paulsen.'

That was all Richardson needed to hear. His right hand disappeared behind him and returned with a revolver.

'Don't move,' Richardson warned. With his left hand – his right firmly aiming the loaded pistol at Paulsen's head – he parted his coat to reveal his navy stripes. 'I am Captain Richardson of the Royal Australian Navy and I am placing you and your crew under arrest. You are now a prisoner of war.'

Jürgen hadn't moved since he saw the gun. 'War?' he echoed.

Richardson nodded.

'*Scheisse*,' Paulsen cursed.

Richardson commandeered *Hobart*'s radio and ordered an armed guard of navy reserves placed on standby earlier to board the ship. The Australian kept his revolver pointed at the captain until they arrived, twenty Royal Australian Naval Reserves, all carrying guns.

Richardson moved on to the next part of his mission: he had seized and now it was time to search. The military veteran divided his men into teams and gave them each a section of the ship to scour.

'Nothing is to be overlooked,' Richardson said. 'Look under, over and inside every object in the ship. Every document you find is to be confiscated. I don't care what you think it is, bring it to me.'

Richardson teamed up with Veale. 'We will start with the bridge,' Richardson said.

'What shall we do with this one?' one of the armed guards asked, indicating Captain Paulsen. 'Want us to take him to his quarters?'

'No,' Richardson ordered. 'He stays on the bridge.'

Richardson watched the captain as he searched the bridge, looking for a change of expression to tell him he was close. For a frown or a wince, a snarl or a clenched fist, a reaction to let him know he was about to find something that should remain unfound.

But Paulsen's face remained an unwavering mask.

'Remove the captain,' Richardson ordered the armed guard. 'Escort him to the deck and wait for further command.'

Cabin clear, Paulsen out of earshot, Richardson slammed down a pile of papers. 'Nothing but logs, maps and proceedings,' he said. 'There are no codes. No keys. This has all been for nothing.'

'Maybe the others have come up with something,' Veale said. 'Something that important, well, maybe the captain keeps it in his quarters?'

Richardson turned and pulled open the door. 'Take me to your quarters,' he demanded of the German captain on the deck.

'Of course,' Paulsen replied mildly.

Richardson, Veale and the armed guard followed the captain into the belly of the ship.

'Here,' said Paulsen. 'My quarters.'

'After you,' Richardson said.

The German captain stood at the entrance to the room as Richardson tore up his box-like, metal-walled room, throwing his meagre and neatly packed possessions to the floor. But the search turned up nothing: no codes, nothing that could help win a war. It was Paulsen's reaction as Richardson ripped his way through the room that was more revealing: frowns, winces and snarls. Richardson even caught sight of a tightly clenched fist.

Yes, Richardson knew the codes were close; he just didn't know how to find them.

But, as always, the captain had a plan.

* * *

Richardson returned to the captain's quarters shortly after telling Paulsen that he was finished and returning to Melbourne on *Alvina* and that a small force of armed men would remain on *Hobart* until the authorities determined his fate.

'It could take a while,' Richardson said. 'In the meantime, you are free to do anything other than leave. A pilot will take this vessel to Hobsons Bay and you are to remain on board with your crew until we sort this out.'

Richardson then left empty-handed – or so Paulsen thought.

Instead of taking a left, the Australian captain took a right.

With a guard keeping Paulsen on the bridge – the burly brute suggesting he help the pilot guide *Hobart* into Hobsons Bay – and other guards keeping the crew in their quarters, Richardson darted through a doorway. By the time Veale and the other Examination Service crew had made their descent to *Alvina* and started steaming for home, he was back in the captain's quarters.

Richardson turned on the light and examined the room. He observed the mess he'd made during his frenzied search earlier. But he was now searching for a place to hide. He walked over to the bunk and dropped a knee to look under the German's bed.

'That'll do,' he muttered.

Richardson got down on the ground and shuffled under the bed after turning off the light. He shifted himself further in and hoped he was out of sight as he lay on the cold metal floor, the revolver in his right hand and a torch in his left.

Minutes turned into hours. His eyelids grew heavy, but he refused to fall asleep. He stared into the dark. Then came a noise, a door opening. Then another, the click of a light. Richardson squinted as the dark disappeared, the artificial light blinding him as if it was a full-frontal blast from the sun. He quickly adjusted his sight and focused. He then saw shiny shoes shuffling across the cold hard floor. He was certain they belonged to Captain Paulsen.

Richardson's arms and legs had gone numb and his hands were frozen around torch and gun. He watched the feet shuffle to the other end of the room. He noted they were facing the other way, heels closest to him, so he bravely stuck his neck out and dared a peek.

Paulsen. Knew it!

He watched on as Paulsen pondered the mess. The German started walking towards his desk.

This is it! He's going for it.

Richardson readied himself to roll and spring into action. But the captain didn't go for the code. He turned.

Oh no!

Richardson darted back into the darkness. He pulled his neck back and pulled his body into a ball. He was certain he had been spotted. But Paulsen said nothing. There was no 'Hey you!' or 'What are you doing?' Eyes now shut, he only heard the footsteps that were closing in. He held his breath.

Thump!

Richardson flinched as the captain crashed onto the mattress. The underside sank to just inches from his face. He clenched his fists and turned his already stiff and sore body into a plank.

The German now seemed to be wrestling his pillow and kicking his sheets. Richardson considered giving up. *Maybe there are no codes? Surely he would have gone for them by now.* But he stayed still and in place, his muscles screaming to move.

The German turned and grunted before finally settling, and Richardson too tried to relax. He must have dozed for half an hour or so then startled when a foot hit the floor, the other following fast. Richardson's grip on his gun tightened as Paulsen stepped away from the bed and towards the adjacent wall.

Click!

He cocked his gun, rolled forward a little and saw the German slide back a section of fake wall to reveal a secret safe.

'Halt,' Richardson shouted as he got to his feet. 'Stop right there.'

Paulsen turned and saw the gun pointed towards his face.

'What have you got in there?' Richardson asked, stamping his feet to try to regain some circulation as the German captain surveyed him with surprise and dismay.

* * *

Richardson departed SS *Hobart* clutching a stack of secrets. Among the logs, letters and routes stored in the hidden safe were a two-part German codebook and another book containing the key to the code.

He triumphantly wrote of his find when he returned to shore.

ATTENTION Navy Office, Melbourne.
1. Forwarded herewith the codebook, etc., found on the German SS Hobart *this morning.*
2. As notified by telephone message of yesterday, the captain of the ship first of all denied the existence of the code. This code was however found this morning.
3. I have instructed the customs officer who relieved me of the ship to make a further search of all papers and documents, and report further at a later date.
Captain Richardson.

Chapter 4

THE CODE CRACKER

Melbourne, 12 August 1914

Knock! Knock!

Thring was making notes on an intelligence report when he was interrupted.

'Not now,' he said, using his free hand to wave away the intruder in the doorway.

'Excuse me, captain,' a voice said. 'You wanted to see me.'

Thring threw his pen down and looked up. 'Oh, Richardson,' he said. 'Sorry, I didn't realise it was you.'

Thring already had Richardson's haul sitting on his desk: bound books, paper stacks and foolscap folders.

Richardson hobbled in and sat down on the other side of the desk. 'Sorry,' he said in response to Thring's raised eyebrows. 'I'm a bit stiff. Rough old night sleeping under a bed instead of on top of one.'

'So, what did we get?' Richardson asked, tapping the pile. 'Anything good?'

'Not quite sure yet,' Thring said. 'It's all in German. But I reckon it's something.'

There was another knock at the door and a naval officer with a grasp of German joined them to loosely translate the seized material, which included documents entitled 'Instructions to Shipping as to Their Conduct in a Naval War' and 'The Secret Appendix', as well as charts of South American waters. Eventually the officer paused as he held up two thick books in his hands.

'It's the *Handelsverkehrsbuch*,' said the interpreter, looking up. 'The codebook the German navy uses to communicate.'

Thring knew exactly what it was. The *HVB*, as it was known, was one of three German codes that the Royal Navy was desperate to get its hands on. A code that, if deciphered, could bring down the German fleet. A code that could win the war.

Originally issued in 1913 to all German warships with wireless radio capabilities, naval commands, coastal stations and merchant steamship companies, the *HVB* used 456,976 possible five-letter groups to allow for alternative representations of the same meaning. The book also contained an appendix that featured a silhouette of all the German and enemy warships.

The code was mostly used for communications between the German navy and zeppelins, small ships and merchant ships. The other two codes used by the navy were the *Signalbuch der Kaiserlichen Marine* (*SKM*) and the *Verkehrsbuch* (*VB*).

'Now, tell me exactly what happened,' Thring said after dismissing the interpreter. 'How you found them and where.'

The captain scribbled notes as Richardson recounted his tale of hiding out and the hidden safe.

'Remarkable,' Thring said. 'You have gone above and beyond, Richardson.'

Thring shook the captain's hand, patted him on the back and showed him out the door. Richardson's work was done; Thring's had just begun.

Eager to impress the establishment that had shunned him, the captain's first priority was to tell the Royal Navy of his war-changing find.

'A copy of the *HVB* code has been seized from SS *Hobart*,' Thring wrote before handing his message over to be typed, encrypted in a secure code used by both the Australian and British navies, and finally telegraphed. 'The RAN is in possession of both volumes of the *HVB* and the book that contains the corresponding key.'

Thring further detailed the find and requested instructions to proceed. He also provided details of signals that had been intercepted by stations in the Coral Sea and suspected movements of the menace that was the East Asia Squadron, the German Pacific fleet.

Thring wasn't content with capturing just one code. Hellbent on both redemption and revenge, the former Royal Navy highflyer wanted the *SKM* and the *VB* too.

'Board each incoming German merchant vessel earliest possible moment in plain clothes, suggest as a medical officer with a few men with pistols concealed on them who should understand German,' he wrote in the order that was sent to all district naval officers. 'Keep the chief officer and the captain on the bridge and muster on deck. Allow no one into the captain's cabin and officers' quarters at once and seize and dismantle wireless telegraphy. Transfer crew and officers to another ship as soon as possible and make the most thorough search for secret books and documents, stripping cabins and furniture if necessary.'

Thring conferred with Creswell after issuing his order, which used Richardson's sneaky work as a blueprint.

'We can't rely on the Admiralty,' Thring said. 'It will take at least forty days to ship the code and the key to London.'

'Longer,' Creswell said. 'We will have to bring a ship back before we send it.'

The *HVB* was both too big and too complicated to be encrypted and sent by telegraph. There was also a high risk of having any telegraph message intercepted.

'We need to start using it now,' Creswell went on, thinking of the pile of gibberish already sitting in his office – intercepted messages that could not be read. 'Who knows what we have already missed? Let's get to it. Do you have a plan to proceed?'

Thring thought on his feet. 'We will need a cryptologist,' he said, no rookie when it came to intelligence. 'Someone who can use the key to decrypt code.'

Creswell nodded. 'Got anyone in mind?'

Thring frowned, realising he needed more than just a code breaker. 'We also have the issue of language. They will have to be fluent in German.'

So now they needed not only a genius mathematician with an expertise in code but also one who could read, write and speak the language of the enemy.

'No Germans,' Creswell said. 'I don't care how long they have called themselves Australian, we can't trust a German.'

Creswell turned his attention to one of the other documents included in Richardson's haul, a set of instructions issued by the Union of Hamburg Shipowners that advised merchant ships to set steam for Punta Arenas in Southern Chile and await further instructions in the event of a naval war.

'This intrigues me,' Creswell said, jamming his finger at the rough translation sitting on his desk. 'The merchant ships have been directed to await further orders. This could be where the German squadron is heading, part of a plan to refit the merchant ships and turn them into war cruisers. This could be our chance to destroy von Spee. I'm going to alert the Royal Navy,' he said.

Thring nodded and turned towards the door.

'Try the instructor,' Creswell said.

Thring swung back to the vice admiral at his desk. 'Excuse me, sir?'

'At the naval college,' Creswell said. 'Wheatley, his name is.'

'In regards to?' Thring asked, still completely in the dark.

'The code,' Creswell said. 'He's a genius. Set up the naval college in Geelong. I seem to recall him mentioning something about an interest in code, some sort of scientist. A mathematician maybe?' Creswell took a moment, shuffling a pile of papers as he thought. 'And I think he speaks German,' he said. 'He spent some time over there.'

'I'll bring him in.' Thring went straight back to his own desk and picked up the telephone. 'Put me through to the Royal Australian Naval College, please,' he said to the operator. 'Yes, Geelong.'

Geelong, Victoria, 13 August 1914

Frederick William Wheatley was scratching away, chalk in hand, numerals, letters and symbols appearing on the blackboard at breakneck speed, when he was interrupted by the administration lady.

'I expect answers when I get back,' Wheatley said, pointing at the white scrawl that could have been anything from hieroglyphs to a train timetable to the uninformed, a couple of his students included. 'Not a word out of anyone while I am gone.'

Born in South Australia, as a teenager Wheatley had risen to the rank of captain in a scout-style organisation called the Senior Cadets, where he'd demonstrated a love of both maths and the military and dabbled with codes. He'd subsequently gained a strong reputation as an educator following stints at Prince Alfred College in Adelaide, King's College in Goulburn and then as headmaster at Rockhampton Grammar School. This combination of early military training and success in education made Wheatley an appealing candidate when the Royal Australian Navy began setting up its own training establishments and looking for people to run them.

In 1910, after travelling to Australia from London to advise the freshly formed Federation on naval infrastructure and development, Admiral Sir Reginald Henderson had personally made the trip to Rockhampton with William Creswell, then director of Commonwealth Naval Services, to try to recruit Wheatley. Henderson and Creswell had told Wheatley of the plan to establish a Royal Australian Naval College where over a hundred cadets would be educated at a time. 'You are the sort of man we should have as headmaster,' Creswell had said. 'I will let you know when things develop.'

Wheatley had been disappointed when he was overlooked for the headmaster's role after being invited to Melbourne for an official interview in 1911. In the end, the job had gone to a gifted mathematician from London University named Frederick Brown, on the recommendation of his friend Senator George Pearce.

Wheatley had rashly resigned from Rockhampton Grammar School in anticipation of the role, a row between his wife and another staff member, which included an allegation of a slap, expediting his departure. Having already returned to South Australia with his wife and two young daughters, Wheatley had initially been at a loss when told he would not be the first headmaster of the naval college, but he soon came up with another plan.

'Oh, well,' he told his wife. 'This gives me time to further my knowledge. Fancy a trip to England?' Wheatley had decided to pursue his interest in the ionisation of gases through studies at Lincoln College, Oxford. But just before he and his wife set off for England, Wheatley was summoned to Melbourne by Creswell. He caught the overnight train from Adelaide following the surprise call.

'Things are unsatisfactory with Brown,' Creswell had said. 'We need you for this. Will you please consider taking a position at the college following your studies in Oxford?'

Wheatley agreed and managed to draft the academic syllabus and college regulations for the soon to be opened establishment before leaving for England.

After earning a Bachelor of Science from Lincoln College, Wheatley returned to the naval college as the senior instructor of mathematics and science, joining the college full-time in 1914. He had included a course on code in the syllabus, being aware that military intelligence was a growing business.

While in Europe he had also travelled Germany, and that's why he found himself now sitting in Captain Thring's office after taking his call and almost immediately making the two-hour trip to Melbourne from Geelong.

* * *

'I was conducting research work in physics at Oxford last year,' Wheatley told Thring when the captain asked about his trip to Germany. 'I was invited to Germany to confer with a professor about the work in which I was engaged.' Wheatley paused for a moment. 'Did you hear about my experience with the German army?'

Thring shook his head. 'Go on,' he said, intrigued.

'I met the Crown Prince, Admiral von Tirpitz and General von Hindenburg,' Wheatley said. 'All the bigwigs.'

'You don't say?' Thring replied. 'Remarkable.'

'Oh yes,' Wheatley said. 'The professor was called up to attend army manoeuvres while I was staying at his house. He asked me if I would like to go along with him. Of course, it wasn't that simple unfortunately, given that I was a foreign national. He had to obtain consent, which I thought would be a problem, but it was no bother at all. Turns out the professor was a personal friend of the Kaiser.'

'Kaiser Wilhelm?' Thring asked.

Wheatley couldn't tell if the captain was impressed or disbelieving. 'Yes,' he said. 'He called him personally to make sure I was approved for the trip. Anyway, I travelled through the Black Forest with the German army for a month.'

Wheatley watched for a reaction. There wasn't one.

'So that's where you learned to speak German?' Thring asked.

Wheatley shook his head. 'No,' he said. 'I studied German in school and university. But that trip to Germany certainly improved my language skills. I was able to have several lengthy conversations with the Crown Prince, Admiral von Tirpitz and General von Hindenburg in the month that I accompanied them.'

Thring looked at Wheatley thoughtfully for a moment before rising and leaning over his desk.

'So what's this all about?' Wheatley asked. 'Am I to write a German syllabus? I'd rather stick to maths and science if it's all the same.'

Thring picked up a leatherbound book and handed it to Wheatley. 'I have been told that you are familiar with code,' Thring said.

Wheatley examined the cover. 'This is the German *HVB*,'

he said, 'a cipher the Imperial Navy uses for all communications with its merchant fleet. Extraordinary.'

Thring smiled. 'I take it that is a yes?' he responded.

Wheatley laughed. 'May I?' he asked, his eyes directed towards the book.

'By all means,' Thring said. 'Take your time.'

Wheatley spent the next twenty minutes thumbing his way through the book, oblivious to everything except the letters, numbers and diagrams printed on each page.

Eventually Thring could contain his impatience no more. 'What do you think?' he asked. 'Can you use it to decipher encrypted messages?'

'As long as they are messages that have been encrypted using the *Handelsverkehrsbuch*,' Wheatley said with confidence, before pointing to another of the books on Thring's desk. 'And if that is the current version of the key it should all be quite straightforward.'

The captain finally smiled.

'You will be required to produce translated copies of the books and send them to Britain,' Thring said. 'But given the time it will take to prepare and then ship them, I would also like you to decode messages at the same time. We could be sitting on something of vital importance.'

And with that Wheatley became an intelligence officer for the Royal Australian Navy, a military cryptographer and Australia's chief code breaker.

He was handed the book, the key and a stack of intercepted nonsense. He would get cracking while his superiors waited on orders from London.

Melbourne, 13 August 1914

Wheatley attacked the instruction book first, the book that contained the key to the code. He would attempt to wrap his mind around the decoding process while translating the book for the copies he was required to make.

'Everyone will be able to decode the messages once you translate the instructions,' Thring had told him. 'Then you'll be able to resume your duties at the naval college.'

Wheatley pulled out a fresh notebook and a pen. 'Object of the Code Book,' his translation began. 'Codebook (*HVB*) is used for sending out secret wireless or telegraphic messages as well as secret flagging and more signals in peace and war. Its frequent use is strongly desired not only for the intercourse of merchant ships with warships but also for merchant ships with one another and with their owners for business telegrams, so that the passages met with in the handling of the codebook are attached with the necessary proficiency.

'The *HVB* is given out to all German warships and torpedo boats fitted with wireless telegraphy, staff of the Admiralty in Berlin, owners, agents and all ships of these owners fitted with wireless telegraphy, and all training ships.'

Wheatley paused. Self-explanatory. Straightforward.

'Classifications or Divisions of the Codebook,' Wheatley wrote, continuing to translate. 'The codebook contains in its several pages, arranged alphabetically, letters, syllables, numbers, names, words, joined words and sentences. The codewords printed in the column "KABEL" are ten-letter pronounceable words which in international telegraph communication underlie the reading of prearranged speech. Every codeword consists of a five-letter root and suffix. Read list one for the rules according to which the codewords are arranged and for guidance for deciphering mutilated codewords.

'The communication groups are arranged alphabetically, they differ from one another at least in one letter, no letter appears twice in any one group. For the use of codewords or communication groups, see Part A.'

Wheatley chuckled, remembering the captain's words. 'Everyone will be able to decode them?' he mused, speaking to no one but himself. 'Everyone? Ha.' He now knew he wasn't returning to the college anytime soon.

'Part A,' he continued to write. 'Pages v to xi contain instructions for communication according to the merchant ships codebook. Part B. Pages xiii to xxi and 1 to 26 contain lists of statements that are self-contained. Part C. Pages 27 to 117 contain geographical names, proper names, letters and syllables for spelling. By the help of these letters and syllables, proper names can be expressed.'

Wheatley sighed, the reading proving tiresome and tough. He continued to plough through the document, the document proving confusing for even an expert. He pondered some of the instruction for thirty minutes, looking for sense.

Wheatley kept on going, writing the explanations and examples. He knew it would be gibberish to most.

Wheatley now thought he would never be returning to teaching.

'Examples of Telegrams,' Wheatley translated. 'The steamer on the voyage to Hong Kong wishes to send the following news to the chief of the squadron, whose flagship lies in Tsingtao harbour and who cannot be reached by direct wireless communication through the coast wireless station. "16 July, 10 am, I met in the Straits of Formosa 4 English armoured cruisers steering northwards with great haste. Among them was the *Invincible*."

'The signals will be: password – HAVAN. For admiral – HANIB UNYRU. 16 July – MICEE XUFOL. 10 am – RYOFO IHAVE. Have met – HEXUL AGEBI. Straits of Formosa – DICOK EVOCA. 4 – HANIB OVUPY. English armoured cruisers – BEHAK IPOHE. With great haste – LAXIP EZATE. Of the invincible type – BEHAK IPYSA.'

Clear as mud.

He finished the handwritten translation of the entire key before taking a deep breath. 'Here goes nothing,' he said.

He wasn't filled with confidence following the pages and pages of complicated instructions, but he would now attempt to crack a code.

Wheatley took the first paper from the stack sitting on his new desk.

'HDGEG FPWDH,' he read. 'EKFGH HDBOA, LKJDL KPNDA.'

What could it mean? Was it a secret direction from a warship? Did it reveal the location of von Spee's Pacific fleet?

He grabbed the hefty codebook and attempted to find out. Papers strewn across the table, ink-covered scraps of confetti on the hardwood floor, Wheatley had his answer six hours later. It was a message about a storm. A merchant ship warning another merchant ship of high seas, lightning, and the possibility of a squall. There was no mention of a location, not that the Royal Australian Navy would have been particularly interested in hunting down a cargo ship even if there was.

Wheatley looked at the pile in front of him, each page covered in alphabet soup, and let out a sigh. Late afternoon had long passed into evening and it was now night. The futuristic metal lamp on his desktop, sleek metal and saucer-like, was blazing.

'And that's just one message,' he muttered.

The *HVB* code was much more complicated than he had first thought, and certainly more time-consuming to break than he'd anticipated.

The codebook he had was essentially a dictionary of words. The words were each assigned a ten-letter code in two groups of five. Without the key, the message looked like nonsense: VOFSF CDPGU. But even with the code, extracting their meaning was no easy feat.

A one-part code was the most widely used and convenient form of decryption, and compiling a codebook for one was also relatively simple. Jumbled words are assigned to real words, usually in some sort of order. Extracting sense from gibberish was also straightforward for a mathematically inclined mind, a matter of searching for the codeword and matching it with a real word.

Unfortunately for Wheatley, the *HVB* was a two-part code. Far more secure, and far more difficult to crack, there were two books instead of one. Instead of revealing the true meaning of the jumbled word in the first book, a number was listed alongside the entry. That's where the second book came in.

After trawling through almost uncountable combinations of letters to find a match to the code in a message, Wheatley found a ten-digit number instead of a word. He then had to take that number and search through all the ten-digit combinations in the second book until the code he had started with became a word, a phrase, the name of a place, a ship or a position on a map.

But he knew it would get easier. Common words and phrases would often be repeated. He would soon become familiar with recurring five-letter groups that would be code for frequently used words. His knowledge of German would also help him find patterns and speed up the process. Knowing the peculiarities of the language, like the fact that verbs usually come at the end of a sentence in German, he could make educated guesses before starting his search. For example, if he was attempting to decipher a word that came before a full stop, he could search the corresponding verbs in his key.

But it would all take time, practice and most of all experience; for now it was tiresome and tedious.

He picked up the next message: HASDH RANSD, KPMAD INSDF. Almost four hours later he had more useless information, this nothing more than banter between a couple of bored cargo-ship captains. Wheatley had skipped dinner for this. He had sat at his desk scouring the pages of the *HVB* and making notes without even taking a bathroom break. And for what? To learn life can sometimes get dull on the high seas, even during a war.

He looked at the paper on top of the stack: KDLFA UYPLE, HSDFE MLPQA, JQPXM POPUI, ASLHJ WTRYD, LPOPQ AAAPO, GDHSH OOYTY, ALPQC NNMMB, XCGDT PLQWP, GFHJK LCJFD, DSYFO NCBYS, LSJDD PASDF, FFDHO GHGEP, JWIVN YTPFS, RSDOD, OFJSF, OMLJK CVGFD, QYTPP AAAAL.

The chair screeched across the hardwood floor and a few papers fell to the floor as Wheatley pushed away from the desk and stood. It was time to take a break.

Standing in the Navy Office kitchen, Wheatley chewed slowly on a ham sandwich as he daydreamed about finding a piece of information that could simultaneously help win the war and make him a hero. By the time he returned to his office he had again convinced himself that this laborious and mind-melting work had meaning. The prospect of finding a needle in this haystack would keep him going. He randomly grabbed another paper from the pile.

Throughout the night Wheatley continued with the same system, haphazardly plucking code then systematically searching for its meaning. He got faster with every decryption as he found patterns in both the keys and the codes. The translations were still trivial but by sun-up he had worked his way through the papers strewn across the floor.

And then he found something.

'*Scharnhorst* to proceed to the Mariana Islands,' the decryption read.

Again the instructor sent his chair screeching, but this time with excitement rather than exhaustion.

He found Thring asleep in his office.

'Sir,' he said as he gently prodded the exhausted man. 'Sir … Wake up, this could be important.'

Thring muttered some nonsense before coming to.

'Here,' Wheatley said, 'Take a look at this.' He handed Thring the decoded message.

Thring rubbed his eyes before reading the transcription, handwritten next to the *HVB* jumble. 'Could be,' Thring said, now fully awake. 'It could be very important.'

A crescent-shaped archipelago north of New Guinea and east of the Philippines, the Mariana Islands were an ideal place for the German fleet to meet and regroup. Sheltered and hidden there from the enemy, they could resupply, strategise and even launch an attack on Australia.

'This could be our chance,' Thring said.

Chapter 5

SEA DOGS

Simpson Harbour, German New Guinea, 11 August 1914

But HMAS *Australia* was by now almost at its original destination. On the evening of 11 August it steamed through darkness infinite.

'I can't see a damn thing,' complained Captain Stephen Radcliffe. 'It's pitch-black.'

Face illuminated by gauges, dials and buttons glowing green, orange and red, the rear admiral winked. 'Good,' Patey said. 'That means they can't see us.'

HMAS *Australia* barely made a wake. Locked on quarter speed, she crept through the rolling sea.

Radcliffe squinted. 'Nothing,' he said. 'Not a damned thing'.

Below the bridge, sailors lined the deck. They too looked into the dark. They saw only death.

'What are we doing?' asked a midshipman. 'This is suicide.'

Every swell that hit the bow was a mine. Every wave that crashed onto the deck was an explosive-laden shell.

Some imagined being trapped below as the ship was sinking. Drowning. Others looked into the dark and saw fire. Burnt to death.

Patey could see only victory. 'Full stop,' he ordered.

The ship was soon still and quiet.

'Drop anchor,' Patey commanded.

The clank of metal chain hitting hull shattered the silent night. The men on the deck winced as they imagined the noise as machine guns.

Patey waited for the fleet to assemble, watching first as HMAS *Sydney* slowed and then came to a stop. 'Good,' he said.

He nodded as HMAS *Yarra*, HMAS *Warrego* and HMAS *Parramatta*, all freshly painted as black as the night, fell into line.

'Good,' he said again. 'All set.'

It was time to destroy von Spee and his fleet. Nothing could match the might of HMAS *Australia*.

* * *

Rear Admiral George Edwin Patey had been with *Australia* since the very beginning. An English immigrant, like most of the navy brass, he had piloted the ship through Sydney Heads in 1913 for its historic launch. With Creswell by his side, Patey and the entire fledgling force of seven warships had been greeted by a crowd of 300,000 lining the shores and docks, climbing trees, cheering and waving flags, some even moved to tears.

'Since Captain Cook's arrival, no more memorable event has happened than the advent of the Australian fleet,' said Minister for Defence Edward Millen. 'As the former marked the birth of a nation, so the latter announces its coming of age.'

Patey had proudly ordered 'fire' that day, HMAS *Australia* unloading two rounds from her guns into the harbour. He was also the man honoured at a who's who of Australia dinner at the Town Hall that night.

Notes in one hand, weight shifting from his left foot to his right, Patey addressed the powerful crowd.

'I thank you very much for the kind words of welcome and encouragement which you have addressed to us this evening,' he said. 'And I thank you all for the manifest reception. I may as well tell you at once that I am no speaker, I am sorry. I understand that you expect your admiral to be able to talk, but if you will try to overlook this failing of mine, I, on my part, will promise to do my best in other ways, which, in the end may prove more useful to you.

'Our splendid reception in Sydney Harbour this morning, I understand, was something more than a personal welcome to myself and those under my command. I take it as a mark of the great importance which Australia attaches to the development of her new navy, and with that view I am completely in accord.

'No one entering Sydney Harbour for the first time, as I have done today, could fail to be impressed by its beauty and its great capabilities, and also with the warmth of your welcome, and I can well understand why it is that Sydney has always been regarded with so much affection in the navy.

'Now I can say that I have never looked forward to my appointment with quite so much interest and pleasure as I do to the command of His Majesty's Australian fleet. I believe the scheme worked out by Admiral Henderson for creating an Australian navy to be a sound one and well thought out, and I therefore enter into it wholeheartedly.'

* * *

That speech was a distant memory now and so was that day. Patey's next fire order would be issued to kill – not to entertain a crowd.

HMAS *Australia* had rendezvoused with the four other ships on 9 August in deep water south of New Guinea. From there Patey and *Australia* had led the way north to St Georges Channel in the Bismarck Archipelago. It was there he ordered an army of men to paint every inch of the three 246-foot destroyers black. But not before revealing his plan to his senior staff. 'All indications are pointing to the probability of the German ships *Scharnhorst*, *Gneisenau* and *Nürnberg* – and perhaps *Planet* – being in the neighbourhood of Simpson Harbour on the island of New Britain,' Patey said. 'Either there or at Matupi Harbour to the east.'

Patey and his intelligence staff had gone through all the wireless interceptions that had been sent to them from the Navy Office in Melbourne. Even as far back as 1 August when signals expert Balsillie had estimated *Scharnhorst* was 300 miles northeast of New Guinea, Patey had predicted von Spee and his gang were en route to the German station at Rabaul on the northeastern tip of the island of New Britain, headquarters of German New Guinea. 'It is the perfect base from which to mount an attack on Australia,' he said. 'Simpson Harbour has been built to supply coal to big ships. That's where they are going. And that's where we should meet them.'

Now, after a message received the day before, he was sure. 'The German squadron is estimated to be in latitude 8°S and longitude 162°E,' the signals report had said. Patey immediately tried to recall the light cruiser HMAS *Melbourne* but neither it nor HMAS *Encounter* would make it in time for an attack.

Patey continued explaining his plan, calling it 'Operation Order No. 1'. 'I intend to make an attack on those ports with the object of torpedoing any ships there and destroying the wireless station,' Patey had told his fleet, assembled at St Georges Channel. 'On arrival at our meeting point, *Sydney* will take charge of the destroyers and will proceed to Simpson Harbour at twenty knots. Should the enemy's heavy ships be met with force outside, the destroyers are to attack at once. Having reached the harbour entrance, *Sydney* will remain there in support. The destroyers will proceed into Simpson Harbour and attack any men-of-war found there. They will rejoin *Sydney* after delivering their attack.

'The main objective is the enemy's heavy ships. Should no men-of-war be found in either harbour, the destroyers are to land a party and destroy the wireless telegraph station reported to be at Rabaul.'

He'd told the fleet they would steam at fourteen knots in an easterly direction under complete wireless silence until they were ready to make their final approach for an attack at 9 pm.

'The sun will be down,' he said. 'But the moon not yet up. We will have eighty minutes of total darkness.'

* * *

That time had come and now, early on 11 August, they were anchored about three miles off Praed Point at the entry to Simpson Harbour, *Sydney* positioned to provide cover. Patey gave the signal and sent his blackened destroyers into the dark.

The crew of *Sydney* watched on as *Yarra* split from *Parramatta* and *Warrego* and bore north, heading solitary to find and destroy anything that happened to be docked in Matupi Harbour. Then they saw *Warrego* and *Parramatta* make straight for the western side of Simpson Harbour. Soon all that could be seen of the ships was the white wash they left in their wake. Then nothing, the dark all-devouring.

Yarra went sight unseen into Matupi Harbour, stealthily passing the wooded slopes that led to the Turaangua volcano. With three eighteen-inch torpedoes in tubes and one four-inch gun loaded, it was ready to unleash hell. But the fire call never came. The dark concealed only jungle.

'All clear,' said Stewart Keightley, lieutenant in command.

All forty-seven crew exhaled.

In Simpson Harbour, *Warrego* and *Parramatta* were just beginning their search. Chugging past the mangrove-choked shore, they headed towards the towering wooden wharves, six eighteen-inch torpedoes in tubes and two four-inch guns ready to create carnage.

Commander Claude Cumberlege saw a light. Brilliant and bright, it was now flashing.

'A lamp signal,' he said.

Fingers hovered over buttons as *Warrego* closed in, all on edge after spotting what they thought to be an enemy ship.

'Stand down,' Cumberlege said as he almost crashed *Warrego* into Rabaul wharf. 'It's a goddamn bushfire.'

He radioed HMAS *Sydney*.

'All clear,' he said.

'All clear,' followed William Warren, lieutenant in command of *Parramatta*.

A combined crew of ninety-five exhaled.

Anchored out at sea, Admiral Patey waited for the thunder that would never come. He shook his head as *Warrego* and *Parramatta* rejoined *Yarra*, torpedoes still in tubes. He sent all three destroyers to search nearby Talia Bay. They only found mangroves.

Pagan, Mariana Islands, 11 August 1914

'Speed is ten knots,' said the German gunnery lieutenant. 'Heading is sixty-two degrees. Distance to target is 5,500 yards.'

Von Spee stood on the stern of *Scharnhorst*, arms folded, watching on as the six-man gun crew went to work. Metal wheels and levers were pulled and pushed, turned and twisted.

'Fire!' yelled a sailor.

The twelve-yard metal shaft of the gun recoiled like a rocket in reverse as smoke gushed from the barrel. The crew didn't wait for a splash. With the shell still in the air travelling at 800 yards a second, they frantically prepared for the next round of fire.

'Fire!' the sailor ordered again, a fresh 550-pound shell shoved into the side-loading breech.

Von Spee remained expressionless as the two rounds missed the co-ordinates of their imaginary target – for this drill, an Australian torpedo boat.

'Raise elevation by two degrees,' the gunnery lieutenant said.

Metal wheels and levers were again adjusted.

'Fire,' came the order yet again.

Von Spee nodded after the new round landed dead on target, the imaginary Australian destroyer smashed to bits.

The German admiral had ordered the artillery practice as soon as *Scharnhorst* had arrived at Pagan, a volcanic island in the Mariana Islands archipelago.

'All hands on deck,' von Spee had commanded, sending the 788 enlisted men and fifty-two officers on board the flagship of the German East Asia cruiser squadron to their stations.

The natives on the island, harvesting coconuts for a German-owned company, dropped to the ground when the barrage of blasts began. All eight SKL/35 naval guns on board *Scharnhorst* – four in twin gun turrets at the centre of the deck, one twin on the fore of the ship and another twin on the aft – erupted at once. With an officer observing each gun and the artillery director watching all from high above, they unleashed shell after shell on the imaginary Australian fleet.

With the wash from the bombardment still lapping the shore, von Spee summoned the artillery director.

'Targets all destroyed,' he reported. 'The rate of accuracy was sixty-eight percent.'

Von Spee wasn't happy. 'Not good enough.' A former artillery officer specialising in heavy gunnery, von Spee demanded artillery excellence. 'We won't win the Kaiser's shooting prize again at that rate,' he said. 'We will practise again tomorrow, and every day after that until I am satisfied.'

The threat of HMAS *Australia* and her fleet had not only prompted a series of drills but also forced von Spee into a strategic rethink. Australia was no longer a poorly defended country with ports that could be taken easily. The Melbourne to Fremantle route could no longer be harried and then attacked. Even most of the resupplying ports mentioned in his war plans were a no-go, potential targets for the Australians to attack.

'The cohesion of the cruiser squadron, including the auxiliary cruisers, imposes a very difficult if not impossible demand on the supply of coal,' he wrote in his diary. 'Thus a division of the force must be considered through which the different trade routes can be threatened. The armoured cruisers should remain hidden as long as possible, so the enemy is constantly required to reckon with an encounter and accordingly detach a strong force. The seeking out of the enemy only comes into question when we are superior.'

And right now, he knew they were inferior, thanks to the news provided by his Sydney spy, so von Spee had ordered his fleet to regroup for a rethink, to rendezvous in Pagan, a coconut island in the middle of nowhere. He also called on all available colliers, supply ships and passenger liners.

Von Spee's fleet assembled off the coast of Pagan on 11 August, *Scharnhorst* arriving first, followed by the cruisers

SMS *Gneisenau* and then SMS *Nürnberg*, the latter back from San Francisco. A collier called *Titania* steamed in next and then two auxiliary cruisers, *Prinz Eitel Friedrich* and *Cormoran*.

Last to arrive was SMS *Emden*.

Simpson Harbour, German New Guinea, 12 August 1914

The dawn shed fresh light on the failure.

'All clear,' Captain Cumberlege radioed in, the destroyers having been sent back into Simpson Harbour for a daytime search.

There were no ships. No Germans. All that was to be found was a charred grove of palm trees, thanks to the fire he'd thought was a ship.

'Received,' Patey said. 'Move to stage two. Locate and destroy all enemy wireless stations. I repeat, locate and destroy all wireless stations.'

'Received,' Cumberlege replied.

Armed with binoculars and telescopes, a crew of sailors stood on the deck of *Warrego* studying every inch of the surrounding landscape. They scoured the area around the town of Rabaul first, a small settlement built behind the wharf. Established in 1884 as a German colony and the capital of German New Guinea, it encompassed a court, a post office, a hospital and a sprawling line of residences.

But there was no radio tower.

Next they studied the scrub-clad face of the volcano. They saw bougainvillea, grevillea and leatherleaf.

But they didn't see a tower.

'Come on, lads,' Cumberlege shouted. 'The thing should stick out like dogs' balls. It's a twenty-five-ton tower, not a needle in a haystack.'

'It's not here,' said a sailor, lowering his binoculars. 'It must be on the other side of the island.'

It wasn't.

They were back in Simpson Harbour after a two-hour cruise around New Britain, having examined every ridge, rise and crevice. They saw lizards and frogs, but no tower.

'Really,' Patey snapped when he saw them re-entering the harbour, 'what's going on?' He snatched up the radio and asked for a mission update.

'Sorry,' Cumberlege said, 'we can't locate the tower, sir. We are going to search the harbour again.'

'Negative,' Patey commanded. 'Send in a landing party.'

Cumberlege docked *Warrego* at Rabaul wharf at 9 am and his crew swapped their binoculars and telescopes for rifles and revolvers. They left the safety of the battleship and walked into the unknown.

'We are at war with these people,' Cumberlege said. 'Don't forget that Germany is now your enemy.'

There was no need to remind the men. They knew full well they could become the first Australian casualties of this fresh and frightening war.

But there wasn't a soul in sight.

Guns drawn and pointed, they walked towards the biggest and most official-looking building. The door was locked.

'This is the Royal Australian Navy,' Cumberlege shouted after knocking. 'Please open the door or we will be forced to break it down.'

A frail man, elderly and dressed in a suit, obliged. One hand already raised, he put the other in the air as soon as he opened the door.

'Please,' he said, 'we offer no threat.'

Cumberlege and the landing party were led to the most senior German official in the outpost colony. The man introduced himself, extending his hand. 'I am the district officer, Mr Tölke. What is it you want?'

Cumberlege asked him about the tower. Told him they wanted to know where the German wireless station was.

'Wireless station?' Tölke repeated. 'I know nothing about this. I am just an administrator on an island of farmers and merchants. How would I know what a wireless station looks like?'

'Because it is a twenty-five-ton tower,' Cumberlege said. 'About fifty-five yards high. I don't think you could miss it.'

'Well, why are you asking me then?' Tölke said.

Cumberlege stormed towards the official. 'Where is it?' he shouted. 'Do you want that big ship waiting in the harbour to level your town?'

'*Nein*,' Tölke said. 'But I can't help. There is nothing here of that description.'

Cumberlege kept pressing but got the same response – *nein*, *nein* and *nein*. He only stopped the inquisition after Tölke presented him with a handwritten affidavit.

'I state on my honour that there is (a) no wireless station within fifty miles of Rabaul,' he wrote, 'and (b) that there are no troops of any sort in Rabaul, and (c) that no resistance will be offered to any landing force.'

The rear admiral did not take the news well. 'No ships,' Patey yelled. 'And no wireless station. What in God's name is going on? What the hell am I doing here?'

Commander George Hyde was standing closest to Patey. 'Just following orders, sir,' he said.

With a clenched jaw and a filthy look, Patey told him he had asked a question that did not require an answer.

'Sir,' a sailor interrupted. 'You'd better take a look at this.' He passed Patey a note.

'Six enemy ships lying near Rabaul,' the translated note said. 'They are supposed to be about to destroy the wireless station or to bombard Rabaul and Herbertshöhe. Dare not send more.'

'It was sent from the station we believe to be in Rabaul, sir,' the sailor said before Patey could ask.

Patey's palm went crashing onto the table. He was tired of the games. He sent Cumberlege back to shore with a message for Mr Tölke, the district officer with all the *neins*.

'Tell him to give this to the governor,' Patey said. In the message Patey demanded all signals be stopped immediately. He also demanded to know where the wireless station was. And he threatened to fire on the settlements of Simpson Harbour if his demands were not met.

'To the admiral of the British warships now visiting Rabaul and the neighbourhood,' came the written reply. 'The administration of the town of Rabaul is in the hands of the undersigned as district officer. With reference to the letter handed to me for delivery to the governor, I have to state there is no wireless station in or near Rabaul. I am not in any position to exercise any influence on the management of the wireless station (wherever it may be) and in particular I am unable to prevent it functioning in the future.

'The threatened bombardment of the undefended town of Rabaul would be contrary to all international law. I have forwarded this letter to the governor and will let you know as soon as it arrives.'

Patey clenched his fists. 'This is a complete waste of time,' he said. 'We should be looking for von Spee, not some wireless station.'

The station could be on any one of the ninety-seven islands surrounding Rabaul. And the fleet was running as short of coal as Patey was of patience.

Tail between legs, the Australian Squadron steamed out of St Georges Channel at 4.30 pm.

Pagan, Mariana Islands, 12 August 1914

Von Spee had spent the previous two days meeting with commodores and captains. The enlisted men loaded supplies onto the ships, performed now daily artillery drills and slaughtered livestock, pigs and cows, which were then quartered before being thrown into freezers on the ship. Drinking local coffee on the shore, von Spee and his officers were going through transmissions, examining trade routes, studying maps, reviewing past plans and making predictions.

'It is no longer our objective to engage the enemy,' von Spee told his most senior men. 'It would mean the destruction of this fleet if we took on the Australian Squadron. *Australia* by itself is such a superior opponent.'

An officer shook his head in resignation.

'This frustrates me to no end too,' von Spee said. 'There is no glory in running away. But what contribution will we make to the Kaiser, to Germany, if the entire East Asia Squadron is destroyed in the first battle? No, we can't engage the enemy, but we can certainly disrupt the enemy. Our focus must now be on ultimately halting trade.'

With the tropical sun, white sand, clear water and coconuts, it was difficult to forecast gloom. But von Spee saw plenty of dark clouds and thunder coming his way.

'We are faced with many difficulties,' he continued. 'Avoiding the Australians is just one. Fuel is our biggest problem in the short term: where to get coal from.'

China was out, he said: the powerful Japanese were surely patrolling the Tsingtao Station now that the world was in a state of war.

San Francisco was out too, he said. What he'd thought would be a constant stream of coal appeared to have been cut off by the Americans, who were proving anything but neutral.

And German New Guinea was too risky, he said, as the Australian fleet would surely head to Rabaul.

Von Spee had spent the best part of two years setting up coal supply stations throughout the Pacific in anticipation of war. And in the space of a few days, and right when he needed them, his carefully planned and planted resources could not be harvested.

'Our plan to attack shipping in the Pacific will be reliant on German steamers providing us with coal from the Philippines and the Dutch Indies,' von Spee said. Coal could sporadically be obtained from remote anchorages, but not without risk and travel. 'But with support from our colonial bases, intelligence from our wireless stations and information from merchant ships, I think we can still conduct a cruiser mission in the Pacific.'

'What about Japan?' asked a commodore.

That was the million-dollar question. While he was confident that the expanse of the Pacific would hide him from HMAS *Australia* given enough fuel, he knew no ocean was big enough to conceal him from both the Australians and the Japanese.

The Imperial Japanese Navy was a fast-growing force with over a hundred ships, most notably two sister dreadnoughts, *Settsu* and *Kawachi*. Von Spee's fleet would not stand a chance against Japan and Australia.

'Admiralty are of the opinion Japan will remain neutral unless we attack a British territory in East Asia,' von Spee said. 'But intelligence received from our China Station suggests they are already moving on Tsingtao. An officer in Shanghai has reported that steamers have brought in Japanese reservists from Canton and Hong Kong for forwarding to Tsingtao.'

Von Spee knew there was every possibility of Japan joining the war. Having signed an alliance with Britain in 1902, Japan was already responsible for protecting Britain's interests in Southeast Asia.

'But for now, they remain neutral,' von Spee said.

Von Spee did not tell his commodores and captains that he had already requested that a coal supply in Chile be made available to his fleet. He didn't show them his diary, where he had written: 'Should Japan's neutrality change it may prove a necessity to leave the East Asia Station and either conduct cruiser warfare in the Indian Ocean or around South America.'

He dismissed all the officers but one after ordering them to make preparations to conduct shipping raids in the Pacific.

'Commodore,' said von Spee turning to Karl von Müller, commanding officer of SMS *Emden*. 'Do you have a suggestion?'

Von Müller did.

'Sir, I would like to ask permission to detach *Emden* from the squadron,' von Müller said, 'to mount an attack on shipping in the Indian Ocean. At the moment we don't have a presence off the west coast of Australia, and supplies will continue to flow in and out of Australia even if the east coast is sufficiently interrupted.'

Von Spee nodded – the commodore had a point.

'And having a presence in both the Pacific and Indian oceans may force the Australians, or the Japanese should they become hostile, to split their fleet.'

Von Spee continued to nod, another good point.

'Very well,' he said. 'Make arrangements to disguise *Emden* as a merchant ship.'

'I thank you, your excellency, for the confidence placed in me,' von Müller said.

Later that night, von Spee snatched up a telegram brought to him by a nervous-looking cryptologist. He steadied himself before lurching back towards his lamp. With a flick of a switch he had light. 'Tokyo,' it said. 'Declaration of war – withdrawal to Chile as enemy fleet appears departing for Pacific. Naval Attaché.'

'Where is the rest of it?' he yelled.

The cryptologist flinched. 'That was all of it, sir. The message was incomplete.'

Von Spee didn't need the rest of the message to know his worst fears had just been realised: Japan had entered the war.

He dismissed the code breaker and then limped his way from the bridge, a sudden blast of pain making him grab at his leg. 'Infernal heat,' he muttered, blaming the tropics for the ripening of his rheumatism. Von Spee entered his quarters and closed the door – he needed calm and quiet, well aware that the decision he was about to make could determine the fate of his fleet. He hobbled towards his desk, diary open and waiting. In the end he didn't even need to take his seat. He opened his door and – rheumatism forgotten for now – marched back to the bridge.

'We are abandoning the Pacific,' he said. 'Send word to Berlin.'

Von Spee got back to his diary later that night. He knew he could no longer stay in the Pacific and be of service to Germany. He would be hiding, not fighting. 'Only by proceeding to the east will we have some chance of obtaining coal from neutral territories,' von Spee wrote. 'I cannot see how we could obtain enough fuel to transfer to the Indian Ocean. Passing through the British-controlled Malay Archipelago is also filled with peril. Either course will see a temporary abandonment of cruiser warfare. We will have to be content in the short term to provide service. Our presence and the uncertainty of our whereabouts may still be effective in disrupting trade.'

Von Spee lamented the difficulty of heading west. It would be in the Indian Ocean that he could be most productive in disrupting trade given its frequency there. That was where the glory was. But he just couldn't see a way to get there. Not an entire squadron anyway. He would leave the spoils to *Emden*.

He sat silent in thought then put his diary away and replaced it with a clean sheet of paper.

'Great laurels are not to be achieved given the conditions,' he wrote in a letter to his wife, Margarethe. 'One does one's best. Whether my present plans are correct, only the future will validate. The night is no one's friend and the thoughts that come to one are not exactly uplifting, but I hope that everyday life will accustom us to them.'

Bougainville, New Guinea, 13 August 1914

Joined by *Sydney*, HMAS *Australia* resumed its hunt for von Spee. After refuelling with coal and oil at Rossel Island, the two battleships headed north to search.

They were stalking the sea passages around Bougainville when a message arrived from Melbourne and was rushed to Rear Admiral Patey.

'It's about *Scharnhorst*, sir,' the wireless operator said.

Patey grabbed the message and read it aloud. 'A decoded message sent from Yap to *Scharnhorst* is as follows: "*Scharnhorst* to proceed to the Mariana Islands".'

'When was this message intercepted?' Patey demanded. 'And how was it decoded? Who decoded it?'

The operator could only answer one of the fast-fired questions. 'The message was intercepted from Yap on 3 August. It appears the message has just recently been decoded, but how and by whom I don't know.'

Patey shook his head, wishing he had been given this message earlier. Before steaming into Simpson Harbour. Before finding just mangroves and forest fires.

'It could be a decoy,' said Captain Radcliffe. 'An attempt to lure us away from their colonies in New Guinea. Sending us northeast would give them their chance to resupply and make a run for the west.'

Patey considered the proposition. 'Then why would they encrypt the message?' he asked. 'My concern is that the message is now ten days old. Let's get the latest from Yap.'

The signals operator returned later that day. 'Yap is down,' the operator said. 'It was destroyed by the China Squadron yesterday.'

'Really?' Patey replied.

The station had been blown to bits. In a move designed to cut von Spee and his squadron off from Berlin, the British Royal Navy commander-in-chief in China, Admiral Sir Martyn Jerram, had destroyed the communications hub.

Patey shook his head. The station that linked Tsingtao with all the German islands had been constantly sending and receiving messages since the outbreak of war. Much of Patey's intelligence and the suspected movements of the German squadron had been garnered from Yap.

Jerram had wiped out the station in a bid to cut Germany off from the rest of the world. He had succeeded in stopping the talk. But he had also stopped Australia from listening.

'Contact Admiralty,' Patey ordered. 'Request permission to head to the Mariana Islands to pursue the German East Asia Squadron.'

The request was denied.

'What?' Patey replied, dumbfounded by the response when it came through later that day.

The Admiralty had new orders for Patey.

'It's over,' Patey said of the search for von Spee. 'For now ...'

Central Pacific Ocean, 14 August 1914

Von Spee was in the dark as he steamed towards the Marshall Islands – both figuratively and literally.

Now northeast of New Britain, Yap had gone silent. Nothing from the wireless station since 13 August. Connected by an undersea cable to Shanghai and Tsingtao, it was the only direct link to Berlin in the Pacific.

'Destroyed,' he told Captain Gustav-Julius Maerker. 'It appears the Yap station has fallen into enemy hands.'

He knew Japan had entered the war. He knew Tsingtao was lost. He now knew he was on his own.

'It is pointless to manoeuvre here against Britain, Japan, France and Russia,' said Captain Maerker. 'Not even the Admiralty staff know where we are. Certainly we are already given up for sunk.'

'I know where we are,' von Spee replied. 'And I know what we can do. We will never give up. And we will never stop fighting. We don't need the Admiralty to tell us what we know needs to be done. Perhaps we can gain news from a captured enemy ship.'

* * *

Born in Copenhagen in 1861, Maximilian Johannes Maria Hubertus Reichsgraf von Spee, the fifth son of a Danish mother and a Prussian father, Count Rudolf, had left the family estate in Lucerne, Switzerland, when he was seventeen to join the Imperial German Navy as a cadet. Tall, lean, blue-eyed and serious, he'd served at the German naval base in Kiel until he was commissioned as a lieutenant at sea and sent to West Africa on the gunboat SMS *Möwe*.

During his time in Africa, he was part of the mission that saw Germany sign treaties with local rulers to create the colonies of Togoland and Kamerun. Von Spee became the port commander of Duala in Kamerun in 1887, and it was during his time there that he was first struck down by rheumatism. Sent back to Germany to recover, the then twenty-eight-year-old married Margarethe Baroness von der Osten-Sacken. He became a father to two boys and a girl before being appointed to the staff of Vice Admiral Otto von Diederichs, commander of the East Asia Squadron, in 1897.

Von Spee was involved in heavy action during the Boxer Rebellion in China in 1900 and the leadership, bravery and potential he showed during the conflict kick-started a rapid-fire rise through the ranks that would see him become the commander of the East Asia Squadron in just twelve years. He held command on several ships and served as a chief of staff for the North Sea Station, where he reported directly to the Kaiser. He was also the deputy commander of reconnaissance forces for the High Seas Fleet before he raised the flag on *Scharnhorst* in 1912 to depart on a tour of the Southwest Pacific with sister ship *Gneisenau*.

In short, he had held prestigious post after post. Von Spee had also become an international statesman and the face of Germany in the Pacific. He had met Asian leaders including the Japanese emperor and the first president of the Republic of China. Von Spee had been heading to tour German New Guinea when Archduke Franz Ferdinand had been assassinated.

Those handshakes, bows and sips of sake were now forgotten. He no longer had any friends in the Pacific – he and his squadron were on their own. Without radio, only limited coal, the Japanese to his west and the Australians to his south, he was going to run the gauntlet to get to Cape Horn. From there he would attempt to return to Europe for reassignment.

'I am quite homeless,' von Spee wrote when he returned to his diary. 'I cannot reach Germany. We possess no other secure harbour. I must plough the seas of the world doing as much mischief as I can until my ammunition is exhausted, or a foe far superior in power succeeds in catching me.'

Port Moresby, New Guinea, 17 August 1914

Rear Admiral Patey had abandoned his search for von Spee after receiving a direct order from the Admiralty to escort a New Zealand force to Samoa for a mission to invade and occupy Apia. Since 1900 it had been the capital of German Samoa. Nearly 200 German and American sailors had lost their lives in the port in 1889 when a cyclone ripped through the Pacific outpost. The Scottish writer Robert Louis Stevenson died in 1894 on his very own Treasure Island after settling in Samoa in what would be the last years of his life.

'Isn't the objective to destroy the Pacific squadron?' Patey asked. It was, at least according to every correspondence he had received from the Admiralty until then. 'Then why are we being asked to babysit?' he complained. 'Why are we being asked to occupy a territory that could be useful to the squadron when we can just eliminate the squadron?'

The move did not make sense to Patey, nor to anyone else in Australia for that matter. It seemed political at best, a land grab at worst.

But orders were orders.

Steaming out of Port Moresby on 17 August, *Australia* and *Melbourne* set off to meet the New Zealand convoy in Noumea and escort it to Apia.

Despite the latest orders, Patey refused to give up on finding von Spee. He was on a mission, determined, dogged and even desperate to be remembered as the man who took down the German legend and his fleet.

He requested and then examined signals reports, hoping to find something that would force the Admiralty to change its mind.

'With reference to the intercepted telegrams received at the various radiotelegraph stations during the last few days,' the latest report said, 'I submit the following observations: *Scharnhorst*, using the call signals ASB, CI, DASV and IO, was last heard on 17 August. She then appeared to be a considerable distance off on the north-northeast of Thursday Island, probably 1,500 miles at the very least.

'A new station using the call OB, first heard on 16 August, I suggest is Angaur Station using increased power. This station has been heard communicating with the call NQ or QN practically continuous through the night of 17 August. The station has been working with the call sign OI, the *Scharnhorst*.'

Patey pored over maps, attacking them with protractors and pencils. He then decided all was not lost. 'They are heading to Samoa,' he said. 'We can get them yet.'

He prepared a telegram for the Admiralty. 'There appears to be no doubt that the Germans are collecting large supplies of coal and are concentrating somewhere northeast of New Britain,' he wrote. 'I believe the main body will make across the Pacific either east or southeast, possibly visiting Samoa and Tahiti. Probably auxiliary cruisers will be left to work from a base in either the Pacific Islands or China. I believe the main body will eventually head to the American coast.'

He went back to his intelligence reports after ordering his message be sent to the Navy Office in Melbourne and then on to Britain.

The next report made reference to various telegrams from Darwin, Port Moresby and Thursday Island – but it was all in German.

'Does anyone read German?' Patey yelled. 'What am I supposed to do with this?'

'We will get hold of a translator, sir,' came the reply.

Marshall Islands, Central Pacific, 19 August 1914

The freshly risen sun was already blazing down on the once Spanish and now German colony of Eniwetok in the Marshall Islands, located just north of the equator. On a dirt track leading to one of the few buildings on the island, two second lieutenants followed in the long shadow cast by Vice Admiral von Spee.

Despite the heat, and the importance of the man they followed, the officers looked cool and calm. Even in the Arctic the presence of von Spee would normally be enough to make senior officers sweat, but these two lieutenants at sea – the lowest rank of officer in the German navy – were completely at ease.

The younger of the two, boyish and thin, pushed at an ornate oak door when the unlikely trio reached the church, the biggest and oldest building in the tiny town. 'After you, father,' he said, holding the door open as the admiral entered. 'Brother,' he nodded as the slightly older and heavier lieutenant followed.

Von Spee looked around the room, noting the freshly cleaned pews, the hefty wooden cross hanging above the altar and the kaleidoscope of colour that filled the room, the stained-glass windows making rainbows from sun.

He turned first to his twenty-four-year-old son, Otto, then looked at his twenty-one-year-old, Heinrich. 'This may be your last confession,' von Spee said finally. 'I don't say this to scare you. Given the circumstances and the odds, it is a fact we must face. We may never set foot in a church again, so make your peace and the Lord will have a place for you in his eternal Kingdom.'

Von Spee had been fearing a moment like this since Otto and Heinrich were small children. Privately tutored in a family castle with a world of position and privilege at their feet, the boys only ever wanted to be like their father. Running around the family estate wearing his old navy jackets, oversized and dragging on the ground, they would sit in boxes and pretend they were in ships, his old caps hanging over their eyes. When he returned home from sea they would rush to jump on his lap. 'Did you see any pirates?' they would ask. 'Tell us a story. Please, please!'

And von Spee would tell them of faraway places: tropical wonderlands, emperors he had met, kings and queens. He brought them spears from New Guinea, boomerangs from Australia and silks from China.

Now he gave them advice. 'I don't know how this will end,' he said. 'So be prepared for the worst.'

Von Spee, Otto and Heinrich gave their confessions to a Catholic apostolic vicar. The family's religion was unusual in Prussia and Denmark. Von Spee was devout and his Catholic faith long-standing; he preferred the solace of church to high society. He was not one for lawn parties, banquets or royal receptions.

Confession completed, souls clean and back in the blazing son, von Spee addressed his boys.

'We will soon be split up,' he said. 'This will be the last time we are together for some time.' He turned to Otto, a lieutenant on SMS *Nürnberg*. 'Son,' he said, 'I will be sending the *Nürnberg* to Honolulu with mail. We have been cut off from the Admiralty and news of my plans needs to be sent to Berlin. The rest of the fleet will head southeast.'

'Will we rejoin the squadron?' Otto asked.

'That is up to God,' von Spee replied. He now looked towards Heinrich, a lieutenant on *Gneisenau*. '*Gneisenau* will follow *Scharnhorst*. It is likely we will find battle. We will go proudly and pray for victory. We shall bring glory to our country and Kaiser.' He then looked at them both. 'Enjoy each other's company for now,' he said.

He walked away before they saw the tear in his eye.

Chapter 6

THE WAR ROOM

Melbourne, 19 August 1914

Jens Lyng made line after line. Pushing his ruler right, left, up and down, his lead pencil attacked the page after every move.

'Lyng,' his supervisor interrupted. 'You have been summoned. Someone at the Navy Office wants to talk to you.'

'Finally,' the draughtsman said. Lyng had been waiting for this moment. Ever since he'd written to the Navy Office when the war declaration looked imminent, when he'd told them he'd once held a commission in the Royal Danish Standing Army and had also served in Australia in the Cadet Force.

Born in 1868 in Hasle, Denmark, Lyng had migrated to Australia in 1891 after rising to the rank of second lieutenant during a six-year stint with the Danish standing army. After working as a labourer, land clearer, shearer, secretary and magazine editor, he was now with the naval works branch of the Department of Defence. But he longed to serve with more than a ruler and pencil.

'I would like to volunteer for service should an expeditionary force be required,' Lyng had written shortly after the outbreak of war.

Now, called away from his work, Lyng thought his letter had been answered. He arrived at the Navy Office expecting to meet an administrator; to be given a pen, paper and volunteer form. He was instead taken to the office of the Second Naval Member, Captain Arthur Gordon Smith.

'We have an important role for you, should you be willing to take it on,' Smith said. 'A position has become available that requires a very certain set of skills and I have been told that you have them.'

Lyng was intrigued.

'We have acquired a set of codebooks and we require someone who is both fluent in German and has a military background to translate messages.'

A translator? Lyng had been summoned in front of a captain to be offered a translator gig?

'Sir, I was hoping to serve more actively,' Lyng said. 'I was a second lieutenant in the Royal Danish Army.'

Smith knew he had to land his man. Thring had tasked him with finding a fluent German speaker with a military background and no links to Germany, and Lyng was the only name on the list.

'This position is of vital importance,' Smith said. 'You would be making an immense contribution to both King and country.'

Lyng still didn't looked convinced.

'You will be given an officer's rank,' Smith said. 'And an allowance of twenty pounds a year. I also expect you will be sent to serve on HMAS *Australia*, where intercepted messages will need to be translated immediately.'

The promise of a return to rank and the prospect of active duty sealed the deal. 'When do I begin?' Lyng asked.

'Now,' Smith replied.

Lyng was handed a copy of the *HVB* codebook and told to pack his bag and head to Brisbane. To report to Rear Admiral George Patey on HMAS *Australia*. To go to war.

Melbourne, 20 August 1914

'It's done,' Captain Smith told Thring. 'The translator is on his way.'

'Good,' Thring said. 'That will be all.'

One flame doused, now to the blaze – the bushfire he was fighting with a garden hose. Thring had to find a way to convince the Admiralty to let him go after von Spee.

Control of the Australian fleet had been taken away from Thring by way of a cable on 10 August:

> *An order in council on 10 August transferred the Royal Australian Navy under direct Admiralty control. All vessels, officers and seamen of the Commonwealth naval forces are under the control of the Admiralty until the issue of a proclamation that war no longer exists.*

Every movement of his fleet was to be dictated by Britain.

Officially the hunt for von Spee and the German East Asia Squadron had been suspended after the Admiralty had ordered

HMAS *Australia* to escort an expeditionary force of 1,500 Kiwi soldiers to Apia, Samoa, for an occupation mission.

Unofficially, Thring, Patey and the Royal Australian Navy were still very much chasing von Spee. All intelligence suggested he remained in the Pacific and that he still posed a threat to Australia. A direct attack on the Federation was both possible and plausible.

Wheatley had decoded another message that suggested *Scharnhorst* was in the vicinity of the Mariana Islands. The jumbled message was intercepted on 16 August.

'NULEN EFIFU,' the message read. 'ELAVO BUFEN, DGATI GYGIT, ALYRA RIHDI, AGULE GYGIT, AMICI MARFL, YMEMY FUKOT, AWONO FYROB, OPECO RAVUB, ETONE KELAH, DGYPU NALOM.'

Wheatley had delivered the decryption the next day: 'Following signal heard from Yap to unknown in the cipher code used for communicating between German merchant ships and German men-of-war,' his report read. 'The signal was made at 8.50 pm on 16 August: "Notify at once union with *Gottingen*. Position given auxiliary cruiser *Rajsan* will be 17°N 150°E." Ends.'

The coordinates given were for a stretch of ocean just northeast of the Mariana Islands, the location revealed in Wheatley's previous decryption. The two ships mentioned were suspected to be heading to meet von Spee and become part of his fleet.

Thring got no response from the Admiralty when he sent them his report, the information either dismissed or ignored. Patey still had to steam to Samoa.

While the occupation of Samoa was a distraction, it wasn't a disaster. Patey had predicted the German fleet would head southeast across the Pacific and stop at either Samoa or Tahiti. With Patey in Samoa, the Australian fleet would be in the right place.

Or would they? Thring feared the Admiralty would issue new orders before von Spee arrived. He expected they would want *Australia* to act as an escort for the Australian troops scheduled for transport to Egypt on 1 September. He would need more than signals reports and predictions to convince them that he could destroy von Spee and his fierce fleet. The captain was fast thinking that Frederick Wheatley, his somewhat strange scientist, was his only hope.

Both Thring and Creswell agreed that the capture of the *HVB* code had provided the Royal Australian Navy with an early strategic advantage over the German fleet. Despite the lack of response from Admiralty, Creswell ordered the code-breaking campaign to continue.

'Give your fellow whatever he needs,' Creswell said. 'Give him staff. And give him access to all our intercepts.' It had been decided that Wheatley needed to see all the messages, not just the coded ones, in order to be effective. He needed the full picture.

Thring drafted his latest order:

The Admin in CMO 1254 order all ships to report intercepted messages from 1 August 1914. We have a considerable number of these messages but the call signs are difficult to recognise.

Dr Wheatley could make a clearer report on the subject than anyone else and I recommend that he should be called on to translate all our messages and to draw up a report for the Admiralty.

W.H. Thring

Melbourne, 21 August 1914

Back at his desk, further scratched and splashed with ink, Wheatley trawled through stacks of reports.

'Yes, sir,' he had replied when Thring asked him for a signals report. 'All the way back to the outbreak of war? As you wish.'

He went through all his handwritten notes. There were translations and decryptions, coordinates and conversations. There were also the messages he was unable to decode.

'Not in *HVB*,' he muttered as he looked at the gibberish he could not crack. 'Some other code ...'

He now had to put it all into a report.

Wheatley groaned as he heaved his typewriter from the floor, the cast-iron hunk setting off a fire in his lower back. He shuffled the Royal back into place on his desk, from where it had been moved to make room for all the reports.

Click! Clack!

His fingers sent the stainless-steel hammers hurtling.

Click! Clack!

The rubber letters thudded into the ink-soaked ribbon.

Whoosh!

He flung the carriage back to the right for a new line.

Soon the pile of blank paper to his left was smaller than the pile of typed paper on his right. He looked down at his latest page.

15 August, 7.08 pm. KAN to SCH

Angaur to Nauru (6/600m)

After you -------- must also. If I cannot answer, will you just fire away if you have anything for me.

7.12 pm Nauru to Angaur (6/850)

OK. I have for many messages good connection with G R (Apia) must wait until six for K R (Yap). Please at this time be very attentive.

7.17 pm Angaur to Nauru (4/600)

OK. By you when and where you can. 10/11 words Behuneira Manila send 10,000 bags rice for Frieduchwillelmshafen 2,000 signature Forsayth.

Perhaps you can answer that of Manila or Guam. If danger threatens of being taken by the enemy then quickly beforehand make the wireless apparatus incapable of being used by hiding the important parts, also government station. Destroy all secret papers and cards if attached (or when ordered). Have you pressure?

7.45 pm Angaur to Nauru (5/850)

Italian and Japanese mines laid Dardenelles. Surrounded by large waves.

8.00 pm Angaur to Nauru

Calls missed reply left

Nauru to WA

Listen to me here removal.

WA to Nauru

OK. Please everything before vorescume ehcumczofn.

Nauru to WA

Tell Molber I want notice for removal quickly.

Wheatley continued the clicking, the clacking and the whooshing until the pile of paper on his left was gone.

Melbourne, 28 August 1914

Wheatley's latest stack was all chitchat. Bitter nothings.

'There is little of note,' Wheatley said to Thring. 'No locations. Mostly from merchant ships.'

Thring crossed his arms, the hint of curiosity he had shown when he waved the instructor in now buried by a frown.

'Did anything come of the other messages?' Wheatley asked. 'The one that gave the location of *Scharnhorst*? The other with the details of where the *Göttinger* was going?'

Thring shook his head. He didn't want to have to explain.

'Have you heard of the ABC code?' Wheatley asked.

This time Thring nodded.

'Well, I have come across multiple messages that appear to be ciphered with the ABC code or a variation of it,' Wheatley said. 'There may be something of value in these messages if you can obtain a codebook. Given that it is a commercial code used by merchants, it might not prove difficult to obtain.'

'Well, we best get you one then,' Thring said. 'And don't be discouraged. Your work is showing great promise. I believe it is only a matter of time.'

Captain Thring walked Wheatley out before making another trip to the Navy Office.

'An order, sir?' Naval Secretary Macandie asked, expecting Thring to ask him to type and send another cable.

Thring shook his head. 'A letter,' he said.

One of Macandie's sixteen clerks typed while Thring dictated.

DEPARTMENT OF DEFENCE
NAVY OFFICE, MELBOURNE
28 August 1914
SECRET
The Secretary
Department of External Affairs, Melbourne

From May code signals which have been intercepted, it appears that German war vessels are using a German edition of the ABC code for communicating with their consuls and others.

This office has been unable to get a copy of the code referred to and are very anxious to obtain one as some of the signals are no doubt important.

It is probable that the more important German shipping agents and the German consuls have this code.

The Naval Board would be glad if your department can suggest any means whereby a copy of the ABC code could be obtained.

Naval Secretary, on behalf of Captain Thring

'Good,' Thring said, reading it over.

The letter was signed, sent and soon in the hands of Atlee Hunt, Australia's first spy.

Sydney, 29 August 1914

The man who lived in the shadows picked up the phone. 'The ABC code,' he said. 'Can you get it?'

Atlee Arthur Hunt – lawyer, public servant and spy – had started making calls as soon as he'd received his orders from the Navy Office. As secretary of the Department of External Affairs, appointed to the position on the organisation's formation in 1901, Hunt knew exactly what it was they were after.

He had rifled through a filing cabinet after reading his mail. 'Got it,' he mumbled, a copy of the German commercial ABC code in his hand. He fast found out it was useless.

'That's the first edition of the code,' one of his agents had informed him. 'They are now on the fourth edition, possibly the fifth.'

That was when Hunt contacted his network. He instructed his agents to look for the book and then called the head of one of Australia's biggest companies, who also happened to be an undercover agent in Hunt's employ.

On a Burns Philp and Company letterhead, the major shipping line that Hunt had recently and strategically awarded the nation's mail services contract to, came the reply:

PERSONAL

Dear Mr Atlee Hunt,

Referring to your telephone enquiry for a German edition of the ABC code, I have to advise that the same enquiry was being put round by the Defence Department yesterday, and Mr McMaster laid them on to a number of firms. To make certain, I sent a man over the ground again today (omitting any German firms) and have satisfied myself that there is not one here. As a last resort, I rang up an English chum in the Norddeutscher Lloyd office, and he informed me the wireless station had made the same enquiry yesterday, and he replied they only had a small private code in German, but had referred them to Justus Scharff and other German firms. He expressed an opinion that there would not be such a book in Australia, as the firms here would use the English version of the particular edition.

I confirm my urgent telegram today as follows:

'There are several editions of the code mentioned, fourth and fifth editions being principally in use. They are totally different codes although on the same principle. The edition is important, the language immaterial.'

I would also add that a German firm who had the code would be unlikely to admit it and the only possible way would be to search and commandeer. In view of my friend's information, however, I would have grave doubt whether such a book would be found.

Yours truly,
Walter H. Lucas
Cars Burns Philp and Co., Sydney

Hunt's agents came back with similar stories.

'Keep up the enquiries,' he said.

He then sent the Navy Office the news of this rare failure:

SECRET
The Naval Secretary,
Navy Office, Melbourne.

I regret that I am unable to inform you as to where a copy of the code in question could be obtained. I assume that it is not desired to make a formal search under the extreme powers conferred on the Minister of Defence in cases of war. I am, however, informed that we should not be much further advanced if we had the volume as it is only a translation of the English version, that is to say, the codewords remain in the German edition precisely the same as they are in the English but meanings are a German translation of the English meaning.

I have two or three agents enquiring on my behalf in regards to obtaining the current English version while also looking for the German edition. If they have success in securing a copy of the document I shall be very glad indeed to forward it.

Secretary,
Atlee A. Hunt

Melbourne, 1 September 1914

It had now been twenty-seven days since Great Britain had declared war on Germany. September started, winter over, and the world was at war. The declarations had come thick and fast, the Austro-Hungarian Empire declaring war on Russia on 6 August, Britain and France returning serve by declaring war on the Austro-Hungarian Empire six days later, and then Japan plunging Asia into the action on 23 August by declaring war on Germany.

The battlelines had been drawn and blood was being spilled.

In a first fight debacle for the Allies, 75,000 Frenchmen lost their lives as they clashed with the German army in the 'battle of the frontiers', on the eastern border of France and in southern Belgium. Britain also suffered 1,600 casualties in a failed offensive against the Germans in Belgium.

Australia was preparing to send an expeditionary force of 20,000 men off to Egypt. All volunteers, the quota had almost been reached. On the day the recruitment offices opened in Sydney, 10 August 1914, 2,000 men signed on to go to war. Another 15,000 men added their names to the list in just two weeks. They were preparing to be shipped out to fight.

Wheatley's battle had already begun. Sitting behind his desk, now personalised with spilled ink and scratches, he fought his war with a pen. He had been delivered new messages and transmissions stretching back to 24 July. His notebook was fast filling with handwritten notes:

Thursday Island
Scharnhorst *and Yap exchanging many messages from 25 July to 31 July.*

24 July

Berlin to German warship Planet, *Morseby, 4.25 pm:*

CHOER-RAYEA

AYENA-CEROT OMNIL-VALIS CHOER-DIFYP

OLYGE-MATHP

30 July

Berlin to German warship Planet, *Moresby, 6.10 pm:*

GINDI-ENTOF RIABI-DEDCE ROTAL-IUSHO

USETA-PAASI

31 July

8.16 pm: KCA calling APL (Yap to Planet*)*

*8.25 pm: DKT calling ASB (*Komet *to* Scharnhorst*)*

*8.31pm: ASB calling KCA (*Scharnhorst *to Yap)*

*9.17 pm: KCA calling WVNM QRU (*Scharnhorst *to ?)*

10.20 pm: KCA (Yap) sent the following – REALZ-IDIFY

BYGUH-IETED GATAM-UBELA

*10.35 pm: ACB to KCA (*Scharnhorst *to Yap): Gave OK and asked for papers.*

10.37 pm: RCA to ASB (Yap to Scharnhorst*): Go on to 2820 and will send on.*

1 August

2.45 am: KBN to ASB (Nauru to Scharnhorst*): Germania*

MAUIL-ADRYL DELAN-DHERI SHDJF-JUHDS

MDLPD-PPEIO

3.45 am: Telephone call to station no letters.

4.50 am: ASB to KBN: Call only.

11.10 am: From Port Moresby to urgent to Thursday Island. From Berlin German warships: CEUDA-THAAC CESOT-ALUSH – Message not yet disassembled.

And so went the notes; pages and pages, some of the messages decoded, some not. Some of his scribbling in German, some of it in English. Some of it gibberish. Some of it gold, like this one referring to the German warship *Komet*, intercepted by the Port Moresby wireless station: *24th DKT responded he was in Samoa.*

And this, sent from the battle cruiser SMS *Geier* on 25 August: *Use cipher key. Make your position. Keep in connection with Yap and other ships. Have received news war has broken out with Japan.*

He had been told the ABC code was proving difficult to find. He was also told to keep decoding what he could.

Melbourne, 7 September 1914

Thring examined Wheatley's latest report, the instructor sparing him the notes that were only understood by geniuses. Wheatley instead provided what he thought was important information in plain and precise English.

Thring found bits and pieces. The information about a German merchant ship in Sumatra could prove useful, a potential prize. He also now knew that the Germans had been informed about Japan's entry into the war.

But there wasn't much else.

Thring couldn't help but wonder about the information Wheatley could be providing, about the piles of currently meaningless messages sitting somewhere in a room in Whitehall, London.

The Admiralty still had not acknowledged his messages about the seizure of the codebook – or Wheatley's success in decoding the intercepted German messages.

He decided it was time to be more direct. He scribbled a handwritten note that would be turned into a telegram:

We have a secret German codebook and key Handelsverkehrsbuch for intercourse between German merchant ships. It is issued to all German warships, Admiralty, marine stations and leading merchant men. Messages are sent in four-letter groups or in ten-letter groups. In the letter, the first or last group often recurs. Messages for the admiral begin 'OCRP' or 'HANIB UNYRU'. Messages by open cipher begin HAVUB.

Messages to be decoded by the cipher key (only to be used in wartime) begin PCZA or KISAH ACIBA. The general war call sign for German warships is DK and for Merchantmen DH.

In this code, the four-letter war call signs for all German warships begin with D and for Merchantmen with G.

We have decoded many intercepted messages by wireless and can decode any in this code if you cable them to Naval Secretary.

Thring almost spilled his tea when a reply was put on his desk less than hour later.

'We acknowledge,' the Admiralty wrote. 'And we will send all intercepted messages to Melbourne for decryption.'

Chapter 7

FOR KING OR COUNTRY?

Rossel Island, New Guinea, 8 September 1914

Towering emerald peaks were capped by cloud, swirling marshmallows in a dozen shades of white – ivory, pearl, alabaster, porcelain, chiffon and lace.

Lyng had never seen anything like it. 'Magnificent,' he breathed.

The Danish immigrant turned Australian navy translator had arrived at Rossel Island, off the coast of New Guinea, after twenty-one days at sea. After accepting his assignment – lured by the promise of pay and rank – Lyng had travelled to Brisbane by train.

'Is it all like this?' he'd asked a fellow passenger as the steam train neared the border of New South Wales. 'All this brown? This dry?'

Australia was in the midst of a drought. One of the driest winters on record had levelled fields. Wheat lay wasted, trees had been stripped bare. The drought accounted for some of the 20,000 who had volunteered to go to war. By now the quota, which the government originally thought was ambitious, had been filled. Thousands of men had even been rejected. Too old. Too young. Too short. Too skinny. And many, both the accepted and rejected, had made their way to the city-based recruitment offices from failing farms. The offer of six shillings a day – rain, hail or shine – was hard to resist. Quota quickly filled, the government added another 10,000 men to the 20,000 they had promised.

The fellow passenger had nodded. 'Mate, it's as dry as a dead dingo's donger out here. All these poor bastards are losing their shirts.'

Lyng's rattling ride through the rain-starved countryside had finished in Brisbane, population 152,000. From there he was transported to Moreton Island.

'This is it?' Lyng had asked, pointing at the vessel he was to board. 'This is the warship?'

It wasn't. Lyng's voyage began on HMAS *Berrima*, a P&O passenger liner sequestered for the war. Refitted and armed, the auxiliary cruiser was now a Royal Australian Navy transport ship. Lyng was one of 1,500 men jammed on the ship, which before war claimed a capacity of 600, for the two-day trip to Townsville.

'I am supposed to be on HMAS *Australia*,' Lyng had told an officer as they arrived in the north Queensland port town. 'I have orders to report to Admiral Patey.'

'Settle down, cobber,' said the lieutenant pointing to HMAS *Sydney*, a Town-class light cruiser. 'You'll see him soon enough. That ship will take you to HMAS *Australia*.'

Eighteen days later, after almost three weeks of swells, seasickness and cabin fever, Lyng was standing on the deck of HMAS *Sydney* staring at the cloud-capped peaks of Mount Rossel.

At the eastern end of the Louisiade Archipelago, 500 miles from Port Moresby, Rossel Island was a jungle paradise, with white sand beaches, crystal clear waters and overgrown rainforest. Armed with a rough copy of the codebook and high expectations, Lyng was led off *Sydney* and towards HMAS *Australia*, the biggest ship he had ever seen.

'You must be important,' said Captain John Glossop, the commander of HMAS *Sydney*. 'Not too many civilians have business with the commander-in-chief. Come on then.'

'Who?' Patey asked when Glossop introduced Lyng to Patey.

'Mr Lyng,' Glossop repeated.

Patey remained expressionless. He was somewhere else.

'I have been sent by the Navy Office in Melbourne,' Lyng interrupted.

Patey was still unresponsive.

'I have the codes,' Lyng continued. 'I am the translator.'

Patey was suddenly back from wherever his mind had been. 'Too late,' he snapped. 'Nothing to translate. They've gone. We missed them. The transmissions have stopped.'

Patey had just read the latest signals report:

From particulars extracted from intercepted telegrams between 6 August and the current date. I submit the following particulars.

DASV – Scharnhorst – *Last heard 17 August. She passed beyond the range of Commonwealth stations in a northeasterly direction.*

DI – German war vessel – Last heard working with Geier *on 25 August.*

DAKG – FU – Geier – *Not heard since 26 August.*

DAFZ – Emden – *Nothing heard since 27 August.*

FT – German war vessel – Not heard since 27 August.

KCA – KR – Yap – Last heard 8 August. Heard being called repeatedly since that date by German and other vessels but no reply.

NQ – Planet – *Also uses QN – Would appear to be the same as RN. See RN.*

OM – German station – position unknown. Last heard 25 August.

RN – I am of the opinion this is an assumed call of Planet. *Last heard on 28 August. Her position on the date would appear to be 146 E. and 4 S.*

Mr John Graeme Balsillie
Engineer for Radiotelegraphy

Gone. Vanished. Not heard from since 27 August. Thirteen days. Almost two weeks.

'I'm preparing for redeployment,' Patey said. 'I'm sure you will be of some use, but not to me.'

Patey was still seething, certain he had lost his chance to go toe-to-toe with von Spee.

Marshall Islands, Central Pacific, 8 September 1914

His torch blinked before it gave up. 'What's wrong?' von Spee asked. He shook it like a baby attacking a rattle. 'Come on,' he said, each jiggle forcing a burst of bright. He smacked the failing torch against the ship's wall. 'Good,' he said, as a steady stream of light resulted.

The metal-on-metal thunderbolt of aluminium torch hitting steel ship was still echoing through the belly of *Scharnhorst*.

'It's nothing,' von Spee said as doors began opening. 'Go back to sleep.'

'Yes, sir,' came a voice from the dark.

Von Spee turned and pointed the now working torch towards the face. 'At ease,' he said as he saw the shocked sailor saluting. 'Get some rest.'

The sailor looked half-dead, a standing, saluting corpse, von Spee thought, as he turned and continued his midnight mission.

The admiral emerged from the non-commissioned sleeping quarters looking like he belonged in a graveyard too.

'They are right,' von Spee said when he returned to the relative comfort of the commissioned officers' deck. 'It is dark and hot. No good. They look exhausted.'

The threat of HMAS *Australia* had sparked the spiral.

'Australian Squadron heading in full strength to the colonies,' said the message they had intercepted from Nauru on 17 August. The enemy fleet was close.

'All doors, portholes and openings are to remain sealed at all times,' von Spee had ordered in response, putting defensive measures in place. 'The ship is to be kept dark at night. No lights.'

So now the ship was stale, stagnant and sullen. Dark, gloomy and depressing.

And, Christ, was it hot.

The tropical heat – humid and relentless, combined with boilers and engines, soot and steam – had turned the ship into a floating furnace. Sailors were sweating and complaining about lack of sleep. Portholes shut, doors closed, the hot air could not escape. They suffered in the sauna. Others became claustrophobic, shaking, gasping and eventually darting to the deck.

And then there was the dark, gloomy and depressive. Thoughts of death and despair were encouraged by it.

'Formalities will have to be relaxed,' von Spee told Captain Felix Schultz. 'All messes are to be integrated. The officers, the non-commissioned and the engineers will eat together.'

Von Spee knew what his men needed and when. They both respected and responded to him – firm but fair was how he was described. He could make a sailor who had done good work smile and one who had done bad work shit his pants. His spittle-laden sprays were legendary. They were mostly set off by inaccurate or insufficiently prepared reports and usually directed at junior officers. Imposingly tall and broad-shouldered, he would shout, scream, point and punch the air and his piercing blue eyes would turn red.

But while being strict, methodical and orthodox, von Spee was also perceptive and personable. He had once been a cadet. He had worked his way to the top. He had developed empathy.

'Increase rations too,' von Spee continued. 'Both food and rum.' The last thing he needed was discontent or, heaven forbid, a mutiny. But if ever there was cause …

There had been no good news since departing Pagan on 14 August. Nothing at all had come out of Yap. He had been cut off from Berlin. *Australia* and her squadron were close, the intercepted message from Nauru plunging the commander into a do-or-die game of cat and mouse. And he was commanding the SS *Mouse*.

War with Japan had also been confirmed on 24 August, when Apia had sent out an open broadcast. 'It is quite pointless to remain in east Asian waters,' von Spee wrote later that night in a letter to his wife and daughter. 'And so we will move on from here. To where I don't know. To what I have no idea.'

And then news had finally been delivered from Berlin. SMS *Cormoran*, a newly converted cruiser that had joined the squadron on 28 August, brought a dispatch from the Admiralty:

The cruiser squadron intended, in the event of war with Great Britain, to proceed from the South Seas to Tsingtao. It may be assumed that it is now in east Asiatic waters. The news of Japan's impending entry into the war makes its position hopeless. It is impossible to judge from here whether the squadron will be able to choose against which enemy it will deal its dying blows. If the choice does not rest with it, it is useless to issue any orders. If the choice does still rest with it, an attack on Japanese forces or on their communications would seem advisable.

It would undoubtedly be the best plan if there were any chance of saving Tsingtao, but as that appears to be out of the question, it is useless to issue orders in this case also. Further we are ignorant of the commander-in-chief's dispositions regarding coal supplies and, judging from his often repeated utterances, it may be taken for granted that he will attempt to bring the enemy to action.

Whether he engages the British or the Japanese must depend on their relative situations, and any interference on our part might be disastrous. The commander-in-chief must have complete liberty of action as hitherto. If he succeeds in beating the British before the Japanese have time to come in we should regard it as a great achievement.

Even if he were able, contrary to all probability, to transfer his activities to another ocean, it would be wrong for us to interfere with his freedom of action.

Should he succeed in reaching the Atlantic Ocean he might damage the British far more seriously than in the Far East and might also contrive to maintain his squadron there for a longer period, thanks to former preparations. In view of the above it is better to send no instructions to the commander-in-chief.

The Kaiser, von Spee's personal friend after serving under his brother Prince Heinrich as staff officer during the China war, also sent a message: 'God be with you in the impending stern struggle.'

Von Spee had been both shaken and inspired by the correspondence. The impending doom was disturbing as it appeared Captain Maerker was right after all: even the Admiralty had all but written them off as sunk. 'Dying blows' and 'hopeless', they had said.

He had also been roused. The Admiralty was sure he would engage an enemy. Bring them 'to action', they said, 'a great achievement'. They had faith in him.

It was there and then that von Spee had decided he would go out in a blaze of glory. Help his Kaiser and country win the war. Or die trying.

He had penned a letter to the Admiralty, not knowing if it would ever be read. 'I shall proceed to Chile,' he wrote. 'Arriving at Juan Fernandez on 15 October.'

The admiral then split his fleet, first dispatching *Nürnberg* to Honolulu with the mail. He then ordered *Cormoran* and the *Prinz Eitel Freidrich* south to disrupt trade in Australian waters.

'For the glory of Germany,' he said. 'There are great prizes to be won.' Von Spee would put his trust – and the care of the 840 souls on board *Scharnhorst* – in God.

After coaling in Eniwetok Lagoon, a secluded German settlement in the Marshall Islands, von Spee had taken his armoured cruisers and five supply ships to another colony in the Marshall Islands.

Now, approaching Christmas Island, in the northern Line Islands, on 8 September, von Spee was summoned to the radio room. He had already noted an improvement in the men's mood after announcing the relaxed conditions earlier that day.

'Sir, *Nürnberg* has just sent word,' Captain Schultz said. 'The enemy have captured German Samoa.'

En route to Hawaii with the mail, *Nürnberg* had taken the opportunistic move of stopping at Fanning Island to cut the enemy's Fiji–Honolulu cable. It was there that they had learned that the New Zealand and Australian forces had combined to take Samoa. They'd got word to *Scharnhorst* before severing the cable.

'Admiral Patey?' von Spee asked. '*Australia*?'

Schultz nodded. 'We believe the Australian fleet was involved.'

Von Spee summoned Schultz and Captain Maerker from *Gneisenau* for an emergency meeting when they arrived at the island. The admiral was strictly business during the chat.

'This Australian force will need constant provisioning,' von Spee said. 'An attack on ships at anchor in Apia might have good results. We will engage enemy ships and acquire provisions and coal.'

Von Spee's plan was motivated by more than the prospect of acquiring fuel and food. He hoped to find warships. He hoped to find Patey. He hoped to go to God with glory.

Apia, Samoa, 14 September 1914

As *Scharnhorst* neared Samoa, each and every gun was inspected. All the bolts tested and tightened, screws turned clockwise. Fresh oil coated on every sliding part. Nothing would stick. Nothing would jam.

The ammunition was methodically inspected and then stacked: 250-pound, 150-pound and 22-pound shells put in pyramid-like piles after being deemed watertight.

The night glasses were fixed. The signalling equipment tested. Each station was wiped, swept and cleaned. Spotless.

Below deck, the 1,212-pound torpedoes were heaved into firing tubes. The sailors had checked all 201 inches of the mean metal before loading and locking.

The chief engineer, flanked by the torpedo officer, toured the ship. He checked every station. Every shell. Every gun. He nodded when he was happy. He yelled, pointed and invoked hell when he was not.

The chief medical officer also toured the ship, the doctor not checking guns but making sure the first aid stations were stocked and adequately armoured, makeshift metal partitions erected to stop the wounded from taking further fire. The doctor counted dressings and swabs. Made sure the scalpels were sterile.

The first officer was also roaming *Scharnhorst*. 'That's a fire hazard,' he shouted as he pointed towards an ammunition box. 'Remove it now. Keep all the gangways clear.'

They were now ready for action. To destroy or be destroyed. Few could stop thinking about HMAS *Australia* and her twelve-inch guns.

SMS *Scharnhorst* and her sister ship, *Gneisenau*, steamed towards Apia. Von Spee held high hopes of landing a blow for Germany. Under the light of his lamp, he studied his map. 'That's close enough,' he said, pulling his head away from the charts and looking towards Captain Schultz.

Schultz nodded before ordering his crew to kill the engines and then the lights.

'Now we wait,' von Spee said.

He walked from the bridge to the side of the ship, grabbing a rail and staring towards the sea. He could see nothing. All was black, the night at its darkest just before dawn. Floating off the coast of Apia, out of sight from the shore, the crew of *Scharnhorst* were still and silent.

That's when God got to work. First, He splashed purples and pinks, His brushstrokes broad, His canvas the sky. Then came the oranges and yellows, suddenly spectacular and brilliantly bright.

'Half speed ahead,' von Spee ordered. The sunrise would be the signal for his attack to begin. He would steam west with the sun glaring bright behind his back. With Apia positioned on the eastern side of Samoa's second largest island, anyone looking from the shore to the sea would be staring directly at the rising sun and *Scharnhorst* would be a narrow silhouette. Von Spee would fire his torpedoes from the shadows.

The four eighteen-inch torpedo tubes on *Scharnhorst* were loaded and ready to be fired. So were the four on *Gneisenau*. Von Spee was hoping to fire before he was spotted. He could send them hurtling towards the sun-blinded enemy ships from a distance of 4,050 yards at a speed of 26 knots. He was hoping that the payload, 388 pounds of TNT, would be delivered before they even knew he was coming. He wouldn't stand a chance against the might of HMAS *Australia* in a toe-to-toe fight. But with the element of surprise he was in with a slugger's shot.

Motoring across the glassy sea towards whatever lay in wait, *Scharnhorst* was mostly silent, no one speaking unless an order had to be administered or acknowledged. Even the ship seemed to be holding its breath.

'Land ahoy,' came the call.

Von Spee pressed his binoculars hard into his eye sockets and saw Samoa slowly revealed. Just a thin green blur on the horizon at first, browns and yellows soon following. Eventually he saw more than colours: trees, cliffs and sand. What he didn't see was ships.

'They're not here,' von Spee muttered.

Both disappointed and relieved, he kept the men at their stations as Apia came into full view. The harbour was deserted except for a solitary ship, a three-mast American schooner. There was, however, a British flag waving proudly at the top of a tall pole on the shore.

'What are your orders, sir?' asked the captain. 'Are we to storm the island and retake her for Germany?'

Von Spee quickly thought through his options. 'We leave,' von Spee replied. 'We make to the northwest … for now.'

The sight of the British flag angered von Spee, but retaking Apia would be pointless. He might have been able to overwhelm an Allied force – the number of which he could only guess at – but he wouldn't be able to leave an occupying force of his own. He needed all his men to man his fleet. Apia would have been left free for the retaking.

He also had no desire to destroy Apia. He didn't want to level the colony just because he could not reclaim it for himself. He thought of the lives that would be lost; there would be soldiers, settlers and natives – his shells did not distinguish. Many of the men, women and children on the island were German citizens.

No, he didn't want Apia. He wanted HMAS *Australia*.

'I would have fought them gladly,' he wrote in his diary that night. 'But the nest was empty. I do not believe I will come into contact with enemy warships in the near future.

'I refrained from ordering a bombardment,' he continued. 'There were houses by which a few groups of people – conjectured by some to be soldiers – were gathered, and among them were natives with children. At 10,000 yards the wireless was too distant so I had to be content with jamming the signals. The results that promised were not delivered.'

Pacific Ocean, northeast of Australia, 17 September 1914

Patey tossed and turned as HMAS *Australia* steamed into the night. He had tried his left side, his right side, his back and even his stomach. No position on his sweat-soaked mattress would allow for sleep.

He tried to silence his mind. *Think nothing. All black. Oblivion.*

He was soon stuffing the pillow under his neck and slamming his back into the bed. Patey could not force away his thoughts, the what ifs. His mind was racing, a torpedo out of its tube. It had all begun after he was ordered to leave Samoa …

Patey had found the two New Zealand transports *Moeraki* and *Monowai* off the coast of Noumea on 21 August as planned. The transports had been escorted to Noumea by the French cruiser *Montcalm* and the three British cruisers *Psyche*, *Philomel* and *Pyramus*.

'We have heard of enemy ships near Samoa, sir,' the captain of *Psyche* told him. 'Two big cruisers are said to be patrolling the coast. It could be *Scharnhorst* and *Gneisenau*.'

It was music to Patey's ears. 'Let's hope so,' he said.

Patey took control of the three-nation fleet. 'We are to proceed with extreme caution,' he said. 'We must take note of the warning and expect to encounter the enemy.'

Patey ordered *Psyche* to lead, travelling eight miles ahead during the day and two miles ahead at night. She would act as a lookout, a forward flank. The rest of the fleet was told to follow in two columns, each a mile apart. HMAS *Australia* would lead one column, the next best-equipped ship, *Montcalm*, the other.

'*Australia* will lead the attack if we are required to engage,' Patey said. '*Montcalm* and *Melbourne* will follow. The rest are to escape.'

They encountered no battleships on the way to Samoa. No cruisers and no torpedo boats. Just blue sky and scorching sun.

A solitary ship confronted them when they entered Apia Bay at 7.45 am on 30 August, an unattended three-mast American schooner. Patey gave the nod for *Psyche* to land and deliver his orders: surrender the colony or else. Patey wasn't expecting 'or else'. With a population of 37,500, of which only 500 were not natives, Patey estimated the colony could muster a fighting force of a couple of hundred at best. They would be up against 1,400 well-armed and well-trained Kiwis and the twelve-inch guns of HMAS *Australia*.

There were no surprises when a man who announced himself as the acting governor of German Samoa emerged at 10.15 am with a response.

'We will offer no resistance,' he said. 'And there are no mines. I have also ordered all transmissions to stop.' He asked for some time to draft a written response.

Patey agreed.

'I leave it to Your Excellency to take possession of the Protectorate of Samoa,' the acting governor said in the handwritten document that was delivered at noon. 'I beg to observe that Your Excellency must also take over responsibility for the life and property of the European population.'

The Kiwi forces were on the ground in Apia by 2.30 pm, all 1,400 ferried to land without incident. The British occupation of German Samoa was made official the next morning when the German flag was taken down from the courthouse and replaced with the Union Jack. The moment was marked with a 21-gun salute, kicked off by the twelve-inch guns of *Australia*.

Patey had completed his mission for the Admiralty – the one he thought was political at best, a land grab at worst and not in the slightest bit strategic. Now he could get back to the business of winning a war. He and his twelve-inch guns would lie in wait.

But just three hours after German Samoa was officially made British, Patey was issued with a new set of orders. A telegram told him he was to escort an Australian expeditionary force from Queensland to Rabaul.

'No!' he shouted. 'Have they lost their blooming minds?'

Patey sent back a message reminding the Admiralty that big German cruisers were still at large and had not been located. Patey was convinced the German fleet was on its way to Samoa.

'Their destination must now almost certainly be South America where coal supply would be guaranteed by nominally neutral but de facto pro-German Chile,' Patey wrote in a message to the Navy Office. '[Von Spee's] way to the Indian Ocean is blocked by both the Japanese and Jerram's fleet. There is to be no chance of coal in the west. We have had the opportunity to bring von Spee to action. I feel for sure he is in the vicinity.'

The Admiralty disagreed. 'He is probably somewhere off northern China,' they wrote. 'He will be covered off by Jerram.'

Patey contacted Admiral Martyn Jerram directly, suggesting the China Squadron and Australian Squadron combine for a sweep of the Caroline Islands and Marshall Islands to find von Spee. Jerram declined, agreeing with the Admiralty. Patey was sent from Samoa.

* * *

That was when the sleepless nights had begun. The tossing and turning. The pleading for the oblivion of black.

Think nothing. That's it. Nothing.

Finally, he could feel himself starting to drift.

Bang! Bang!

'Sir,' came the cry after the assault on his door. 'Admiral, you need to see this.'

Patey snapped to attention without even knowing if he was asleep or awake. He opened the door.

'Sorry, sir,' said the sailor, proffering a telegram.

Patey turned on the light at his desk and read. 'Situation changed by the appearance of *Scharnhorst* and *Gneisenau* at Samoa on 14 September,' the note said. '*Australia* and *Montcalm* to cover

Encounter and expeditionary force from attack, and then search for the two cruisers. *Melbourne* to be used at the rear admiral's discretion. *Sydney* to return for convoy of Australian troops to Aden.'

Patey didn't know whether to laugh or cry. All he knew was that he wouldn't sleep. He was back in the hunt.

'Rabaul?' Patey queried when his next order was sent through later that night: to proceed to Rabaul and cover the expeditionary force of Australians on its mission to occupy the German colony. 'But *Scharnhorst* is in Samoa,' Patey complained to no one in particular. 'That is three thousand miles east of New Guinea. They are not coming back.'

Patey still maintained the German fleet was sailing east. He felt sure they were heading to South America, that they would refuel and resupply before making a run for home.

But the Admiralty insisted the Germans would be heading west, back to New Guinea to stop the Australian occupation and then on to the Indian Ocean to attack trade. Patey's objections were ignored.

When HMAS *Australia* arrived in Rabaul at 4.30 pm on 19 September, Patey was told to wait and watch as a force of 1,523 Australians continued the occupation mission that had started on 11 September. His role was to cover the Australian Naval and Military Expeditionary Force from a possible sea-led attack.

But he didn't want to be providing cover. He wanted to be *leading* an attack …

Chapter 8

SECTION E

Melbourne, 17 September 1914

'Wheatley's report, sir,' said the secretary.

'Good,' Thring said. 'Put it there.' He pointed to the only vacant space on his desk. Thring wiped his eyes, only recently opened after yet another night spent in his office. He took a swig of tea before reading Wheatley's summary, thankfully separate from the blow-by-blow list of every signal intercepted since the start of the war:

Report of Intelligence Branch, Navy Office, Melbourne, on wireless messages of German origin intercepted by Australian shore stations during the week preceding the outbreak of war.

At the outbreak of war the German Pacific Squadron (flagship Scharnhorst*) was amongst the islands to the north of New Guinea. From 25 July to 31 July the German wireless stations at Yap and Tsingtao were very busy interchanging messages between Berlin and* Scharnhorst. *Unfortunately, the* *text of these messages was not taken by our stations, the only record being that the German stations were interchanging traffic.*

Thursday Island, Port Darwin and Port Moresby all notified the head office in Melbourne of this interchange of traffic.

At times, there was apparently some difficulty in getting Scharnhorst *through Yap and Tsingtao, as on 30 July and 1 August messages were transmitted from Berlin to Thursday Island to be sent through Port Moresby radio to* Planet, *which at that time was on the north coast of New Guinea. These messages were then forwarded by* Planet *to* Scharnhorst *and also by* Planet *to Nauru and* Scharnhorst *replied to Yap. Messages continued to arrive in this way for* Planet *until 3 August but on this day they were not transmitted by Port Moresby. On this day the Germans were also making use of the Dutch stations to get into communication with* Geier, *which was evidently cruising in the Dutch Islands. These messages were mostly intercepted by Broome and Port Darwin.*

The same message was frequently being sent in different directions. On 2 August 8.20 pm a message of 19 words was sent from Berlin to Deutscher Kriegaschiff Planet *Nauru and intercepted by Port Moresby. On 3 August at 9.17 pm the same message beginning Berlin No.23 19 words via Yap 2 August was sent by the Dutch station Sitoebondo to* Geier *and intercepted by Broome.*

Again on 3 August at 12.10 am a message was sent from Planet *to Nauru 10 words to Admiral Berlin, also at 12.52 am from* Scharnhorst *to Yap 12 words to Admiral Berlin. Both these messages at 10.40 pm that night were sent by Sitoebondo to* Geier.

For days after the outbreak of war Scharnhorst *was receiving and sending messages from and to Yap and Tsingtao. These were all in the same code, which was evidently a code for the use of men-of-war and important land stations only. It differs very considerably from the* Handelsverkehrsbuch *which was used when men-of-war communicate with merchant vessels.*

Thursday Island and Port Moresby were the best stations for intercepting messages to the north of New Guinea, and Broome for messages from the Dutch Indies.

It may be noted that the receipt of these messages altered the whole movement of the Australian fleet. It was clearly indicated from these messages that the German fleet was to the north of New Guinea and the sailing orders of the Australian fleet were in consequence entirely changed. It had originally been arranged with Admiralty that Australia *should proceeded to Singapore via the south of Australia and sealed orders to this effect were on board, but on receipt of the intercepted enemy messages these orders were cancelled and the whole fleet was ordered direct to New Guinea to get in touch with the enemy and bring him to action if possible.*

Although this was not brought about, it is probable that the presence of HMAS Australia *and cruisers prevented a raid on the coast of Australia.*

Thring was ruing the opportunity missed and he hoped the Admiralty, suddenly interested in *Scharnhorst* following a shock appearance in Samoa, would be too. He ordered a copy of the report to be sent to Jerram and another to Whitehall.

Maybe with this they would take his work seriously. But then again, maybe not …

Melbourne, 18 September 1914

The morning was proving busy for the naval secretary.

'Excuse me, sir,' he said, opening Wheatley's door after a series of progressively louder knocks had failed to provoke a response.

Wheatley was asleep, slumped over the aftermath of a paper storm, typewriter back on the floor.

'Sir,' he said again, this time louder. 'Sir, sorry to disturb you but they are here.'

Wheatley stirred.

'Mr Wheatley,' the secretary said as the instructor lifted his head. 'The ladies are waiting for you in the foyer.'

Wheatley shook his head, suddenly wide awake. 'Ladies?' he said. 'What ladies?'

'Your staff,' the secretary replied.

'Staff?' Wheatley replied. 'Oh. Right. Jolly good.'

Wheatley straightened himself, flattening what little hair he had left with his hand, tucking his shirt back into his pants and reknotting his tie.

'Ladies?' Wheatley muttered as he left his piles of mess.

The instructor had been told he would be getting help. 'You won't be able to get through it all on your own,' Thring had said, after telling him of Britain's plan to send all of their interceptions to Melbourne for decoding. 'I'll get someone in to assist.'

He was expecting an assistant. Just one. A mathematician maybe. A man most certainly.

Wheatley walked into the foyer. 'Oh my,' he said.

His maybe mathematician, certainly a man, was a small army of skirts and cardigans. He counted eight.

'I think I am going to need a bigger office,' Wheatley chuckled. 'Hello, ladies. Welcome aboard.'

Wheatley and his staff of eight were moved into a large room later that day.

'You all read and write German, I take it?' Wheatley asked.

They all nodded.

'And I'll need you to sign this,' Wheatley said. He held up a document and read it out loud. 'I hereby solemnly swear that I will at no time during the course of the present war divulge the nature of the work upon which I am engaged in the Navy Office or discuss outside the office any of the details connected with the work.'

One by one, the new employees signed their names. Wheatley picked up his pen and signed his own name at the bottom as a witness.

And with that Australia had its first crew of code crackers. They called themselves 'Section E'.

Melbourne, 19 September 1914

Wheatley burst through the door, a smile on his face and a pile of pages tucked under his right arm.

'I did it!' he exclaimed. 'I have decrypted the message, sir, and I think it may be rather important.'

Thring smiled. 'I knew you would,' he said. 'Bring it over here then. Let's see what we have.'

Wheatley passed over the message sent by *Scharnhorst* he had five days ago told Thring he couldn't crack.

'It's *HVB*,' he'd said when Thring had presented him with the coded message intercepted in the mid-Pacific. 'But it is not quite right. I can't make any sense of it.'

Thring had told him not to give up. 'This could be it,' he'd said. 'This could be the piece of information we need. I have seen what you can do; your work is extraordinary. I have faith in you. Now have some faith in yourself.'

Wheatley had straightened his shoulders. 'Very well,' he'd said. 'Let's just hope your faith is not misplaced.'

It wasn't.

Now Wheatley, standing tall, handed Thring his paper stack. The captain couldn't hide his excitement. He grabbed at the papers and frantically started flicking through them.

'What am I looking for?' Thring asked.

He was thumbing his way through a pile of handwritten and barely legible notes. There were letters, numerals, scribble and scrawl. Words had been crossed out and replaced in both German and English. And then there was the code, meaningless letter groupings littering every page. They had been attacked with circles, crosses and angry black lines.

'The final page,' Wheatley said. He had given him pages instead of just one, hoping the captain would appreciate the process.

Thring flicked to the last page of the document.

'There.' Wheatley pointed.

Thring found the plain English and read. 'This is it,' he exclaimed. 'You've done it.' He looked down at the page again, rereading it just to make sure. 'By George, this is something indeed,' Thring said.

The message revealed that the entire German East Asia Squadron was set to rendezvous at Easter Island, the most southeastern island in Polynesia. Von Spee had ordered colliers in South America to collect coal and meet him at the Chilean outpost. He was going to sail around Cape Horn.

'I'm sorry it took so long,' Wheatley said. 'I fear I may be to blame for a missed chance.'

'Not at all,' Thring said. 'Even if we can't get them at Easter Island we now know where they are going.'

The message confirmed the predictions from both Patey and Thring that von Spee was heading to South America. That he was not, as the Admiralty had claimed, heading west to the Indian Ocean.

Thring immediately cabled the Admiralty. He told them about Easter Island, about the coal that had been ordered in South America and about what they deduced to be von Spee's plan to steam around Cape Horn.

He then ordered HMAS *Australia* to resume the hunt.

Chapter 9

OPERATION OCCUPIED

Bora Bora, French Polynesia, 22 September 1914

They no longer complained about sleeping in their clothes, shoes, socks and all. They no longer complained about the heat, with doorways, hatches and portholes kept closed. They no longer complained about the daily drills, two hours of every afternoon spent simulating an attack.

By now, as they steamed towards French Polynesia in search of coal, the men aboard *Scharnhorst* and *Gneisenau* had accepted the routine of war.

Von Spee had split his crew into two shifts. Half the ship worked during the day and slept at night, the other half worked during the night and slept at day.

Each shift had its pros and cons. The men who worked the day shift were exposed to the brutality of the equatorial sun, sunburnt and occasionally struck down by sunstroke. Every inch of exposed metal on the ship was turned into a hotplate. The sailors suffered first-, second- and even third-degree burns, flesh melting on railings, door handles and ammunition. Working the crow's nest often proved fatal. With no escape from the sun, dehydration turned into delirium. No one knew until it was too late and no one caught them when they fell.

The men on night shift were not burnt or blistered during the day, they were baked. In closed quarters, doors and portholes tightly shut to block any incoming shells, they sweated more than they slept. The thermometer reached 104 degrees Fahrenheit in the shade. Fully clothed – shoes, socks and all – they tossed, turned and prayed for sleep. God rarely answered.

The men lay awake and thought the worst, waiting for a shell to rip through the side of the ship. They imagined being trapped in their metal box as they drowned.

When darkness finally fell and night swallowed the heat, the men on night shift were forced to work without any form of artificial light. Already sleep-deprived, they manned guns, climbed ropes and read maps by moonlight. They stumbled, and bumped and bruised themselves, a regiment of zombies.

Grabbing an hour of sleep here and there, von Spee worked both day and night. He wanted the men to see him leading the way – up, about and willing to do whatever it took.

'Not far now,' said Captain Schultz. 'Battle stations?'

Von Spee nodded.

Schultz set off the alarm. Those asleep were woken. Those awake would not sleep.

* * *

Eight days earlier, SMS *Scharnhorst*, SMS *Gneisenau* and their crew of colliers had performed a U-turn and headed east after attempting to trick the Allies into thinking they were heading for the Indian Ocean. Once dark, well and truly out of sight, they had turned to their true heading.

'Here,' von Spee had said, pointing at a map. 'This is good.'

The admiral was indicating Suvorov Island, east of Samoa. A former Russian colony, the lagoon atoll was now a British pearl-shell farm.

'There will be no guns,' von Spee said. 'But lots of coal. Here. We go here.'

'*Scheisse*,' von Spee exclaimed when they reached Suvorov, the admiral surprising those within earshot at the rare profanity. As predicted, there were no big guns and no shooting, and lots of coal stores in sight – the big buildings used to hold the precious commodity brimming with black. But there was also nowhere to anchor. The island was just eighty acres, and no ship bigger than twenty-five feet could enter its harbour, which was really just a lagoon.

Von Spee looked at the lagoon and then at his map and swore again. Frowning in concentration as he stroked his bearded chin, he steeled himself for the decision he had to make. He returned to the bridge.

'We will not attack,' von Spee said. 'We leave immediately.'

'But, admiral,' Schultz said, 'what if they report our position?'

Von Spee turned back towards the island and stared. He imagined the inhabitants, mostly natives, all civilians. 'They will not suffer for our mistake,' he said. 'If they do report us, then so be it.'

Von Spee returned to his map. He soon fingered their next destination.

'Papeete?' asked Captain Schultz.

Von Spee nodded. 'I intend to sink any enemy warships which may be found in Tahiti, commandeer coal and requisition food supplies. Forcible measures will be taken in case the demand for supplies is not complied with. The targets will be the first positions from which the enemy opens fire, then defended targets, arsenals and public buildings. We must have the armed cutters ready to take the requisitions. Minesweeping gear will be needed too.'

'Very well,' Schultz replied. 'I will prepare the ship for battle.'

'Not just yet,' von Spee said. 'We will be making a stop on the way. Take the flags down instead.'

* * *

That stop was Bora Bora. A colony of France, Bora Bora was a Pacific paradise. Turquoise sea and white sand, it had been annexed by the French in 1888 along with several other islands that became known as French Polynesia.

Von Spee wasn't there to attack but to trade.

After removing the flags from the ship to hide that they were the enemy, he sent his best French and English speakers to shore. Pretending to be traders, they fooled a French police officer, who welcomed them with open arms, mistaking the

English-speaking German for a British admiral. A town official presented him with a flower bouquet.

The German actors used gold to pay for pigs, poultry, eggs, fruit and vegetables. French officials asked them for news of the war. Had the Allies had any victories? Would it soon be over? Were there Germans in the Pacific?

A large French flag was hoisted in a farewell salute from the shore. In reply, *Scharnhorst* raised the German naval ensign. Von Spee laughed as he imagined the red faces and profanities.

As they steamed away, von Spee blocked all wireless signals coming out of Bora Bora, jamming the system with static so the French colonists could not warn anyone of the devious Germans who had come with gold instead of guns.

Telling Schultz he could now prepare the ship for battle, von Spee set a course for Papeete. The capital of French Polynesia, located on the island of Tahiti, Papeete was the biggest French base in the Pacific. The unsuspecting officials in Bora Bora had revealed Papeete was storing 5,000 tons of high-quality Cardiff coal. They had also warned that it was guarded by coastal batteries and a battleship.

Von Spee edged towards the port, ready for a fight. All hands were on deck – more than 1,600 men, the combined crews of *Scharnhorst* and *Gneisenau* – as the volcanic island of Papeete was revealed.

The twelve-yard metal barrels of the 8.2-inch SKL/40s sought targets as they approached, and the 550-pound shells were loaded. Soon eight of the gigantic guns were aimed at Papeete.

More levers were pushed and pulled, wheels were turned. Another sixteen guns were aimed at the island, the SKL/35s locked, loaded and ready to fire.

The artillery director, watching from high above, gave the signal. And with that they unleashed hell.

The guns barked, a pack of ferocious dogs let loose in paradise. A series of explosions silenced the tropical birds, the sound of the ocean lapping the shore replaced by gunfire.

The blitzkrieg of shells took out a battleship, the French gunboat *Zélée* sunk. The French returned fire from the shore, the coastal batteries launching to life. But they were not in range and the shells fell short.

A fresh round of fire from *Scharnhorst* destroyed the French guns. A brushfire started next to the rubble and ruin.

Von Spee nodded after the attack, all French defences down. The spoils of war awaited.

'Over there,' Schultz said. 'Look.' The captain was pointing at a rising cloud of black.

'*Scheisse*,' von Spee swore again.

It turned out that Papeete had been warned about a potential raid from the Germans. They had prepared for an attack by placing incendiaries in and around their coal stores. They'd been lit as soon as the Germans had fired. The plume climbed fast and high, ghostly ash fingers soon reaching towards the 7,000-foot peak of the dormant volcano that towered over the island.

A further barrage came from shore, white puffs of smoke appearing from amidst the trees. Von Spee's gunners were quick to destroy the previously unseen French batteries. They too were reduced to rubble.

'Shall I order the landing?' Schultz asked.

'No,' von Spee said shortly, his frustration evident.

With no coal to acquire, the stores still sending black smoke high into the sky, von Spee ordered the raiding party to retreat. He set a course for the French Marquesas Islands, 850 miles to the northeast.

Rabaul, German New Guinea, 26 September to 3 October 1914

The occupation of Rabaul was officially proclaimed on 26 September after the Australian Naval and Military Expeditionary Force overcame almost 300 soldiers to claim the German colony for the British Empire. Six Australians were killed during the campaign that saw a total of forty-two dead.

Patey was now free to hunt von Spee.

Scharnhorst had last been seen on 14 September in Apia, Samoa. By the time *Australia* was ready for sea in three days' time, the German ship could be anywhere in the Pacific between South America and Australia.

'In all probability, they are not in the Marshalls or the Carolines,' Patey wrote. 'The presence of two Japanese squadrons in that area should ensure they stay away from this area. That would leave them to: a) attempt to reach the Indian Ocean via Malaysia, b) attempt to reach the Indian Ocean around Australia, c) operate in Australasian waters, or d) make for the coast of South America and thence reach the South Atlantic.'

Patey was almost certain von Spee and his fleet would take the last option. But he needed something more than a hunch to be able to act. 'What about the message?' he asked at a meeting to decide the next move for *Australia*. 'The intercept decoded in Melbourne? Surely that is proof enough.' He knew it wasn't.

As soon as the message had been decrypted, Commander Thring had sent through an order for *Australia* to steam to Fiji. Thring had travelled straight to Sydney and arranged for the fastest colliers he could find to meet Patey in what was the nearest friendly port to von Spee's suspected position. The colliers would set off with enough stocks and supplies for *Australia* to hunt von Spee to the edge of the earth. But once again the Admiralty had dismissed the intelligence. They had overruled Thring and ordered *Australia* to stay in Rabaul until the occupation had been accomplished.

'Thring has also provided intelligence that large supplies of coal have been bought by Germans from San Francisco,' Patey had said. 'Surely this puts it beyond doubt?'

It didn't.

The Admiralty were certain von Spee had gone north from Apia and would soon encounter the Japanese. Patey too was ordered north.

'Pick up wireless with the Japanese,' he was told. 'And then arrange to cooperate.'

So Patey steamed north. He left New Guinea behind on 1 October and went looking for the Japanese.

'Sir, we are intercepting signals from the Japanese,' a radio operator said later that night. 'They are within range.'

'Tell them we are here,' Patey said. 'That we request a location to rendezvous.'

The operator returned an hour later.

'Well?' Patey asked. 'What did they say? What's the heading?'

The operator stood silent.

'What is it, man?' Patey asked.

The operator summoned the courage to speak. 'I have a message, sir, but it is not from the Japanese,' the operator said. 'They are yet to reply. But I don't think it really matters if they do or not.' The operator's tongue was again tied.

'Spit it out,' Patey demanded.

'It's the Admiralty, sir,' the operator said. 'We have new orders.'

The Naval Board had received news of a fresh sighting of *Scharnhorst* and *Gneisenau*. Shortly after midnight on 27 September, it had learned that the two German ships had attacked the French port of Papeete on 22 September.

'We are to head back to Rabaul, sir,' the operator said. 'And we are to await further instructions.'

Again, Patey didn't know whether to laugh or cry. His suspicions had once more proved correct and he had now been pulled off a pointless rendezvous with the Japanese. But how much time had they wasted? How long would it take to prepare the fleet in Rabaul? They would already be upon von Spee had they departed for Suva when Thring had given his order.

Further instructions came on 3 October as they neared Rabaul. 'It is very probable that *Gneisenau* and *Scharnhorst* may repeat attack similar to that at Papeete,' the Admiralty order read. 'Therefore, they may be expected to return to Samoa, Fiji or even New Zealand. Make Suva your headquarters, search for these cruisers in those waters, and leave Simpson Harbour as soon as possible to search.'

Now it was time to cry.

Easter Island, southeastern Pacific, 12 October 1914

The tear that he had refused to let Otto and Heinrich see outside the church in the Marshall Islands returned as he saw the incoming ship.

'It's *Nürnberg*, sir,' said Captain Schultz. 'She's back.'

Von Spee had not dared hope he would see his eldest boy again. He had watched *Nürnberg* steam away from Eniwetok almost certain he and *Scharnhorst* would soon be sunk. The sight of *Nürnberg* returning, with his son aboard, was a moment of both joy and pain.

He had sent *Nürnberg* – and Otto – away privately hoping the ship would be spared, that both the ship and his son would see out the war as couriers. But now, with *Nürnberg* returning after receiving orders to rejoin the fleet from Admiralty while in Hawaii, he and both his boys would face the same fate.

For better or worse, they would be together.

After a five-day stop at the Marquesas Islands, coal and provisions obtained and legs stretched, *Scharnhorst* and *Gneisenau* and their coal ships had zigzagged their way across the Pacific. Attempting to avoid trading routes, they had sailed on a wide front, the squadron cutting from south to north as they made east for Chilean-controlled Easter Island.

Before leaving the Marquesas Islands, von Spee had sent two supply ships to Honolulu with new messages for Berlin. He'd told the Admiralty of his plan to proceed to Easter Island, and from there onwards to the Juan Fernandez Islands and then to Valparaiso, a port in Chile.

Von Spee had also sent a message to the high consul in San Francisco. He'd told the consul to send 5,000 tons of coal to Valparaiso and another 10,000 tons to other ports throughout Chile. He'd also requested stores from Neuva York and La Plata, Argentina, to be sent to Pernambuco, Brazil, to supply his fleet for the Atlantic leg of the German return.

During the nine-day trip from the Marquesas Islands to Easter Island, a brief connection to a wireless network had delivered the news that *Nürnberg*, *Dresden* and *Leipzig* would reunite with the German squadron at Easter Island. By coincidence more than design, as the Admiralty knew nothing of the squadron's plans, the three ships had been ordered by Berlin to rendezvous at Easter Island. It was a case of same time and same place.

'Please send an invitation to both Otto and Heinrich,' von Spee asked Captain Schultz, the tear well and truly wiped before he turned. 'I would like both of them to join me tonight for a small celebration.'

'What's the occasion, sir?' Schultz asked.

Von Spee held his left hand aloft and pointed to the gold band on his ring finger.

'It is my twenty-fifth wedding anniversary,' von Spee said. 'I believe that is called the "silver" anniversary, although for me it will be very much a sea anniversary, as I am also married to this ship. I wasn't going to celebrate it, but now that both my boys are here, why not?'

Von Spee spent the night smoking cigars and playing cards with his boys. They didn't talk about tropical wonderlands, emperors they had met or kings and queens. But they did speak of one faraway place: home.

'Here's to your mother,' von Spee said, raising his glass. 'The love of my life. I can't see or talk to her on this day, but I will write to her tonight.'

Schultz interrupted them following the toast. 'For you, sir,' he said. 'A little something from me and the crew. It is not much but it's a token of our respect and good wishes.'

The captain presented him with a finely crafted chocolate – a rare delight – delivered on a silver dish. Not one to usually show emotion, von Spee grinned from ear to ear, a rare smile for a rare kindness.

He retired to his cabin following his unexpected dessert to make good on the promise to his wife. 'Despite the demands of war there is still time for human touch,' he wrote. 'It is not often and fleeting but I suppose its absence makes it so much more special when such occasions should happen. Tonight was such an occasion. The constant uncertainty of what is to come aggravates the loneliness of command. The evenings here are extremely tedious, as we extinguish the lights. It is too hot to sit in a closed room and everything is uncomfortable. We cannot escape the coal grime.

'I long for news of you all but that is a forlorn hope. I am missing you and the social contact very much. I suppose this is a small sacrifice we have to pay for these great times in which we live.'

He then told his wife of his bold bid to deliver himself and her sons back to Berlin.

'May God wish it so,' he wrote.

Suva, Fiji, 12 October 1914

Rear Admiral Patey and his squandered squadron had arrived in Fiji. 'Japanese Admiralty have been asked to agree to the following arrangements,' his latest order had said. 'Japanese Second Squadron to cruise north of latitude 20°S and west of 140°E. Japanese First Squadron to cruise north of equator and west of 140°E. Australian Squadron to cruise and search south of equator and west of 140°W and to include the French islands. All of these squadrons should communicate whenever possible with each other and with their respective admiralties, and will, by their movements, assist each other's operations.'

Patey was an attack dog bound by a leash. Tethered to Suva, he could only go as far east as Papeete before his master would pull the chain and yank him on back.

But Patey had continued to collect intelligence. He'd never relented from studying his maps, and he was now more adamant than ever that von Spee was heading to South America. By now almost there.

Patey had again messaged the Admiralty. If he couldn't change their mind maybe he could suggest a better alternative, one that would put him in a position to strike once their position in South America was utterly and definitively proved.

The gun emplacement at Fort Nepean, Port Phillip, south of Melbourne. This six-inch coastal gun fired the first shot of World War I – a warning blast aimed at the departing German merchant ship SS *Pfalz* – on 5 August 1914. Bombardier John Purdue, who pressed the fire button, is fifth from the left in the back row. *(Australian War Memorial, A01184)*

Following the warning shot, SS *Pfalz* was persuaded to return to Portsea. Subsequently requisitioned by the Royal Australian Navy, *Pfalz* was converted to a troopship, renamed the HMT *Boorara* and sent to the Mediterranean to support Allied forces. *(State Library of Victoria)*

Vice Admiral Sir William Creswell was the Royal Australian Navy's inaugural chief, or First Naval Member, from 1904 to 1919. *(State Library of South Australia, B 11220)*

Captain Walter Thring and his wife, Lydia. Thring was instrumental in turning the Australian Navy into a world-class force. *(Royal Australian Navy)*

A naval college instructor at the start of the war, Dr Frederick Wheatley was plucked from obscurity to become the Australian Navy's chief cryptologist. *(Royal Australian Navy)*

Admiral George Edwin Patey, commander of HMAS *Australia*, felt the British Admiralty stymied his attempts to engage the German Pacific fleet. *(National Portrait Gallery)*

HMAS *Australia* in Sydney, 4 October 1913. The ship was ordered in 1910, built in Glasgow and commissioned as the Royal Australian Navy's first flagship. Wielding far greater fire power than any of the German Pacific ships, it was greeted with fervour by the Australian public and seen as a powerful symbol of nationhood. *(Royal Australian Navy)*

The British Admiralty ordered HMAS *Australia* to support a New Zealand expeditionary force as it attempted to invade and take over the former German colony of Samoa in August 1914. Allied soldiers raised the British flag in the capital, Apia, on 30 August. *(Alamy)*

Vice Admiral Graf Maximilian von Spee, head of the East Asia Squadron, the German fleet in the Pacific. Von Spee was considered to be one of the world's best naval tacticians. *(Alamy)*

Rear Admiral Christopher Cradock led the British fleet that was soundly defeated by von Spee's ships at the Battle of Coronel, Chile, on 1 November 1914. *(Getty Images)*

The German East Asia Squadron's flagship, SMS *Scharnhorst*, docking at Valparaiso, Chile, after its triumph at the Battle of Coronel. Measuring almost 150 metres in length and displacing more than 11,000 tons, *Scharnhorst* had a crew of 52 officers and 788 men. *(Alamy)*

On his arrival in the neutral town of Valparaiso, von Spee was greeted by German residents. Despite their warm welcome, von Spee ordered that his victory at Coronel not be celebrated and that, instead, flowers should be laid around the settlement's docks to honour the dead. *(Alamy)*

After replenishing its coal supplies, the German fleet set sail from Valparaiso in mid November 1914. At that point, von Spee's plan was to head across the Pacific, round Cape Horn and make a dash across the Atlantic Ocean, back to Germany. *(Alamy)*

After the German cruiser SMS *Emden* took over a communications station in the Cocos Islands, HMAS *Sydney* was sent to investigate. In the subsequent battle on 9 November 1914, *Sydney* destroyed *Emden*, forcing the German crew to flee their ship in lifeboats, as seen here. *(Alamy)*

A resident of the Cocos Islands watches HMAS *Sydney* depart after its victory over *Emden*. *Sydney* lost just three crew, compared to 134 German dead. The victory was seen as a triumph for the fledgling Royal Australian Navy and widely celebrated. Recovered pieces of *Emden* are on display today in the Australian War Memorial, Canberra. *(Australian War Memorial, H12447)*

The German fleet off Chile in November 1914 en route to the Falkland Islands. The photograph was taken from the deck of the *Dresden*. Up ahead are the *Nürnberg*, *Leipzig*, *Gneisenau* and *Scharnhorst*. *(Alamy)*

A contemporary illustration of the Battle of the Falkland Islands, which took place on 8 December 1914 and is still marked by a public holiday in the Falkland Islands. Those killed in battle numbered 1881; all except ten were German. The Allied victory effectively eliminated the German naval threat in the southern hemisphere. *(Alamy)*

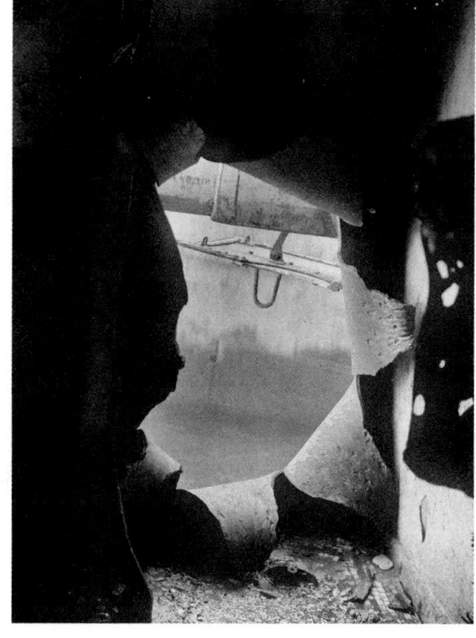

Damage suffered by HMS *Kent*, one of the eight British ships that took part in the Battle of the Falkland Islands. No ships were lost on the Allied side, while four of the eight German vessels were sunk and two captured and subsequently scuttled. *(Imperial War Museum, Q45917)*

Towards the end of the Battle of the Falkland Islands, Maximilan von Spee went down with his flagship, *Scharnhorst*. His two sons, Otto (at left), a member of the crew of SMS *Nürnberg*, and Heinrich (at right), who served aboard SMS *Gneisenau*, also lost their lives. *(Alamy)*

German sailors from SMS *Gneisenau* adrift in the ocean after the Battle of the Falkland Islands. The photograph was taken from the British ship HMS *Invincible*; in the background HMS *Inflexible* stands ready to bring survivors aboard. *(Wikimedia Commons)*

'If Germans intend remaining in Pacific Ocean, it is possible they have established a collier base at Marquesas Islands,' Patey wrote in his message to the Admiralty. 'Or if they intend to go to America and return westward later on, it is possible also that colliers might be left at Marquesas Islands. Therefore, it might be worthwhile to visit Marquesas Islands and return to Suva.

'Should it become definitely known that the German squadron has gone to South America, and if Admiralty decided to send the Australian fleet after them, the following suggestion is offered: route proposed to follow, Marquesas Islands and Galapagos Islands. If only *Australia* and *Sydney* go a rendezvous should be arranged with *Newcastle* and *Idzumo*.'

Patey received the Admiralty's reply on 14 October: 'It is decided not to send Australian fleet to South America,' the Admiralty wrote. 'Without more definite information it is not desirable to proceed as far as the Marquesas Islands.'

Patey's neck reeled, the chain yanked hard. 'What more can I do?' he exploded. 'The world is at war and we have been chasing ghosts for three months.'

Still he refused to give up.

Patey was sure it was only a matter of time until von Spee and his squadron were spotted off the South American coast. He had Thring's message about the rendezvous in Easter Island. He had Thring's message about 15,000 tons of coal being ordered from San Francisco.

'Keep all the colliers stocked, manned and at the ready,' he ordered. Patey would make sure his fleet was ready and able to steam halfway across the world at a moment's notice. He had ordered his fastest collier, *Mallina*, to be filled to its 6,500-ton capacity and to remain by *Australia*'s side at all times. He also had his bigger but slower colliers ready and waiting.

They would have to give chase.

'Everyone is rather fed up,' an officer wrote in a letter to his wife. 'We are doing nothing and we are all very sick and tired at not being allowed to cross to South America. Perhaps there are, after all, some of our armoured cruisers from the southwest coast of America waiting for them. They would just be in time if they were, but it would spoil our game completely.'

Chapter 10

SUPERENCIPHERMENT

Melbourne, 19 October 1914

Thring clenched his fists so hard that the skin covering his knuckles almost threatened to tear.

'Is this really how they are going to tell us that we were right?' he asked, shaking the document as he handed it to Vice Admiral Creswell.

Creswell looked down and read aloud. 'Please telegraph to Intelligence Centre, Montevideo, addressed Vivitur, Montevideo, confidential call signs for following German men-of-war: *Scharnhorst*, *Gneisenau*, *Emden*, *Nürnberg*, *Dresden*, *Leipzig*, *Geier*, *Karlsruhe* and *Eber*.'

The Admiralty had just asked the Navy Office to provide the decoded call signs for the German squadron to an intelligence station based in South America.

'So they finally believe that von Spee is headed to South America?' Creswell asked.

'What else could this message mean?' Thring replied. 'They have put their South American stations on alert.'

'Did anything else come through?' Creswell asked. 'Have they orders for Patey?'

Thring shook his head. 'Nothing,' he said. 'But I assume they will be coming. Let's just hope he can get there before they wreak havoc. Anything from the minister?'

'Nothing of significance,' Creswell said. 'They are growing tired of the situation, but nothing can be down for now. It's going to be the Admiralty running the show until the end of the war.'

Like both Thring and Creswell, the newly elected Australian government had concerns with the Royal Australian Navy being run from a room on the other side of the world. Former prime minister Joseph Cook's bold gamble to dissolve parliament in response to the blocking of all bills in the Senate by Labor had backfired in spectacular fashion when Australia went to the polls on 5 September. Going up against Labor leader Andrew Fisher, who had previously served two terms as prime minister, Cook lost in a landslide. Fisher and his Labor Party won forty-two out of seventy-five seats in the House of Representatives and thirty-one out of thirty-six seats in the Senate.

Following the defeat, Cook admitted to getting a 'jolly good licking', which was in no way helped by a memorable speech made by Fisher before the outbreak of war. 'Turn your eyes to the European situation,' Fisher had said. 'And give your kindest feelings towards the mother country at this time. I sincerely hope that international arbitration will avail before Europe is convulsed in the greatest war of any time. All, I am sure, will regret the critical position existing at the present time, and pray that a disastrous war may be averted. But should the worst happen after everything has been done that honour will permit, Australians will stand beside our own to help and defend her to our last man and our last shilling.'

When he was sworn in to serve his third term as prime minister of Australia, he made good on that promise, raising 30,000 volunteers to be shipped off to Alexandria in Egypt to join Britain in her fight.

With the new government came a new minister for defence; king-first-and-country-second Millen was replaced by George Pearce. He had served in the role during Fisher's previous two terms, so both Thring and Creswell were familiar with this Australian-born son of a blacksmith.

Pearce had campaigned for Australia to be in control of all her military affairs before the Commonwealth Liberal Party won office in 1913. But the following plan had been agreed to by the former government before he was returned to office:

On the receipt of a prearranged cablegram from the Imperial authorities, the Australian government would place the Naval Board and the naval services of the Commonwealth directly under the control of the Admiralty. The sea-going fleet would then become a squadron of the Imperial [Royal] Navy, taking orders either direct from London or the British officer under whom they were placed. The Naval Board would be placed in the position, with regard to the Admiralty, of a naval commander-in-chief at a British port, and would take orders

> *direct from the Admiralty, informing the Commonwealth government of those orders. Any important orders issued to Australian ships, or orders involving help that the board could give, would be communicated to the board by the Admiralty, and other naval officers in high command anywhere would communicate with the board exactly as they would with fellow officers of similar rank.*

Pearce's hands were tied.

'We just have to keep up the good fight,' Creswell said. 'Keep the intelligence coming and keep at 'em.'

Thring rolled his eyes as he thought of the latest decryption that the Admiralty had ignored after Wheatley had come bouncing into his office on 5 October.

'We have another one,' Wheatley had said. 'More proof that they are heading to Easter Island.'

The message had been intercepted by a station in Suva at 8.15 pm on 4 October. Using the call sign 'FODA', an eight-word message beginning with 'KISAH ACIBI' had been transmitted from one unknown ship to another. The message was sent on to Melbourne after no one in the newly formed 'Room 40', the Admiralty's version of Australia's Section E, could crack the code.

Enter Wheatley and the women of Section E. For the past sixty-eight days the instructor had spent every waking minute with his head in the *HVB*. His all-female team had assisted him by taking notes, typing letters, and bringing him food. Some nights he had even fallen asleep reading the leatherbound book.

Having committed chunks of pages to memory, he could now look at five-letter groups of nonsense and see real words: names of ships, common phrases and frequently used terms.

He decoded the new message that was considered indecipherable by his Room 40 counterparts in just twenty minutes.

'*Scharnhorst* to *Dresden*,' the decryption read. '*Scharnhorst* is on the way between Marquesas Islands and Easter Island, present position 130°W.'

The remainder of the message had been mutilated in transmission.

'Proof indeed,' Thring had said. 'This isn't just *about* the *Scharnhorst* – it is *from* the *Scharnhorst*.'

'I'm sorry that the message is incomplete,' Wheatley said. 'That is how it was presented to me. The wireless station only picked up the first part.'

'It doesn't matter,' Thring said. 'The longitudinal position is all we need. We know where they are headed.'

It was time to unleash the sea dogs. To release Patey and *Australia* from their chain.

Or so Thring thought.

Having directed Patey to Suva on 3 October following the German attack at Papeete, the Admiralty had told the Royal Australian Navy that the order was to stand. They were still adamant von Spee and his squadron would head back west to attack their bases in the Pacific.

Yet now, just five days after refusing the Royal Australian Navy's latest request to send the Australian Squadron east to hunt down and destroy the German fleet in South America, the Admiralty had requested intelligence – not ships – be sent to Uruguay.

Melbourne, 26 October 1914

'What a curious collection of ships,' Thring said, looking at the latest message from the Admiralty.

With HMAS *Australia* all bark and no bite, locked in a Pacific cage, Thring had boldly asked the Admiralty of their plan to deal with von Spee should he and his fleet suddenly appear in South America. He queried how they would bring down one of the great naval tacticians and his fearsome fleet.

The Admiralty informed Thring that *Good Hope*, *Canopus*, *Monmouth*, *Glasgow* and *Otranto* were operating on the South American east coast. The Admiralty considered this fleet of five ships, commanded by Rear Admiral Christopher Cradock, plus some minor reinforcements, would be a more than sufficient force to deal with von Spee and the German East Asia Squadron should they attempt to round Cape Horn and make a run for Europe.

Thring and Creswell disagreed with the Admiralty. The flagship of the 'curious' fleet was HMS *Good Hope*, a fifteen-year-old ship with a top speed of twenty-three knots. The *Drake*-class armoured cruiser was equipped with two 9.2-inch guns and sixteen six-inch guns. It would be up against the eight 8.3-inch guns, six 5.9-inch guns and eighteen 3.5-inch guns of both *Scharnhorst* and *Gneisenau*.

Half the guns on board *Good Hope* were also useless, most of the six-inch guns mounted on broadside batteries so low that they couldn't be aimed high enough to hit anything but water. Of her crew, ninety percent of the men aboard *Good Hope* were reservists, who had only fired one full practice shoot since the ship had departed Portsmouth on 2 October.

Only the war had stopped HMS *Monmouth* from being condemned. A fourteen-year-old ship, seventy feet smaller in length than *Good Hope*, she was recommissioned at the outbreak of war and rushed into service without being welded into fighting trim. She would have been sent to the bottom of the ocean had it not been for the assassination in Sarajevo. The effective broadside of *Monmouth* in a seaway was only seven six-inch guns.

Built in 1909, *Glasgow* was the fastest and newest of the fleet. With a top speed of twenty-five knots, the Town-class light cruiser was manoeuvrable. But the ship was only equipped with two six-inch guns and ten four-inch guns. *Glasgow* also wore light armour, less than an inch thick in weak spots on the deck.

HMS *Otranto* was a 12,000-ton merchant liner that had been requisitioned for the war. Converted to a cruiser that was intended to protect shipping lanes in Britain, the five-year-old vessel had been armed with eight 4.7-inch guns. *Otranto* wore no armour. None.

And then there was *Canopus*, a slow but well-armed and well-armoured ship. Launched in 1897, the pre-dreadnought vessel carried two twelve-inch, twelve six-inch and ten three-inch guns. As on *Good Hope*, the crew were largely reservists. But unlike *Good Hope*, *Canopus* had not even had one fire test.

Christopher Cradock, known as Kit, would be the Royal Navy admiral who would go toe-to-toe with von Spee should the German squadron sail into the South Atlantic. The 52-year-old was considered one of the best officers in the Royal Navy after proving both courageous and capable during the Boxer Rebellion. His 'curious' fleet, however, was cause for concern.

Thring could not decide if the Admiralty were arrogant or simply stupid.

He sought and found Wheatley. 'I need you to get to these with haste,' he said, a fresh stack of coded transmissions tucked in his hand. 'There may be a message in here that could stop a catastrophe.'

He told Wheatley of the lambs being sent to slaughter.

Suva, Fiji, 27 October 1914

Patey was prepared, his 590-foot-long deliverer of death ready to depart. Every gun on HMAS *Australia* was oiled, manned and seemingly begging to shoot shells at German steel.

He could only imagine the type of destruction HMAS *Australia* could inflict, having never taken the destroyer into battle. Her four twin twelve-inch guns – the largest of any ship in any fleet – sixteen four-inch guns and two eighteen-inch torpedo tubes had only ever been fired at test targets. Patey looked at the men operating them – young, fit, and well trained – and saw victory.

HMAS *Australia* was made for war, and now, with the world at war, she was being made to wait.

Patey had been informed that 'Kit' Cradock and his curious fleet would deal with von Spee should the German squadron appear in South America. Patey thought Cradock's fleet was more than curious. He thought it was suicidal.

Melbourne, 26–28 October 1914

Wheatley, getting straight to the codes, wondered what the random letters would reveal. An order from Vice Admiral von Spee? The location of Scharnhorst? The final destination of the fleet? Whatever the jumble of code on the two pages of paper handed to him by Thring said, it had to be important.

'This has come directly from the Admiralty by way of Montevideo,' Thring had said. 'They couldn't make sense of it, but they are in a big hurry to find out what it says.'

Wheatley wondered why the Admiralty had not deciphered the message themselves. He had made a single translated copy of the *HVB* and sent it to Whitehall. Surely they had the book by now? It had been sent on a steamer travelling directly to London at the end of August. The cryptanalytic department Whitehall called Room 40 was headed by the director of naval education, Alfred Ewing, and Wheatley wondered whether they had chosen a naval educator because of the success Australia had enjoyed with a certain college instructor. He couldn't help but think so.

'Ready for some work, ladies?' Wheatley asked as he returned to Section E. He pointed to the stack of code delivered to him by Thring. 'I'll need all my translations typed with haste. And I may need you to lend your minds if I end up in a muddle.'

Wheatley's assistants did more than type. When he was stuck and could make no sense of the jumbled-up words, his female force would become code breakers too. He would often ask them to take a look at his notes and see if there was something he had missed, or something he could not see. They also offered vital support and encouragement.

With his team on notice, Wheatley retreated to his office to attack his stack. His desk had slowly transformed from mess to meticulous since the start of this code-cracking caper. From the random chaos of the start – files thrown on the floor and paper stacks reaching towards the roof – his office now resembled a surgery. He only had the tools he needed for the job: a lamp, blank paper, pencils and pens, a rubber and, last but not least, the codebook that Captain Richardson had seized at gunpoint.

Even his notebooks were neat. Once covered with random letters, thick black lines, doodles and the odd profanity, the foolscap folders now contained only crisp and neatly written decodes. All legible, no failures or fuss.

He had reduced what was infuriating work at first to a process. He was now a mechanic, replacing and installing letters instead of spare parts. He sat down at his work bench, flicked on the light and started on the latest codes, thinking it wouldn't take long.

Four hours later the room was wrecked, a hailstorm of scrunched paper on the hardwood floor. Files lay scattered, pens and pencils everywhere. Wheatley was also a mess, his hair sticking up in every direction. There were coffee stains on his white shirt, which was untucked and damp with sweat. His foolscap folder was full of squiggles and scrawl; the only legible words on the hundreds of pages he had filled were ones like 'Why?' and 'What?'.

Wheatley ripped yet another page from his notepad, scrunched it into a paper ball and threw it onto the floor with the rest. He fell face first onto his desk, brow bashing the closed codebook to punish himself as much as it. He knew the *HVB* contained the answers, but he had run out of questions. He just could not crack the message from Montevideo.

It was made up of random letters in groupings of five. He was sure the code was the *HVB,* but once again the key had been changed. And this time he could not see an obvious solution.

DGASF SDFWE. He had started with the first five-letter groupings in the message. Writing the two non-words down, he went to his book but couldn't find anything that remotely resembled the seemingly random combination of letters.

He wrote down the next groupings, LMPGF LDSMG, before going back to the book, hoping the first two groupings had been recorded wrongly. *A dodgy line? A dodgy operator?*

But again, the combination of letters was nowhere to be found in the *HVB*. He checked all 300 entries – over fifty word combinations on each page, starting with A and ending with Z – in case the first letter had been changed. But there wasn't a combination of letters that matched what he had at all.

He repeated the process for the next grouping and then the grouping after that.

He was certain that this was the *HVB* code but he couldn't decode it with the key he had.

Wheatley pulled his head up from the book and glanced down at his soiled shirt, wondering how long he had been wearing the once-white button-up. Was it three days or four?

He then wondered how long it had been since he had seen his family: his wife, Alice, and his three children, Vivian, Phyllis and Ross. Was it a week? More?

All he knew was that he had spent two days working on the code given to him by Thring on 26 October.

Like Thring, Wheatley had a foldout bed in his office. He had spent the last two nights there. That wasn't unusual. Most days he missed the last train from Melbourne to Geelong, forty-six miles away. He loved Geelong, but right now he wished he and his family lived in Melbourne. He missed home-cooked meals and his wife's touch. He missed helping his girls with their homework. He missed playing cricket with his son.

Geelong had welcomed Wheatley and his young family. Local dignitaries had presented him and his wife with membership to various clubs; the former headmaster with the double degree had been embraced immediately as a pillar of the community. Wheatley had become fond of the yacht club, a popular place for navy types. He imagined being there now, knocking back a beer, his biggest problem a tardy student or a pile of papers waiting to be marked. He then imagined going home to his wife, another glass of beer and dinner waiting, unmarked exams and disagreeable students fast forgotten.

Wheatley sat for a moment and smiled, holding onto thoughts of friends and family for as long as he could. But his mind was soon invaded again by random letters, begging him to turn them into sense.

He gave up, and decided to turn to his female team.

'All yours,' he said as he put down a pile of paper on the nearest desk, which happened to be occupied by Irene Williams. 'I'm out of ideas.'

Miss Williams placed a hand on the pile. 'Is it *HVB*?' she asked.

'Almost certainly,' Wheatley said.

'Maybe they've used a superencipherment,' Williams suggested, 'added another layer of code?'

Wheatley smiled. 'By golly,' he said. 'That might just be it.'

Irene Williams smiled, blushed even.

'You'll have my job soon,' Wheatley said.

Half kicking himself for not seeing the obvious and half chuffed that he had been given a solution, Wheatley strolled down the hall to see Thring. 'They've used a superencipherment,' he announced. 'They've recoded the decryption with another key that, unfortunately, we don't have.'

'Well, crack it then,' Thring said. 'I won't accept anything less.' He handed Wheatley another message, fresh from Montevideo. 'Something is happening,' Thring said. 'And you are the only one who can tell us what and when.'

Chapter 11

CORONEL

Valparaiso, Chile, 1 November 1914, 3 am

The German East Asia Squadron had arrived in Chile without incident, ducking and weaving across the Pacific, and was now anchored off Valparaiso. The South American country was officially neutral, but thanks to a large German population and a century of unofficial support, Chile was rooting for the Kaiser.

Von Spee stood alone on the deck of *Scharnhorst*, the darkness a familiar friend. Unable to sleep, thoughts of destruction and death unshakeable and keeping him awake, he had escaped the cabin he feared would become his coffin.

He contemplated the path ahead, playing out the fight to be fought. He imagined glory, the pride, the joy and the victory parades. And he imagined defeat, fire, water and corpses.

'If it comes to battle,' he had said to his crew when they hit the South American coast, 'and I think it will, we will put our trust in God and hope for victory. It will not be easy and we will need some luck, but I believe that whatever is demanded of this ship, whatever comes our way, we will succeed.

'There is something uplifting in the thought that the whole nation stands shoulder to shoulder for the common good. They stand as one and they stand with us. We shall put our trust in God that we have victory.'

Von Spee thought his men were ready for war. He had seen it in their eyes, heard it when they spoke. They no longer complained about the heat or the dark, the closed hatches and doors.

He was certain he was facing a fight. Soon to round Cape Horn – with its winds, waves and icebergs, a cemetery of ships – von Spee and his fleet would then enter the Atlantic, home to the Royal Navy. This route, forced upon him by a lack of fuel, the Japanese fleet and a ship called *Australia*, would take him straight into hostile seas. Eventually he would run the gauntlet between Iceland and the home of the enemy, Great Britain. Of course, he had to get that far first.

In the South Atlantic, von Spee would have to evade any British fleets on patrol. He had no doubt that a formidable force would be on the prowl, protecting – and being supported by – the British colonies in the region. The most powerful navy in the world would be hunting the waters around the Falkland Islands and stalking the ocean around the islands of Saint Helena and South Georgia. And they would be waiting to strike in the South Sandwich Islands too.

He did not expect to meet them in a place called Coronel.

* * *

Knock! Knock!

'Admiral,' came a voice after the pounding. 'Sir, *Göttingen* is back with news.'

Von Spee had just drifted off to sleep. The dark thoughts of earlier taken away by the South American sunrise, the admiral had gone back to grab an hour or two. He'd managed ten minutes.

Knock! Knock! Knock!

'Sir,' the man with the heavy fist tried again. 'Captain Schultz has ordered all hands on deck.'

'Yes,' von Spee boomed. 'Yes, yes, yes. I acknowledge. Stand down. Tell Schultz I am coming.'

Von Spee, fully dressed when he had gone back to bed, was standing on the *Scharnhorst* bridge with Schultz only minutes later. The rising sun showed up every crack and line on his face.

'Admiral,' said the captain. 'The British. They are here.'

He handed von Spee a message that had been sent by a supply ship, SS *Göttingen*. 'British light cruiser anchored in Coronel Roads at 1900 on 31 October,' the message said.

'It's HMS *Glasgow*,' Schultz added. '*Göttingen* is lucky she wasn't sunk.'

Von Spee had sent SS *Göttingen* to Coronel – a port about 300 miles south of Valparaiso on the coast of Chile – to send and receive signals. The ship had also been asked to search for a German sailing vessel that was rumoured to be in the area. Signals sent and received and about to go looking for the mystery ship said to be making for Santa Maria Island,

Göttingen had pulled anchor and was set to steam when a 430-foot cruiser rounded the northern head and entered the Chilean port.

'It's British,' the captain said as he put down his spyglass. He thumbed his way through his identification guide, the pages packed with the silhouettes of ships. He identified the hulking piece of steel as the Royal Navy Town-class light destroyer HMS *Glasgow*. A 4,800-ton British warship, she was packing six-inch guns and torpedo tubes.

Despite his lack of sleep, von Spee was now wide awake. 'Prepare *Scharnhorst* and *Gneisenau* for battle,' he said. 'And bring the other ships back from their patrols. This is a godsend.'

Suddenly von Spee had gone from hunted to hunter.

'And bring me everything we have on HMS *Glasgow*,' he ordered.

Von Spee smiled as he read the reports. German intelligence had last spotted *Glasgow* cruising with a ragtag fleet in the South Atlantic that were no match for *Scharnhorst* and her sister, *Gneisenau*. For *Leipzig*, *Dresden* and *Nürnberg*.

'They must not know we are here,' von Spee said. 'They would have sent a stronger fleet. Surely?'

This could be his chance to get home. To return to his wife and daughter. To save the thousands of souls on his ships. He predicted he could evade whatever else lay in wait in the Atlantic if he wiped out this British fleet.

Von Spee prepared the ship for war.

Again, every gun was inspected, bolts and screws were tightened. All moving metal parts were re-oiled. The ammunition piles were stacked and deemed live and watertight, ready to be shoved into barrels and shot into the sky.

Once again, the medical staff set up their stations, but this time they were certain there would be blood. They made sure they had enough antiseptic and that scalpels and saws were sterile and sharp.

The torpedoes were already in their firing tubes. The air valves had been checked and their flood tanks filled. With their breech doors closed tight, the torpedoes were ready to deliver the 330-pound warhead they wore as a nose.

As von Spee joined the chief engineer and the torpedo officer to check every station on the ship, he noted the mood of the men. 'This is exactly the atmosphere I wish for my ship,' von Spee wrote. 'Their mood is quiet and calm. They are soldiers who have come to terms with their lives. They await battle with a joyous expectation.'

Von Spee thought of his sons going through the same checks on the other ships and wondered how they felt. He hoped they were not afraid. And he prayed he would see them again.

Under the rising sun, the fleet set steam south, course set for Coronel.

* * *

By 10 am, the wind rising from the southeast had chopped up the sea, the smooth water replaced by rolling waves and sea spray. The morning was warm and clear except for some patches of fog, the ghostly white swirls soon to be burnt away by the summer sun.

Scharnhorst and *Gneisenau* ploughed through the rising swell, speed set at fourteen knots. The two metal behemoths – these cities in the sea – were led by *Dresden*, while *Leipzig* played the part of lookout and powered away ahead, and *Nürnberg* had been dispatched to mount a closer inspection of the coast.

Von Spee was expecting to find *Glasgow* still anchored in Coronel Bay, now about 200 miles away. The admiral was planning an ambush on the British ship as she left the port. Or maybe he would follow her and be led to the rest of the fleet. He would soon decide.

Boom!

Von Spee flinched, the blast of a gun a rude shock. He snatched up the radio.

'Come in, *Leipzig*,' von Spee said. 'Report your status.'

The bridge was deathly silent as they waited for the response.

'We are stopping a merchant ship,' came the reply. 'We sent a shot over her bow.'

'British?' von Spee asked.

'They are flying a Chilean flag, but we will check to make sure,' the operator responded.

The crew from *Leipzig* had soon boarded the four-masted barque. They found no British on board, just Chileans and piles of wood.

They sent the timber ship and its terrified crew north before resuming their trip south.

* * *

The radio barked at 4 pm.

'This is *Dresden*,' came the call from the lead ship. '*Dresden* to *Scharnhorst*, we have spotted smoke southeast of our position. Do we have permission to investigate?'

Von Spee nodded and the authorisation was issued.

The radio barked again at 4.17 pm. '*Dresden* to *Scharnhorst*,' came the call. 'We have another column of smoke. I repeat, we now have two ships.'

The radio barked again at 4.25 pm.

'We now have a third,' came the call. 'I repeat, a third smokestack has been spotted another fifteen miles away.'

Von Spee felt a surge of both nerves and excitement.

'We have identified the first ship as HMS *Glasgow*,' the *Dresden* radio operator confirmed. 'I repeat, the ship previously unidentified is HMS *Glasgow*.'

Stumbling upon *Glasgow* about 150 miles northwest of Coronel was a surprise for von Spee, considering he thought the light cruiser would still be anchored in Coronel Bay. But the British ship had left the port earlier that morning and was on her way to rejoin the rest of the Royal Navy fleet.

Another ship was soon identified.

'The second ship is *Monmouth*,' the call came again from *Dresden*. 'I repeat, we have identified the second of the ships as HMS *Monmouth*.'

The sea was now dark green and ominous. The gentle dawn breeze had become an afternoon gale, churning up the ocean. Foam-crested waves smashed into *Scharnhorst* as she steamed south, the ship pitching and bucking like a bronco.

Von Spee ordered more fuel to be thrown into boilers. He increased his speed from fourteen knots to twenty and the engines that had been chattering now screamed. The extra power sent *Scharnhorst* hurtling into the oncoming waves. They broke over the bow, spray and saltwater slapping the deck. Sailors were soaked.

'Make sure we are not outmanoeuvred,' von Spee said. 'We must cut the enemy off from the coast.'

The radio barked again.

'We have a fourth ship,' *Dresden* reported. 'A fourth ship has joined the rear of the line. We have identified the ship as the auxiliary cruiser *Otranto*.'

Von Spee frowned at the sight of what was essentially a merchant ship plated with light armour and given a couple of guns. *An auxiliary cruiser? How odd.*

For now, the admiral was only interested in the ship at the front of the queue. The ship that was leading the British charge. The ship he and *Scharnhorst* would fight.

Von Spee snatched his binoculars up and looked towards the first funnel of smoke. *Dresden* continued to lead the line, the ship plunging in and out of the swell. He could only make out a slight silhouette through all the spray.

'More power,' he ordered. 'Faster.'

The boilers were refilled and the ship shuddered, engines pushed to the limit. The stream of smoke pouring from the funnel thickened. *Scharnhorst* soon powered past *Dresden* and to the front of the German queue.

Von Spee looked into his binoculars again, now only having to contend with the still sizeable spray caused by his own ship. He studied the silhouette.

'That's HMS *Good Hope*,' he said. 'The flagship.'

Von Spee didn't need to thumb through the pages of a handbook to know the ship leading the motley crew. Von Spee had memorised all of the British ships.

'Prepare for battle,' he ordered.

* * *

A two-hour game of cat and mouse saw the warships draw level. The opposing ships formed two single-file lines, now both heading south. The German battle line led by *Scharnhorst* was closer to the coast. About 20,000 yards further out to sea, *Good Hope* fronted the convoy of British ships.

In a side-on fight that would be fought ship to ship, it would be *Scharnhorst* versus *Good Hope*, *Gneisenau* against *Monmouth*, *Leipzig* facing *Glasgow*, and *Dresden* against *Otranto*. At the tail of the German line, *Nürnberg* would choose which of the one-on-one fights she would make unfair.

'They are going to engage,' von Spee said, slightly surprised as he watched his opponents form a battle line. The German admiral had thought the British fleet, outgunned and outnumbered, would flee and had been readying himself for a chase. But instead of scattering, the inferior collection of Royal Navy ships was facing up.

'What is the distance?' von Spee asked.

'Sir, 19,000 yards and closing,' said the navigator.

'Closing?' von Spee asked.

'Yes, sir,' the navigator had confirmed. 'They have altered their heading to southeast.'

'Towards us?' Now von Spee wasn't just surprised but astounded. They were attacking. The British had set a course designed to bring their line closer to the German line. They were manoeuvring themselves into a firing range. They were also manoeuvring themselves into the range of the German guns.

'What is the distance?' von Spee asked again.

'It's 18,000 yards and closing, sir.'

Side by side, ship lined up against ship, the outgunned force was bringing the fight. Von Spee was impressed.

'We are about to face brave men,' von Spee said. 'Good men. There will be no shame in their defeat.'

The sun was now setting behind the enemy.

Perfect.

Von Spee had positioned himself against the coast not just to prevent the British from finding a friendly port in which they might hide. Looking into the setting sun would put him at a disadvantage if the attack came before sunset, but if he timed it just right the British fleet would be perfectly silhouetted by the last of the light while his fleet would be a dark shadow framed by black.

'Distance?' von Spee asked yet again.

'Sir, 17,000 yards and closing,' the navigator said.

Von Spee turned to Schultz. 'We need to strike soon,' he said. 'The sun is almost gone and with it will go our advantage.'

He gave the order to angle the fleet west. He needed to bring the British fleet into the range of his guns before the sun vanished over the horizon and put them all into darkness.

Von Spee kept asking for the distance and eventually was given the answer he sought.

'It's 12,300 yards, sir,' the navigator said. 'We are in range.'

With von Spee's ships in darkness and the British foursome illuminated in the afterglow of sunset, the admiral began the Battle of Coronel at 7.04 pm with a single word.

'Fire!'

The Jot Dora signal was hoisted aboard the flagship; it meant 'open fire'.

Von Spee was still as he watched the opening barrage. 'Ummmmm,' he grunted when it fell short. He then shook his head as he watched eight blowholes erupt one after another, water sent shooting into the air.

'Minus five hundred yards,' the navigator said.

Down on the deck, the sailors manning the guns were turning, twisting and reloading. The fire director was shouting. The pitching ship – rocking five degrees this way and then ten degrees that – sent sea spray into telescopes, and the threat of being shot first made finding range difficult.

'Four degrees,' said the man with the sights, ordering the gun to be raised.

'Damn it,' von Spee said as another blowhole spewed a load of sea into darkening sky. He turned to his aft and estimated the shot had landed about a thousand yards away from *Gneisenau*. The British had returned serve.

'Fire,' came the next order, guns re-aimed and reloaded.

The moon had risen behind *Scharnhorst*, but clouds prevented it from throwing a silhouette over his fleet. Another stroke of luck.

Boom! Boom! Boom! Boom!

Von Spee's big guns were back at it.

Boom! Boom! Boom! Boom!

The eight 8.3-inch SKL/40s fired from left to right, fore to aft.

Von Spee held his breath as the latest round of shells screamed through the air at 850 yards a second, a grim reaper's whistle. A flame lit up the night sky as one of the 250-pound shells went smashing into a ship.

Booooom!

The thunderous crack reached von Spee's ears as a ball of fire rose towards the stars that now littered the new night.

'Hit!' exclaimed Schultz. 'We have scored a hit.'

The third shot fired in the latest left-to-right line had struck HMS *Good Hope*, a 40-calibre round ripping through her bow. The first blow of the battle, the shot wiped out a 9.2-inch turret and crippled the conning tower.

Von Spee looked back down his line. His other ships were at it too, fire spewing from barrels, gunsmoke filling the air.

'*Gneisenau* has scored a hit,' said the *Scharnhorst* fire director over his radio.

Almost in synch with *Scharnhorst*, the same guns and ammunition firing at the same time, *Gneisenau* had sent its own shell screaming into a British ship. Now HMS *Monmouth* was ablaze too, the second best of the Royal Navy ships hit on the foredeck. Her port side had erupted in flames.

Up front, another shell from *Scharnhorst* hit *Good Hope*. Ammunition exploded, more flames.

'Fire!' came the latest order, the fire commander screaming at the men crewing the 5.9-inch guns. As the distance between the fleets was cut, the smaller model version of the SKL/40s came into range.

Bang! Bang! Bang!

The smaller guns were no less frightening, all six of them shooting their 150-pound shells towards targets in a matter of moments.

The men arming the eighteen SKL/35s eagerly awaited their turn. They were hoping to deliver the death blow.

'Their only hope is a torpedo attack,' von Spee said as the flaming *Good Hope* continued east in spite of the damage that had been inflicted. 'They are attempting to get into range.'

The two British ships were listing but continuing to come. The smaller guns, the SKL/35s, would soon be in range, as would the torpedo tubes.

By 7.35 pm the distance was down to 5,500 yards.

The Germans continued their brutal barrage. While the English ships fired and missed, *Scharnhorst* and *Gneisenau* landed shell after shell, deadly blow after blow.

A series of fresh shots hit the burning *Good Hope* in the fore section and then the mid-section. Flames could now be seen rushing from her portholes. Two more shells struck the turret. The aft battery was hit next.

HMS *Monmouth* received an equal belting. As it was limping but still in the battle line, an explosive shell struck its six-inch turret and ripped off the roof. Another series of explosions blew the entire turret off the forecastle. A fire as high as the mast shot up on the starboard side.

'*Monmouth* is leaving the line,' the fire director said.

The British ship was crippled and out of the fight. Now it was five against three, and one–nil to von Spee. The crew of *Scharnhorst* cheered.

The battle took another turn when the hopelessly outmatched auxiliary *Otranto* withdrew. Facing certain destruction, she had zigzagged, then darted.

The crew of *Scharnhorst* cheered again.

Both *Dresden* and *Leipzig* attacked HMS *Glasgow.*

Bang! Bang! Bang! Bang!

They scored hit after hit.

At 7.50 pm a mighty blast rocked *Good Hope*. Exploding fuel and ammunition sent a flame 200 feet into the sky.

No one actually saw *Good Hope* go down. The fires simply went out and she disappeared into the dark. Then there was still smoke but no ship.

The Germans searched for survivors. They found none.

* * *

'Chase the enemy,' von Spee shouted into the radio, as the wounded *Monmouth* fled. 'And attack with torpedoes.'

Nürnberg hurtled towards the black smoke. A series of flashes further lit the way, ammunition exploding on *Monmouth*.

'Full speed ahead,' the captain yelled.

The fully fit and flying *Nürnberg* quickly closed in on the damaged destroyer. She found a wounded animal in the last throes of life. Listing fifteen degrees to her port side, *Monmouth* was almost entirely engulfed by flames. The British guns that faced *Nürnberg* were now inoperable.

'Range?' Captain Karl von Schönberg asked.

'One thousand yards,' came the reply.

'Fire,' von Schönberg said. 'Finish her off.'

A fresh barrage from *Nürnberg* hit the mark. Sparks flew into the night sky like fireworks as every shell banged into the steel deck of *Monmouth*. A towering flame of orange erupted as another hit blew up an ammunition pile.

'Wait,' von Schönberg ordered after the first round was delivered. 'That might be enough.'

The listing ship then started to turn. Slowly but surely, *Monmouth* crept around until she was facing the German vessel.

'She is going to try to ram us,' von Schönberg said. 'Order another round of fire.'

A brutal series of blasts followed, all the short-range shots hitting. The list went from fifteen to twenty degrees. Then from twenty to thirty. From thirty to fifty.

And then she capsized.

'Cease fire,' ordered the captain.

HMS *Monmouth* went down with her flag still flying. She

sank to the bottom of the Pacific Ocean, taking her broken guns and 734 souls with her.

'Have sunk enemy cruiser,' said the cable sent by von Schönberg to *Scharnhorst*.

'Bravo, *Nürnberg*,' came the reply.

Valparaiso, Chile, 2 November 1914

Von Spee got back to his desk in his cabin the morning after the battle. Dust still settling, he attempted to recount the event in a letter to his wife.

'Yesterday was All Saints' Day and for us a lucky one,' von Spee wrote. 'I was heading south along the coast when I received news that an English cruiser had entered the small coastal harbour of Coronel. I contemplated taking it. When I was informed that two ships had been sighted, I ordered the other cruisers to rejoin me, for it was clear that they were the enemy.

'I began to narrow the distance and at five miles opened fire. I had so manoeuvred that the sun in the west would not hinder our sight. My ships fired quickly and had great success. *Good Hope* and *Monmouth* experienced many fires on board, and on the former there was a tremendous explosion, causing it to appear like a firework against the dark evening sky, glowing white with green stars showering down above *Scharnhorst*.

'As darkness fell I had narrowed the distance to 4,500 yards and then turned, renewing fire. The guns had battled for fifty-two minutes. *Nürnberg* gave a heavy broadside and finished *Monmouth* off with artillery fire. *Monmouth* sank, and unfortunately the heavy seas prevented any attempt to save its crew.

'So we have won and I thank God for the victory. We were protected in a marvellous way, and have no losses to complain of.'

Others aboard the ship were not so decisive when it came to expressing their feelings in the letters they wrote. Many struggled to deal with the mass death they had inflicted.

'Our target was the *Monmouth*, the second ship of the enemy line,' wrote a captain on board *Nürnberg*. 'Not long since, in February 1913, we had fraternised with her officers at Hong Kong, and in all friendliness drunk the health of our respective sovereigns at meals.'

Von Spee's son Otto also wrote a letter to his mother, recounting his role in the attack from onboard *Nürnberg*. He also revealed why the crew did not rescue any survivors. 'At 2035 the lookout reported a column of smoke on the starboard bow, for which we at once steered,' Otto wrote about HMS *Glasgow*. 'At first it seemed to approach, then the vessel steamed away at full speed, for although we were going twenty-one knots she rapidly disappeared in the darkness. During the chase, we had occasionally observed a cruiser looking something like *Leipzig*, steering at first a parallel course to us about two miles on the starboard beam, but then keeping away.

'When the other fellow got away from us we turned to the second and found it to be *Monmouth*, heavily damaged. She had a list of about ten degrees to port. As we came nearer she heeled still more, so that she could no longer use her guns on the side turned towards us. We opened fire at short range.

'It was terrible to have to fire on poor fellows who were no longer able to defend themselves. But their colours were still flying and when we ceased fire for several minutes they did not haul them down. So, we ran up for a fresh attack and caused *Monmouth* to capsize by our gunfire.

'The ship sank with flying colours, and we were unable to save a single man, firstly, on account of the heavy sea, which made it impossible to lower a boat, but also because fresh columns of smoke were reported which we hoped were the enemy's and for which we at once steered.

'Eventually we found they were our own big cruisers, also looking for the enemy.'

The full extent of the win soon became clear. Signals intercepted from the enemy revealed that both *Good Hope* and *Monmouth* had been sunk. The ships, and the 1,660 sailors on board, had disappeared without a trace. Every man killed.

Both *Glasgow* and *Otranto* managed to escape. Under the cover of night, the two smaller ships, faster than anything in von Spee's fleet, were able to disappear into the dark.

Von Spee cared little about the lesser ships. He had destroyed the fleet's flagship and her next in line. He had also inflicted the first naval defeat on Britain since the Battle of Lake Champlain in the War of 1812. He would forever be remembered as the man who took down a Royal Navy squadron and beat the British for the first time in 102 years.

He was the King of Coronel.

Von Spee had officially called off the hunt at 10.15 pm on 1 November.

'By the grace of God, a great victory,' he cabled to all his ships in a message that was to be passed on to every member of the crew. 'My thanks and good wishes to the crews. Finally, we have been able to contribute to the glory of our arms.'

When he returned to Valparaiso harbour a hero two days after the battle, the local German population turned out to greet the victorious crew.

A woman attempted to give von Spee a bouquet of flowers.

'No,' von Spee said, refusing the gift. 'You can put them on my grave.'

Von Spee refused to celebrate the death of so many men. He feared he would soon join them at the bottom of the sea.

A post-battle inspection revealed *Scharnhorst* had been hit by two enemy shells – both had failed to explode. *Gneisenau* had been struck four times with each of the hits inflicting only minor damage that could be easily repaired. All the other ships in the German fleet survived without taking a shot. Only three Germans had suffered injuries in the fight. They were patched up, their wounds minor, and sent back into service.

The only real cost of the battle was ammunition. The German fleet had used more than half of its shells, bullets and bombs. There was no prospect of replenishment.

Von Spee sat down to write another letter to his wife. He feared it may be his last.

'There has been great joy for the crew who have shared in this victory,' he wrote. 'I am glad they have celebrated now rather than waiting to get home because who knows whether they will be with us.

'How our next undertakings will develop lies in God's hands, and if I too have a place there then I tell myself that the possibilities are so numerous that I have to prepare for everything.'

Chapter 12

THE DECRYPTION

Melbourne, 3 November 1914

The freshly cut lawn, the grandest of green despite the drought, smelled like summer. The sun shone too, a bright day making the fabulous and sometimes outrageous hats worn by the revellers a must.

Wheatley was stunned by the crowd, more than 100,000 turning up to Flemington Racecourse for the fifty-fourth running of the Melbourne Cup. The men wore their best suits and shiniest shoes. The women came in flowing gowns and smelling of flowers.

He would have to fight his way to the bar. Bash through a mob to place a bet.

'And they were going to cancel this?' Wheatley mused to himself.

The war was now raging in Europe, with fierce fighting taking place in a region of France freshly coined the Western Front. More than 8,000 men had already lost their lives as the combined forces of Britain and France fought to stop a German advance.

And only two days earlier, on 1 November, the first of the Australian troops had been shipped from our shore. Bound for the battlefields of Europe by way of the Middle East, they had walked one by one up the gangways of thirty-six troopships, rifles in hands and slouch hats on heads.

Despite attempts to hide both the date and the place of the launch for fear of attack or sabotage, thousands had lined the streets and the wharfs of Albany in Western Australia to give the troops a fitting farewell. They had kissed and cuddled, waved and cheered. Mums, dads, brothers, sisters, sons, daughters, girlfriends and wives, masking their fear with a smile.

The troops had waved and cheered too. They'd made promises to come home. Said this was not the last kiss.

And then thirty-six ships, led by the flagship of the fleet HMT *Orvieto*, with its ninety-four officers, 1,345 personnel and twenty-one horses, set steam into the great unknown.

Bound first for Aden in Yemen and then Alexandria in Egypt, most of the volunteers steamed out of King George Sound dreaming of action and adventure. They would see the pyramids, ride on camels and sleep under stars in the Sahara. Most had never heard of Gallipoli. Of the Somme. Most had never fired a gun. And all of them would miss the Melbourne Cup.

Fresh from Australia's biggest ever departure of troops, many had called for the Melbourne Cup to be cancelled. Inappropriate, they said. We shouldn't be celebrating when the world is at war, cheering for horses when men have been sent to fight for our freedom. Others argued that the nation could use a distraction. That the war could be forgotten for a day. The Victoria Racing Club ended the debate when it stepped in and promised to donate a third of the profits, or £5,000, whichever was greater, to the war effort.

Wheatley was glad the event had been given the all clear. He certainly needed a distraction; in fact, he was desperate for it. With the fate of a fleet, maybe even the result of the war, resting on his shoulders, his mind was a mess. He was clouded and confused, and could not make any sense of the new code. It was all riddles and no rhyme.

Wheatley had barely slept since stumbling over the code he could not break. He'd been staring at the latest mangle of letters earlier that morning when Thring came into his office.

'You need a break, old boy,' Thring had said. 'Why don't you get out of here for a while?' Thring sniffed at the air. 'I suggest you start with having a wash,' he said. 'Go and clean yourself up and head out for the day. Why don't you get on down to Flemington for the Melbourne Cup?'

Wheatley had raised his elbow and sent his nose into his armpit. 'Urgh,' he said, screwing up his nose. 'I could certainly use a bath. And I suppose a few hours away might do me some good.'

He'd told his team to take a break too. 'Ladies,' he'd announced, 'have the rest of the day off. Forget all this for a while and go and have some fun.'

Washed and shaved, Wheatley had made his way to Flemington. He'd fought his way to the bar and bought a beer before braving the betting ring. A man of science and sense, he'd placed a pound on the three-to-one favourite. The instructor turned navy intelligence man had finished his beer and been back for another by the time the race rolled round.

He'd long forgotten about codes and why he could not crack them. He was no longer a man who could win or lose wars but just another punter who could win or lose a bet. He joined in the revelry and cheered as the horses took off from their gates.

'Go,' he yelled as jockeys whipped and hooves thundered. 'Go, go, go!'

He was bouncing up and down by the time they reached the straight. 'Go on,' he yelled.

He was left shaking his head as they hit the finish line.

'So close,' Wheatley said to another head-shaking punter standing at his side. 'Oh well, you win some, you lose some, as they say.'

The race had been won by Kingsburgh, a twenty-to-one outsider. Wheatley had earlier written the horse off after a last-minute look at the field's form, as Kingsburgh had not been impressive in the lead-up. In fact, she had only ever won once, at a minor meeting at Rosehill.

It appeared that most had joined the instructor in writing off the long shot. The man celebrating most was the horse's owner. As Wheatley crumpled his losing ticket and threw it into an overflowing bin, he wondered how much the owner had won.

He suddenly smiled. 'I've got it!' he shouted. 'By George, I've got it.'

Wheatley had found a winner after all.

* * *

Wheatley had had an epiphany. While throwing his losing ticket in the bin he had wondered if there was a winner somewhere in the trash. Wondered if a careless punter had chucked without checking. What if he could just reach in and replace his losing ticket with a winner?

And that was when it had hit him.

'I think they have simply thrown out some letters and replaced them with others,' he said to Thring when he made it back to the office. 'Rather than issuing a new key, I think they have just used a system of substitution.'

Thring looked at him blankly.

'Okay,' Wheatley said, searching for the easiest way to explain his theory. 'Instead of sending out new codebooks and new keys, almost impossible given the state of the war, I think they have simply shifted the code. Say, every letter in the alphabet has been shifted just one place. So that would mean that to send a message, at first you do everything the same as you would have before. Everything according to the original *HVB*. You look for the phrase or word you want and then you pick out the corresponding code next to it. Let's say the code for the phrase or word you want to send is ABCDE. Are you following?'

Thring shrugged. 'I think so,' he said.

'Alright, so using the original *HVB* you have a code that reads ABCDE,' Wheatley said. 'Now let's say the superencipherment that has been chosen is to shift each letter of the alphabet forward by one. So, for the code ABCDE, A will become B, B will become C and so on. The message that was ABCDE would therefore become BCDEF once it has been superenciphered.'

Thring nodded.

'The person at the other end will get the message BCDEF,' Wheatley continued. 'If he tried to find BCDEF in his codebook he wouldn't. It would appear to be meaningless. But if he knew the cipher had been changed, that the key was that each letter was moved forward one position, he would know all he had to do was move each letter back one, so B would become A, C would become B, and so on. Using this formula, he would end up with ABCDE and that grouping could of course be found in the book. He would be able to find the corresponding word or phrase.'

'Splendid,' Thring said. 'So, all you have to do is move each letter down by one.'

Wheatley laughed. 'I wish it were that simple,' he said. 'That is just a hypothetical – they would never use such an uncomplicated key. It could have been changed in a number of different ways.'

'How many ways exactly?' Thring asked.

'By my reckoning, 52 billion,' Wheatley said. 'That is the number of combinations available. The letters may have been moved forwards or back by one or two positions, all the way up to 26 positions. They could change just one letter, two letters, or all 26. They can also omit letters altogether.'

Thring raised an eyebrow. 'So you only have to try 52 billion combinations? Sounds easy enough.'

'Leave it to me,' Wheatley said. 'I have an idea or two.'

* * *

Wheatley kicked his way through the snowstorm of scrunched-up paper as he rushed into his office. He picked up the chair he had earlier knocked over in a fit of frustration and gently placed it back behind his desk. He reached for the codebook and sat down.

Next he restacked his papers, putting the codes that had come from Montevideo into an ordered pile, oldest first, newest last.

Desk straight, reading glasses and lamp both on, he looked at the random groupings of letters on the first page, the five-letter non-words in groupings of two that had set off the cyclone in his office.

'LIKIS IMOFI,' he wrote, plucking a grouping from the intercepted code and inking it onto a blank page of his notepad.

He opened the *HVB* and gave the capacious book a pat. 'Righto,' he said, speaking to the book like a pet dog. 'Let's see what we can do.'

He started on the first page of the book. Using a ruler, he slid down the page, starting with the first coded word. Ruler pressed firm against paper, he glanced at the ten-letter codes just above where he had stopped and then looked at the gibberish he had written down: LIKIS IMOFI.

He shook his head and moved a line down, repeating the process for four pages. His routine suddenly changed on the fifth page when he nodded his head and picked up his pen.

'1. BABAC ACIBA,' he wrote. He curled his lip and nodded, a silent congratulation, before putting down his pen. He got back to the ruler and head-shaking.

It wasn't long before he was nodding and writing again.

'2. BABAC ANOHA,' he wrote. Again, the pen went down and he got back to his ruler, moving it a line at a time and studying each and every word.

'3. BABAC AZYPA,' he wrote next.

He was on a roll.

He continued, mostly shaking his head but sometimes nodding and writing, until he had worked his way through the entire 300-page book. He looked at his notepad after he finished the exhaustive process.

1. BABAC ACIBA
2. BABAC ANOHA
3. BABAC AZYPA
4. BEKEL ECEFE
5. BEKEL EGYVE
6. BEKEL EHIGE
7. BEKEL ENUME
8. BEKEL ETONE
9. BISIT ICIFI
10. BISIT IHULI
11. BISIT INOMI
12. BISIT ITASI
13. BISIT IVADI
14. CEBEF ECEFE
15. CEBEF EGYVE
16. CEBEF ENUME
17. CEBEF EHIGE

18. CEBEF ETONE
19. CEBEF EZATE
20. CANAT ACIBA

And so, the list went on. Seemingly random groups of letters going all the way from BABAC to ZKJKL. He had filled four pages of his notepad.

He looked at his list and smiled. 'You're here somewhere,' he said.

One of the groupings he had written down held the secret that he was searching for. The key to breaking the code that could change the war.

What seemed completely random entries, plucked from the codebook and written in ink, had been carefully chosen. Each of the entries was completely different, but they were all the same.

Wheatley had studied the first grouping of the code he could not crack.

LIKIS IMOFI.

He had looked for a pattern, something that would help him narrow the odds down from one in 52 billion. It took him only a moment.

He had noted that the second letter – I – was repeated in the fourth, sixth and tenth positions. Using his theory that the original code had been superenciphered with letters moved forward or back, he had reasoned that the original *HVB* code must also share the same trait. The letters may have been changed but the combinations hadn't.

That meant every single A that had become a B would still be an A that had become a B in all the superenciphered codes. If the original code had four A's in it then the new code would have four B's in it. He had identified a pattern that could help him crack the code.

Using the randomly chosen LIKIS IMOFI grouping to test his theory, Wheatley had gone through the entire codebook and written down every single code that contained the same letter in the second, fourth, sixth and tenth positions and now had four pages of code to narrow down instead of 300 pages.

Wheatley pushed the codebook aside and looked at his notebook, studying his neat print for another pattern that could force a cull.

Again, he smiled.

He was fast to find lambs in his letters. While only the 'I' in LIKIS IMOFI was repeated, some of the groupings he had written down contained more than one repeated letter. For instance, the first code he had written down, BABAC ACIBA, contained a repeated letter B in the first, third and ninth positions. And BABAC ANOHA had a B in both the first and third positions.

Picking up his ruler in his left hand and his pen in his right hand, he started moving through the handwritten codes and drew a series of neatly ruled lines, eliminating all codes that had more than one repeated letter.

Wheatley smiled again, wider this time. After starting with a one in 52 billion chance of cracking this adjustment to the code, reason, logic, elimination and a Melbourne Cup epiphany had him on his way to finding the key.

He did a count of what remained on his list and sighed when he realised he had only cut the original tally by thirty-five percent. Spurred by his recent success, Wheatley once again studied the combinations of letters that remained, comparing each of them to the code he was trying to crack, letter by letter. He looked for another pattern. Another discrepancy.

He sighed and lowered his forehead to the desk in exhaustion and frustration. A minute later he was sitting bolt upright and reaching again for the codebook.

He glanced at the reduced list and checked through the codebook, reading the translation that was written alongside one of the codes. It was utter nonsense, a phrase no man would ever say let alone send. *How many of these codes have I actually read? How many are actually used?* He pulled the book closer and straightened his glasses, finding the next translation. It was also absurd.

Wheatley continued reading through the translations and realised that he was seeing most of them for the first time. He had used this book to translate thousands of codes, but thousands of others were ridiculous, things that would never be sent from a warship. There were phrases like 'Do you speak German?', 'Do you have the time?' and 'The weather is warm, so we have decided to swim.'

Wheatley again picked up his ruler and pen, examined all the groupings he had left and continuing his process of elimination by ruling out the ridiculous. What was left was a much-reduced list, though still too many. He smiled anyway.

'Got it,' he said.

Well, not quite yet, but he knew he would. And he did. A few hours later Wheatley wrote what he thought was the solution on a fresh notepad:

A = I, B = L, C = K, D = W, E = O, F = T, G = R, H = F, I = E, K = B, L = C, M = D, N = S, O = A, P = K, R = P, S = Z, T = V, U = Y, V = M, W = N, X = H, Y = U, Z = G

Now he needed to make sure he was right. He decoded the rest of the message to see if it made any sense.

'Have received the following information from Punta Arenas Magellan Straits,' the decoded message read. '*Good Hope* is said to be hidden near Wollaston opposite U place 399 in order to catch German cruiser which is supposed to have a rendezvous there.'

He tried another. 'Keep within the three-mile limit,' the very short message said.

And another. 'Presence of enemy warships *Monmouth* and *Glasgow*,' the decoded message said. '16 October with southerly course in the latitude of Valparaiso. Apparently English warship 920, French warship 508, Japanese warship 502 also on the way to South American coast.'

Melbourne, 4 November 1914, 4 am

Wheatley burst into Thring's office to find the captain sound asleep on his stretcher bed.

'Sir, I've done it!' he shouted as he switched on the light.

Thring groaned as he stirred.

'Wake up, sir,' Wheatley said, shaking his shoulder. 'I've done it.'

'Done what?' Thring slurred as he came to. 'What's the bloody time?'

Wheatley realised he didn't even know what day it was, let alone the time. 'Not sure, sir,' he said. 'But I have found the key. You'd better take a look at this.'

Thring looked at his watch. 'This better be bloody good.'

It was.

'This is about Cradock's fleet,' Thring said. 'They know all about his fleet and where he is. We need to warn them. I'll message the Admiralty. You get back to the messages and see what else is there.'

Thring snatched up Wheatley's handwritten notes and darted to the cable room. He first sent them Wheatley's key by way of an encrypted telegram. With it they could start decoding messages for themselves.

November 1914
The Captain-in-Charge

German ships on the South American coast have altered the cipher key to the HVB *code, copy of which was supplied to you.*

The new key has been discovered and is as follows:

Of the following 48 letters, the odd ones are arranged alphabetically, omitting J and Q, representing the letters in the message, and the even ones the corresponding letters for decoding.

A = I, B = L, C = K, D = W, E = O, F = T, G = R, H = F, I = E, K = B, L = C, M = D, N = S, O = A, P = K, R = P, S = Z, T = V, U = Y, V = M, W = N, X = H, Y = U, Z = G

By direction of the Naval Board

He also sent them a separate communication including the decoded message he thought referred to Cradock's fleet.

Wheatley was back in Thring's room at sunrise with a stack of freshly decoded messages. The captain sat back and went through them one by one.

'*Cardiff* number one wishes monthly stores to be sent,' read the first. 'Government is making difficulties.'

Nothing earth-shattering. He moved on to the next.

'Memphis Punta Arenas,' it read. '2,500 coal steamer *San Sacramento*, formerly Hamburg-American SS *Alexandra*, wireless telegraphy call sign GCKS, telegraphs her departure from San Francisco.'

Again, nothing that confirmed the location of von Spee's fleet, although it was another indication it was in South America, given that coal supplies had been sent from San Francisco.

'16 October, signature Persia,' the next message read. 'The steamer will be in wireless communication from 1 November and intends to reach Valparaiso on 7 November and has on board 7,000 tons of coal and stores for cruiser squadron. The government is making difficulties therefore it is wished that you should order a store ship to meet *San Sacramento*.'

Got you!

Thring grabbed the telephone. 'Get in here, please,' he ordered the naval secretary. 'Yes, now.'

He hung up the phone and turned to Wheatley.

'This confirms it,' he said. 'They are in South America. In Valparaiso.'

'Yes, sir?' enquired the secretary as he walked in following the surly summons.

'Forward this to Admiralty immediately,' Thring said. 'And also to Montevideo. It needs to get to Cradock with haste.'

The secretary turned to leave.

'And come back as soon as you are done,' Thring called after him. 'You are going to be sending more.'

That morning the secretary fired off a succession of cables to the Admiralty, including one from the Germans that showed they knew the location of part of the Allied fleet:

> *Following intelligence received from San Francisco 24 October. Apparently English warship 920, Japanese warship 502 are on the way to west coast of South America. English warships 541, 930, 979, French warship 508 at Apia 5 October.*

And:

> *Following intelligence received from Punta Arenas 15 October,* Good Hope *is hidden opposite rendezvous 399 near Wollaston, 515 and 918 on eastern side of Magellan Straits.*

And:

> *Following intelligence received from Punta Arenas 27 October. English warship apparently Queen class with three funnels, one of which is false, was passed near Punta Arenas going in a westerly direction, bringing the steamer* Benbrookz *under convoy of* Langos. *English squadron lying probably at Corcovado Bay.*

And finally:

> *28 October* Orita *English steamer has left Valparaiso for Coquimbo,* Quillota *for Coronel. Following intelligence from San Francisco 25 October. New directions for cruiser squadron will probably be issued. Kraus Lieutenant of the* Leipzig *died in the bay, heartfelt sympathy.'*

* * *

Now it was Thring who was waking Wheatley.

'We were too late,' Thring said as he walked into the darkened office, curtains drawn, the code breaker asleep on his foldout bed. Wheatley had finally succumbed to tiredness in the afternoon.

Wheatley continued to snore.

Thring pulled back the curtains. 'Frederick,' he said, raising his voice.

Wheatley didn't move.

'Fred,' he tried again, even louder.

Wheatley turned and opened his eyes.

'We were too late,' Thring said again. 'They were wiped out. Cradock is dead. Von Spee got to them.'

Wheatley propped himself upright. 'Where?' he asked.

'Coronel,' Thring said. 'South America.'

'We were right?' Wheatley asked.

Thring walked towards Wheatley and placed a hand on the still waking man's shoulder. 'You were right,' he said.

Wheatley shook his head. 'How many dead, sir?' he asked.

Thring remained silent.

'How many?' Wheatley repeated, raising his voice.

'Too early to say,' he said. 'Looks like *Good Hope* and *Monmouth* were both sunk. They are still searching.'

Wheatley slumped back onto his foldout bed. 'I could have saved them,' he said. 'I should have saved them.'

'We warned them,' Thring said. 'We told them all along. They just didn't listen.'

Wheatley was inconsolable. 'But if I had found that key earlier,' he said.

Thring interrupted. 'Stop it, man,' he said, firmly. 'How long were they sitting on this new code before they sent it to you? How many people at Whitehall tried to crack it and couldn't before they decided to suffer the embarrassment of sending it here to you? This is not your fault.'

Wheatley sat up again.

'And there is still a war to be won,' Thring said. 'Von Spee's fleet is still out there. Now let's get back to it and find him. Let's stop the next Coronel. Let's find him and destroy him.'

Chapter 13

THE BLAME GAME

Suva, Fiji, 7 November 1914

'This has to be a joke!' Patey shouted. 'He can't be serious?'

Patey had just been informed that First Lord of the Admiralty Winston Churchill had asked why HMAS *Australia* was not at the battle of Coronel.

Churchill had reacted fast and hard following the failed fight. He'd asked plenty of questions. But this one was beyond Patey's belief.

'He knows exactly where we were,' Patey said. 'He was the fellow that kept us on the wrong side of the world.'

And so the witch-hunt began. Sixteen hundred and sixty men dead. Two ships sunk. The first British naval defeat in 102 years. The blame game had started and the world wanted to know where the most powerful ship in the Pacific was when 'Kit' Cradock and his underpowered fleet were slaughtered in what was being described as the worst naval disaster in British history.

The denials and accusations had begun on 4 November when, three days after the tragedy, news finally reached the United Kingdom and Australia.

Churchill knew perfectly well that HMAS *Australia* was in Samoa, leashed to an island. All bark and no bite. As First Lord of the Admiralty, the thirty-nine-year-old rising political star had rubber-stamped every decision. Or if he hadn't, he should have.

'I cannot accept for the Admiralty any share in the responsibility,' Churchill said. 'The first rule of war is to concentrate superior strength for decisive action and to avoid division of forces or engaging detail. The admiral showed by his telegrams that he clearly appreciated this. The Admiralty orders explicitly approved his assertion of these elementary principles.'

Admiral of the Fleet Rosslyn Wemyss also refused to accept the blame. 'There is but one field of naval operations extending over all the world, namely, the sea. Thus, it is impossible for a naval commander-in-chief afloat to be the centre whence the strategical direction of naval war radiates. The Board of Admiralty, located in London, is necessarily the centre whence radiate the executive orders as regards operations and movements of ships; and it exercises, as far as the navy is concerned, many of the functions of the military commander-in-chief in the field.'

But Australia and her fledgling navy were not going to take the blame either. The Governor-General took the extraordinary step of sending a letter to the Admiralty after learning of the intelligence provided by Wheatley and the predictions of Patey.

'While reluctant to concern myself with naval strategy, I have to report a prevailing opinion that the loss of our cruisers off the

Chilean coast is the climax of a long bungle in the Pacific,' Sir Ronald Munro Ferguson wrote. 'As to this, as I have intimated, there is sure to be discussion later on. The maxim of seeking out the enemy's ships and destroying them has been ignored. Nearly a month was wasted over Samoa.

'*Australia* was also detained for many days in the Bismarck Archipelago and lastly cruising around Fiji. Had Admiral Patey immediately destroyed the wireless to the north, and then sought out the enemy ships, these would have not been left unmolested for three months, nor, in all probability, would have our military expedition been so seriously delayed.

'Admiral Patey at our interview in Sydney on 2 August was insistent on the need for an immediate and unremitting chase of *Gneisenau* and *Scharnhorst*, and I know he has never swerved from that view.

'There is but one opinion here that the HMAS fleet and the China Squadron have been singularly ineffective and to the remoteness of Admiralty control may be traced the concentrating of German ships off Chile with its lamentable result.

'Have written so much on the naval situation with a view to prepare your mind for the large level of local autonomy which is sure to be asked for when the war comes to an end.'

Churchill refused to accept responsibility.

'Von Spee had no lack of objectives,' Churchill said. 'He had only to hide and to strike. The vastness of the Pacific and its multitude of islands offered him their shelter and, once he had vanished, who should say where he would reappear.

'On the other hand, there were considerable checks on his action and a limit, certain though indefinite, to the life of his squadron. He was a cut flower in a vase, fair to see yet bound to die.

'But so long as he lived all our enterprises lay simultaneously under the shadow of a serious potential danger. Von Spee and his squadron could turn up almost anywhere. On the other hand, we could not possibly be strong enough every day everywhere to meet him.'

Admiral Jerram, who had been in direct contact with Patey, seemed the only one ready to make a concession. 'I was aware that the whole of the Australian and New Zealand squadrons and *Montcalm* were well to the eastward of Australia engaged in escorting expeditions, first to Samoa and then to New Britain,' Jerram said, 'that the best ships of the East Indies Squadron were engaged in escorting troops from India westwards, and that the only British forces on the great trade routes between Colombo, Singapore and Australia were the *Fox* and *Espiegle* near Colombo, and the *Pioneer* near Fremantle.

'I have mentioned the possibility of the Germans going to the Dutch East Indies, and bearing in mind the disastrous results to our trade if they did so, the conclusion was irresistible, that a strong force was needed to work from Singapore.'

Amid the blame there were also tributes for the fallen men and their captain, who despite certain death had turned his ship and steamed into the jaws of defeat.

'Why, then, you will ask me, did he attack – deliberately designedly, intentionally – a force which he could not have reasonably hoped either to destroy or put to flight?' said Arthur Balfour, former prime minster of Britain and current member of parliament. 'I think a satisfactory explanation can be given. Remember what the circumstances of the German squadron were. They were not like those of the German High Seas Fleet close to their own ports, capable of taking in a damaged ship to their own dockyards, and their own protected bases.

'The German admiral in the Pacific was very differently situated. He was far from any port where he could have refitted. No friendly bases were open to him. If, therefore, he suffered damage, even though in suffering damage he apparently inflicted greater damage than he received, yet his power, great for evil while he remained untouched, might suddenly be utterly destroyed.

'He would be a great peril as long as his squadron remained efficient, and if Admiral Cradock judged that his squadron, that he himself and those under him, were well sacrificed if they destroyed the power of this hostile fleet, then I say that there is no man, be he sailor or be he civilian, but would say that such a judgment showed not only the highest courage, but the greatest courage of unselfishness; and that Admiral Cradock, by absolute neglect of personal interest and personal ambitions, had shown a wise judgment in the interests of his country.

'If I am right there never was a nobler act.

'We shall never know the thoughts of Admiral Cradock when it became evident that, out-gunned and out-ranged, success was an impossibility. He must have realised that his hopes were dashed forever to the ground, that his plan had failed.

'His body is separated from us by half the world, and he and his gallant comrades lie far from the pleasant homes of England. Yet they have their reward, and we are surely right in saying that theirs is an immortal place in the great role of naval heroes.'

Melbourne, 8 November 1914

Wheatley delivered his report.

'As requested,' Wheatley said to Thring as he handed over twenty-one foolscap pages of handwritten notes. 'All the movements of the German squadron since the outbreak of the war. I have included all of our intelligence and the cables we sent on to the Admiralty.'

Thring flicked through the thick pile. 'Good man,' he said. 'I'll have it typed up and sent on to the minister.'

Thring dismissed Wheatley before turning his full attention to the report.

'MOST SECRET,' the report started. 'For a long time the whereabouts of *Scharnhorst* and *Gneisenau* was in doubt until they suddenly appeared at Apia on 14 September. That they were in Australian waters was evident from wireless calls that emanated from them, and that they were kept informed of the movements of the Australian fleet by *Planet* and *Komet* was also evident.

'They passed very close to *Melbourne* while she was proceeding from Suva to Nauru during the first week of September. This may be seen from the track chart drawn of their movements and it is confirmed by the opinion of the wireless officer of *Melbourne*, who heard their signals very distinctly on the nights of 7 and 8 September. The appearance of these warships at Apia, and the fear that they might return to Australia to interfere with the transports, caused the New Zealand and Commonwealth governments to make strong representations to the Secretary of State for the Colonies to delay the departure of the troops until a strong escort could be provided.

'The Admiralty was evidently of the opinion that *Scharnhorst* and *Gneisenau* had left these shores permanently.'

Thring skimmed through the pages, stopping here and there to mark an important point.

'No doubt now existed in the minds of the Melbourne Navy Office that the ships were heading east and the vice admiral commanding the Australian fleet was of the same opinion. He wired Admiralty on 3 October and suggested he should move to South America. He was instead sent to Suva.'

He skimmed down further.

'This in conjunction with the decoded intercepted German telegraph, giving the position of *Scharnhorst* on 4 October at longitude 130°W, en route from the Marquesas Islands to Easter Island, confirmed the Australian view of an approaching concentration of German cruisers on the west coast of South America.

'The vice admiral telegrammed the Admiralty on 13 October again suggesting HMAS *Australia* move to South America to pursue the fleet.'

Thring then read Wheatley's account of the code-cracking and what the messages revealed.

'The Admiralty was informed on 3 November,' the report said, referring to Wheatley's success in cracking the codes.

'They congratulated the Naval Board on 5 November. These messages prove conclusively that Germany was violating Chilean neutrality by using Màs Afuera Island as a base.

'On 5 November, the Admiralty announced that rumours had been received of a naval action off the Chilean coast. The Admiralty had no official confirmation, the accounts received resting on German evidence. It was reported that *Scharnhorst*, *Gneisenau*, *Leipzig*, *Dresden* and *Nürnberg* had concentrated near Valparaiso and that an engagement had been fought with a portion of Admiral Cradock's squadron on 1 November.'

Thring took the document to be typed and sent. He soon had a response from the minster for defence.

'A very interesting and valuable record,' the minister said. 'The astonishing thing is that in view of the information forwarded to the Admiralty, which showed that the enemy knew of the disposition of British and Allied ships, that an inferior squadron was permitted to go to its doom. A copy of this report should be forwarded to the Admiralty.'

It was.

Suva, Fiji, 9 November 1914

Patey was still fuming. He was also still hoping to get his chance. Surely he would now be freed from his leash? Show the world HMAS *Australia* had a bite to match her bark.

'*Australia* ready to proceed at once when ordered,' Patey cabled.

'Sail from Suva 10 am,' came the reply.

Australia was back in the hunt.

Patey had been given an order to be part of a multinational fleet that was to destroy von Spee and his squadron. To wipe them off the face of the earth.

The Admiralty would hunt the German fleet wherever they went. Whatever the cost.

From the Chilean coast, the German squadron could proceed round the tip of South America into the Atlantic, they could make north along the coast and take the Panama Canal, or they could proceed north to Canada. The Admiralty would be ready and waiting whatever the route.

HMAS *Australia* was to block the road to Canada. They would follow them into the Atlantic if they took the canal.

They needed redemption. They needed a win. And they would soon get one – not in South America but 1,200 miles off the coast of Australia.

Chapter 14

SYDNEY STRIKES

Indian Ocean, 1,200 miles west of Australia, 9 November 1914

The wait was finally over for the 30,000 AIF volunteers. Most of the men on the ships now steaming their way across the Indian Ocean had rushed into recruitment offices three months earlier. Following a series of delays and false goodbyes they were now nine days into the trip.

As they steamed into the great unknown, over 2,000 miles travelled since leaving Albany, so far the trip was all adventure and excitement. There was coffee and cards, cricket and chess. Even three-course meals if you were one of the ninety-four officers on board the flagship HMT *Orvieto*.

And then, all of a sudden, it got serious, following a cable received out of the blue.

Few of the 30,000 men aboard the mass transport would ever know how close they came to never again setting foot on land. Never making it to Aden or Egypt. To places called Gallipoli, Fromelles and the Somme.

The legend of the Anzacs may never have been born.

Captain Mortimer Silver picked up the cable at 6.30 am. 'Get this sent to Melbourne,' he said as he looked at an intercepted page of nonsense. 'It could be from a German ship but who knows? It is in some kind of code. We need to know what it says.'

Silver, nicknamed 'Long John', of course, did not give the message another thought. As captain of HMAS *Melbourne*, one of three warships protecting the troopship convoy, Silver could not afford to be paranoid.

Cautious? Of course. But they would still be docked in Albany if they'd kept up the shadow jumping.

'Sir,' his second-in-command said ten minutes later. 'We have just had a call from the Cocos wireless station. They claim to have spotted a large ship just off one of the islands.'

The Australian convoy was now fifty-five miles north of the Cocos, a British island chain located about halfway between Australia and Sri Lanka in the Indian Ocean.

Was this more than a shadow? Was it time to jump? Silver settled for a skip. 'Put the officers on notice,' he ordered. 'We may have to enact safety measures.'

He hoped they wouldn't have to.

Silver was handed another cable, this one from the Navy Office in Melbourne.

'SOS,' the message read. 'Strange warship approaching.'

A warship, not a shadow.

'Full speed,' Captain Silver ordered. 'Set a course for the Cocos.'

HMAS *Melbourne* had just begun to pull away from the convoy when the captain changed his mind.

'Stop,' Silver said. 'This one isn't our fight.'

For a moment, red mist descending and a fight up ahead, Silver had forgotten that he was leading the convoy. Right now he was responsible for the safety of these men. He could not leave them. Death or glory awaited, but neither would be his. He reluctantly issued the dutiful order.

'Send HMAS *Sydney*,' Silver ordered, selecting the Australian warship closest to the Cocos.

The speed of *Melbourne* slackened. She was soon back at the front of the unprecedented Australian line, protecting and not attacking.

* * *

First, they spotted the island.

'Land ahoy,' came the call.

And then they spotted the battleship.

'All hands,' Captain John Glossop ordered. 'Battle stations.'

Squinting into his binoculars, the 43-year-old captain could just make out the silhouette of the ship. He could see two masts and three smokestacks. He could also see that she was big.

'Either *Emden* or *Königsberg*,' Glossop said, his best guess given both German cruisers had been operating in the North Indian Ocean. Oh, how he hoped it was *Emden*.

'Ring the engines to quarter speed,' Glossop continued. 'Let's make our final preparations.'

It had taken HMAS *Sydney* almost three hours to steam from the flank of the Australian transport to the Cocos Islands. Raising to full steam a moment after receiving the order from Captain Silver, *Sydney* had powered to the Cocos at twenty knots, glory and fame on the line. The sea was calm, almost flat; they could have run an egg-and-spoon race on the deck.

They had slowed to a near stop by the time she was six miles out from both the Cocos Islands and the ship that had now been confirmed as SMS *Emden*, the German warship responsible for the capture or destruction of twenty-three Allied vessels since the outbreak of the war. In an unprecedented raiding career that had covered 30,000 nautical miles in just three months, SMS *Emden* had destroyed two warships, and sunk or captured twenty British steamers and one Russian merchant ship. Her total haul grossed a staggering 70,825 tons. Leaving Vice Admiral von Spee's East Asia Squadron fleet on 14 August to conduct cruiser warfare in the shipping lanes of Singapore, Colombo and Aden, *Emden* had used cunning, guile and strategy to wreak havoc in Southeast Asia. And now she was in the sights of HMAS *Sydney*.

'She's coming,' Glossop said as he watched *Emden* start to steam. 'She wants a fight.'

The manoeuvring began.

Under clear skies and on calm seas, *Sydney* powered up to twenty-five knots, collision course with *Emden* set. The 456-foot ship shuddered as the fully fuelled engines screamed, coal burning hellishly hot. On the decks, the guns were ready. Hands shook as they hovered over triggers.

Launched in 1912, the two-year-old ship came to the fight packing a gun for every occasion: eight BL six-inch Mark XI guns, one three-inch anti-aircraft gun, one twelve-pound gun, ten .303 machine guns, two 21-inch torpedo tubes and two depth charge chutes.

Glossop roared headlong into the fight, expecting to face a reported armament consisting only of ten 4.1-inch and eight two-inch guns. Feeling confident, Captain Glossop stood over the compass at the fore bridge as *Sydney* zeroed in on SMS *Emden*. He looked around his ship, wanting to savour the moment that preceded his making or breaking. He would soon be a hero or a martyr, nothing in between.

He looked up at his navigation lieutenant, a man named Basil Bell-Salter, lying prone on top of the conning tower. Radio ready, he was his eyes in the sky.

Lieutenant Denis Rahilly stood like a piece of granite by his side. Binoculars to eyes, the gunnery lieutenant was in charge of everything that went boom. He would shout coordinates and judge the distances between splashes and ship when the barrage began.

And then he saw the paymaster, Ernest Norton, a man who wouldn't deliver death but could save a nation all the same. More solicitor than soldier, he stood on the deck holding a metal box that contained all the ship's secrets. Glossop only needed a moment, a quick study of the man, to know Norton would not let him down. He would stand firm under fire and throw the box to the bottom of the sea should the enemy score an unlikely win.

Captain Silver asked for the latest distance between him and his target.

'We're at 11,000 yards and closing, sir,' came the reply.

'We open fire at 9,500 yards,' Glossop said. 'I repeat, first fire at 9,500 yards.'

* * *

The first shell fell just 200 yards short.

'They have opened fire,' came the call from Lieutenant Rahilly just moments before.

The sight of the smoke – a white puff of cloud seen before the blast was heard – came as a shock, given they were still at 10,500 yards.

Water exploded in front of *Sydney*, the spray reaching 200 feet into the sky. Glossop grabbed his binoculars and did a fast study of the enemy ship.

'They have managed to get their guns to an angle of thirty percent,' Glossop said. 'We'd better make ourselves thin.'

The storm started. Meteors made of metal and laden with TNT fell from the sky. Waterspouts sprung up everywhere, to the left and to the right, out in front. Two hundred yards away at first, then a hundred, and then …

HMAS *Sydney* shook.

'We've been hit!' Rahilly shouted. 'A blow to the stern.'

'Maintain full speed,' Captain Glossop ordered. 'Straight ahead.'

The barrage was relentless, water exploding all around the ship as she heaved over the waves caused by the near misses. The vessel pitched and plunged. The men on the deck were soaked, bathtub loads of spray slapping them in the face. Rushing water a foot high slammed into legs.

'Another hit!' Rahilly shouted.

Glossop did not have to be told – he'd seen the blast. A shell had scored a direct hit on them, a closely bunched salvo smashing into a control panel. He watched on as a man limped away from a shooting flame and then collapsed on the deck.

'Range?' Glossop asked, gritting his teeth and getting on with the job.

'Sir, 10,000 yards,' came the reply.

They would have to endure a little more. And they did.

HMAS *Sydney* was hit another fifteen times. Blow after blow, the steel was slapped by hellfire. A shell went smashing into a rangefinder on the upper foredeck, killing a man as Captain Glossop watched. He would have been killed too had the shell exploded. There were chaotic scenes on the deck, men running, fires burning and sparks flying.

They would soon get their chance.

'Fire,' ordered Lieutenant Rahilly the moment they were 9,500 yards away from the still-shooting *Emden*.

Sydney was no longer a punching bag. Her six-inch guns recoiled like a rattlesnake after exploding to life with a thunderous crack. One at a time, the eight cannon-sized guns fired, finally making it a fight.

Only two of the sizzling shells hit, one salvo sailing over *Emden* and another falling short and wide.

The German warship continued her rapid and relentless fire. Outgunned and facing a bigger, faster, better ship, her only chance was to land a long-range knockout.

'They are firing a salvo every three seconds,' said Lieutenant Rahilly.

Emden was also sending three shells into the air at the same time.

'Turn two points to the starboard,' Captain Glossop ordered after the enemy ship turned to the starboard in an attempt to get astern of *Sydney*.

Outmanoeuvring *Emden* and keeping the still-shooting ship at an ideal distance for the arsenal aboard *Sydney*, a fresh round of fire was ordered.

This time they did not miss. A series of explosions rocked *Emden*, her wireless station, steering gear, rangefinder and voice pipe all taken out with separate hits.

Still the shot-up *Emden* kept firing, guns exploding every three seconds. But *Sydney* was also firing fast, raining hell on her rival.

'Another direct hit,' Rahilly said as the front funnel of *Emden* was smashed to oblivion.

The hits kept on coming, *Sydney* landing blow after blow. The foremasts of *Emden* were soon destroyed, fore bridge wiped out too. The smoke pouring from her battered body began to make it difficult to aim.

But it didn't matter. *Emden* was now ablaze, listing and threatening to fall. She was only fighting to live a little longer.

Sydney went in for the kill.

'Fire,' ordered the torpedo commander.

The 21-inch torpedo sped out of the chute, 500 pounds of TNT rushing through the water at over thirty knots.

Glossop watched on as a fresh explosion rocked *Emden*, the torpedo ripping apart her side.

'A hit on the engine room,' Rahilly said.

The German ship had not landed a hit on *Sydney* since the fifteenth minute of the fight.

A fresh round of fire wiped out another two funnels.

And then she fired no more.

'She is heading for land,' Bell-Salter said, the navigation man calling from the tower. 'She is turning and making a run.'

Attempting retreat, *Emden* turned towards the island. Glossop followed the burning ship as she ran ashore, bottom ripped apart by reef before she ground to a screeching stop at 11.20 am. She died in a coral cradle, Glossop firing another two broadsides just to make sure.

Battle done, *Emden* dusted, Glossop sat down to write a letter that would be sent to the defeated captain.

'I have the honour to request in the name of humanity that you now surrender your ship to me,' Glossop wrote. 'To show how much I appreciate your gallantry, I will recapitulate the position. You are ashore, three funnels and one mast down and most guns disabled. You cannot leave this island, and my ship is intact.

'In the event of your surrendering, in which I venture to remind you is no disgrace but rather your misfortune, I will endeavour to do all I can for your sick and wounded and take them to a hospital.'

Pacific Ocean, 11 November 1914

Patey allowed for a small celebration when news of *Emden*'s destruction reached HMAS *Australia*.

'We got that son of a bitch *Emden*,' Patey said. '*Sydney* took her down. Get out the cigars.'

Patey and his fleet had been kept out of the hunt for *Emden* too, the task of stopping the German raider given to Admiral Jerram and the Japanese forces that patrolled the South China Sea. He had been able to do nothing as the reports came through almost every other day of *Emden* taking a ship.

The twenty-three ships taken out had an estimated value of £2,200,000, and in just seventy days. Patey's mate Captain Glossop had done himself and his country proud.

Patey had grinned ear-to-ear, a rare thing for the rear admiral during a time of beaten brows, as he read Glossop's official report:

> *I have the honour to report that whilst on convoy escort duty at 6.30 am on 9 November, a message from Cocos was heard: 'Strange warship approaching.'*
>
> *I was ordered to raise steam for full speed and proceed thither. I worked up to twenty knots and at 9.15 am sighted land ahead, and almost immediately smoke which proved to be SMS* Emden *coming towards me.*

> *At 9.40 am she fired the first shot at 9,500 yards. Her fire was very accurate and rapid to begin with, my foremost rangefinder being dismounted quite early and the after control put out of action by the third salvo, but it seemed to slacken quickly.*
>
> *I kept my distance to obtain the advantage of my heavier calibre, longer range guns. First the foremost funnel of the* Emden *went, secondly the foremast, and she was badly on fire aft. Then the second funnel went, and lastly the third; and I saw she was making for North Keeling Island, where she grounded at 11.20 am.*
>
> *I gave her two more broadsides then left to pursue a merchant ship which had come up during the action.*

'He will be called a hero,' Patey said of Captain Glossop. 'And so he should be. This is a proud day for both him and our fleet. For Australia. This is for us all.'

It was the first battle victory in the short history of the Royal Australian Navy. Patey was proud as punch. And Glossop *was* called a hero.

'Our heroic boys', the headlines read. 'Glossop's Glory. Praise for the *Sydney*'.

Patey was particularly impressed by the empathy shown to a brave and daring enemy. Glossop wrote in the official report:

> *I borrowed a doctor and two assistants, and proceeded as fast as possible to* Emden's *assistance. I sent an officer on board to see the captain, and in view of the large number of prisoners and wounded, and lack of accommodation in this ship, and the*

absolute impossibility of leaving them where they were I agreed that if I received his word that all his officers and men would cause no interference to Sydney *and would be amenable to the ship's discipline, I would set to work at once to tranship them, a most difficult operation.*

The conditions in Emden *were indescribable. I received the last man at 3 pm and then had to go around to the lee side to pick up twenty more men, who had managed to get ashore from the ship.*

Dark came on before this could be accomplished, and the ship again stood off and on all night.

We resumed operations next day, a cutter's crew having to land with stretchers to bring the wounded round to the embarking point; a German officer, a doctor, died ashore the previous day.

The ship in the meantime ran over to Direction Island to return their doctor and assistants and send a cablegram, and was back again at 10 am. We embarked the remainder of the wounded and proceeded for Colombo by 10.35 am.

The total casualties in Sydney *were: three killed, four severely wounded, four slightly wounded.*

In Emden, *one can only approximate the killed at seven officers and 108 men based on statements from the captain.*

I had on board eleven officers, nine warrant officers, and 191 men of whom three officers and fifty-three men were wounded, and of this number one officer and three men have since died of their wounds.

The damage done to Sydney*'s hull and fittings was surprisingly small. In all about fifteen hits seem to have been made. The engine and boiler rooms and funnels escaped entirely.*

> *With such a crowd of prisoners and wounded on board it was impossible to do anything more than barely look after them. The wounded were in a terrible state and had to lay about on the upper deck and passages under what temporary shelter could be rigged. As a consequence, the ship will require careful and thorough disinfecting and cleansing.*
>
> *At Colombo, I was more than thankful to be able to stop and tranship to* Empress of Russia *five officers, four warrant officers and sixty-six men belonging to* Emden *who were wounded. Notwithstanding, I retained nine of their worst cases, as I did not like transhipment.*
>
> *Indeed, if we had not been most fortunately in smooth water I could not have shifted the men.*
>
> *I have great pleasure in stating that the behaviour of the ship's company was excellent in every way and with such a large proportion of people under training it is all the more gratifying. The engines worked magnificently, and higher results than trials were obtained, I cannot speak too highly of the medical staff and their arrangements.*

The praise was not just reserved for HMAS *Sydney* and the Australian men. The Australian press spoke highly of *Emden* in spite of – or maybe because of – the destruction she caused.

'It is almost in our heart to regret that the *Emden* has been captured and destroyed,' the *Daily Telegraph* wrote. 'Von Müller has been enterprising, cool and daring in making war on our shipping, and has revealed a nice sense of humour. He has, moreover, shown every possible consideration to the crews of his prizes. There is not a person who does not speak well of this young German, the officers under him and the crew obedient to his orders. The war will lose something of its piquancy, its humour and its interest now that the *Emden* has gone.'

Patey agreed that von Müller deserved praise for his feats, but he was certainly glad that SMS *Emden* was gone. Now he wanted the rest of the fleet – but again he feared he would miss out. 'He will take the direct route,' Patey said of von Spee and his prediction for the next movements of the German East Asia Squadron. 'He will make for the east coast of South America, around Cape Horn.'

Patey and *Australia* were steaming to Hawaii via Fanning Atoll, along with the collier *Mallina*, which was loaded with 3,000 tons of coal. Once at the American naval outpost, they would refuel and resupply before joining the Admiralty-led hunt.

Patey suspected he would never get the chance to destroy von Spee and his fleet. A broken code would prove him right.

Chapter 15

THE FINAL CRACK

Melbourne, 13 November 1914

It was all hands on deck back in Melbourne. Wheatley's assistants had returned after their brief break, refreshed and raring to go; Section E was back in full swing. Typewriters clicked and clacked. Phones rang. And high heels tap-danced across the floor as files were shuffled and shifted from desk to desk.

Even though Wheatley hadn't been able to stop Coronel, his code-cracking feats had at least been acknowledged by the Admiralty. The new First Sea Lord, Admiral John Fisher, brought out of retirement in a swift reaction to the disaster at Coronel, sent Wheatley a cable congratulating him for doing what they could not. What the men in Room 40 had failed to do.

Lord Fisher also requested that 200 copies of the code and key be made in Melbourne. He wanted one for every ship in his fleet.

'It appears they might be taking us seriously now,' Thring said after tasking Wheatley with organising the copies. 'Apparently this codebook captured in the colonies is suddenly important. Shame it took such a tragedy for them to catch on.'

The task of making 200 copies of the codebook proved almost as difficult as cracking the code.

'Can't be done,' said the first printer Wheatley approached. 'We don't have enough typesetters for a job that big. Not enough that know German, at any rate.'

Wheatley was knocked back by another two printers.

'You could take photographs,' another printer suggested. 'Take a picture of every page and we will bind the prints into books.'

Wheatley considered the option.

'Photographs wouldn't stand up to the sun and the sea,' he said. 'They will be kept on ships and used often. Photographs would fade.'

'Can't help you then, mate,' the printer said. 'You're stuffed unless you want to sit down and type 'em out yourself.'

So that is what Wheatley did, though not exactly by himself. He was given permission to hire another twenty women to add to his workforce. The now enlarged group worked eighteen hours a day, only stopping to go home to sleep. They finished the job in seven days, typing a staggering 180,000 pages to make the 200 books. The original codebook was 300 pages, and each page ended up filling three once typed onto foolscap pages. The sorting, stacking and binding took another three days, Wheatley also enlisting the help of his daughter for the job.

Finally, ten days after being requested, the books were sent out – a hundred to the Admiralty, fifty to the commander-in-chief of the America Station and fifty to the China Squadron.

Melbourne, 14 November 1914

'I think Patey is back in the game,' Thring said to Creswell. 'The latest intelligence reports suggest that von Spee is heading north. It looks like he will attempt to take the Panama Canal or round Canada. That will put him on a collision course with *Australia*.'

Creswell looked surprised. 'Really? I thought Wheatley's information had him going around the Cape. And Patey seemed quite certain that he would take that route too.'

'Maybe Patey is just being a pessimist,' Thring said. 'He has certainly had enough bad luck to warrant it. And yes, Wheatley's information suggested the Horn, but we haven't received any intercepts from the Admiralty since the start of the month. It appears they have been decoding the messages for themselves since we gave them the new key.'

The rush of messages from Montevideo had stopped after Wheatley's superenciphered key had been cabled to the Admiralty. Following a message of congratulations, the Admiralty had gone quiet. Room 40 had apparently kicked into gear.

Thring was holding a rare communication from Whitehall in his hand. 'This says that ten German ships were spotted off Valparaiso on the morning of 13 November,' he said. 'And that eight of them steamed off, heading northwest. This information suggests they are heading away from Cape Horn.'

'Patey will be pleased,' Creswell said. 'Let's hope he gets there in time.'

Thring soon had another message from the Admiralty in his hand. This one, however, was marked for the attention of Frederick W. Wheatley.

'Looks like you are back in business, old boy,' Thring said after he found Wheatley. 'They've sent us one they can't crack.' He handed Wheatley the cable.

The world's number-one code cracker, the man they went to when everyone else had failed, studied the intercepted message that had been sent from Montevideo by way of Whitehall. The message contained eight groups of code.

'They couldn't decode it with the key?' Wheatley asked. 'Either of them?'

Thring shook his head.

'They must have changed it again,' Wheatley said.

'Can you work out the new key?' Thring asked.

Wheatley shrugged. 'I did it once. I don't see why I can't again.'

He got straight to work. After putting on his reading glasses and sitting down at his desk, Wheatley checked the new messages against the original transpositions in the *HVB*. They weren't there.

So Room 40 hadn't made the error of not checking it against the original key. Having confirmed the code was indeed in an altered key, he then checked it against the new key, the code he had laboured over for three days until a betting slip and a race already run had prompted his epiphany.

He had not had a chance to use the key since it had been typed out neatly by his staff and placed in the centre of his desk, as the messages had stopped coming to him after then. All the messages he had decoded before that had been done using his frenetically scribbled version.

Wheatley looked down at the now orderly typed letters. He presumed Room 40 had checked the latest intercept against the newest key, but he needed to be certain. He started with the first letter of the intercept, which was an 'F'. He looked to his list and after a quick consultation he replaced the 'F' with a 'T'. And so he went on, replacing each of the letters in the new code according to the key.

They were eight groupings of five-letter jumbles. He had soon converted the entire message with the key he had used to decipher the last round of messages from South America. He went back to his codebook and looked for a match.

He struck out. The key had been changed again. Now he was certain. He would have to work out the new key, which would be a challenge, but he'd done it before, so it shouldn't be that hard.

He was wrong. There were no significant patterns in the fresh jumble of words. He realised he had struck gold by pulling out 'LIKIS IMOFI' following his Melbourne Cup epiphany. 'LIKIS IMOFI' had four repeated letters. The batch he was looking at now contained only one grouping with repeated letters, and those letters were only repeated once. He attempted to make a list of all the codewords in the book that featured two repeated letters in the same positions but gave up after he'd filled a page of his notepad without even making it three pages in to the 300-page codebook. He would never be able to narrow it down. He would be lucky to reduce his odds from 52 billion to one to 40 billion to one at this rate.

Wheatley reluctantly resigned himself to failure.

'I need a bigger sample,' Wheatley told Thring. 'There just isn't enough of the message to find the key. Tell them to send me whatever they have in that code.'

He spent the next five days staring at the code he could not crack. He wondered if there was another way to find the key. Wondered if there was something he was not seeing.

He couldn't sleep. Every time he put his head down he thought of another Coronel. He couldn't help thinking about what the message that remained a riddle said. What it could potentially stop.

Wheatley was asleep at his desk when Thring found him almost a week later.

'We have another,' Thring said. 'Another code from Montevideo has arrived, this time sent direct. They think it is also in the new key.'

Wheatley snapped from his slumber, suddenly wide awake. 'How long?' he asked. 'How long is the message.'

Thring responded by handing him the freshly telegraphed page.

Wheatley looked down and saw half of the page filled with typed print, all five-letter combinations in groupings of two. He counted them.

'Sixteen groupings,' he said with a grin. 'That's more like it.' He picked up a pen and was immediately lost in a world of letters as Thring backed out of the room.

This time Wheatley didn't find a combination with four repeated letters on the intercept – he found one with five.

'You ripper!' he shouted.

It took him just three hours to work out the new key. Then he drafted a note that would be sent out to the Admiralty:

German ships on the coast of South America have again altered the cipher key to the HVB *code.*

New key has been discovered and is as follows:

A = E, B = T, C = D, D = V, E = U, F = H, G = W, H = Z, I = O, K = F, L = M, M = G, N = B, O = Y, P = K, R = L, S = C, T = X, U = I, V = P, W = N, X = S, Y = A, Z = R.

The letters J and Q have been omitted as not used in code.

He then decoded the first message: 'Have passed three of the enemy while steering SW by S,' the first of the two messages read. 'Request orders of Kosmos Liner *Luxor* to sail at all hazards tomorrow night if necessary.'

He knew the message was important. Thring had told him that von Spee and his fleet were suspected to be heading north. Up towards the Panama Canal. Up towards Patey. The message he had just decoded suggested otherwise. It said they were heading south, down towards Cape Horn. Down towards another unsuspecting fleet.

The second message didn't just suggest but confirmed.

'Advise you not to run into Valparaiso,' the message sent by *Scharnhorst*'s sister, *Gneisenau*, said. 'Cannot understand what news you have from home. How do you propose to come on board? In case of anything happening report my arrival at once.

If it is not possible to conduct further operations then get your clearance for the rendezvous at Abrolhos.'

A quick check of the map revealed Abrolhos to be an archipelago off the east coast of Brazil, well and truly south of the Panama Canal. The message, sent to the German steamer *Eleonore Woermann*, was confirmation of von Spee's route via Cape Horn.

'I think we have them, sir,' Wheatley said. 'I think this is it.'

Thring read the decoded message. 'I think we do too,' he said. 'You've done it again, Wheatley. You will get a medal for this. Everyone will know your name. Everyone will know what you have done.'

Thring wasted no time in sending the Admiralty the message that would give them their revenge and Wheatley his legacy.

Chapter 16

THE FALKLANDS

Cape Horn, Chile, 2 December 1914

Von Spee and his squadron were about to hit fifty-six degrees south, the deadliest latitude in the world.

'Cape Horn,' von Spee said as *Scharnhorst* led the German squadron into the most treacherous stretch of ocean known to man. 'Isn't she something?'

First rounded in 1616 by the Dutch explorer Willem Schouten and named after the city of Hoorn, Cape Horn was a graveyard of ships. Von Spee thought of Charles Darwin's famous quote as *Scharnhorst* rocked and rolled through a standard six-foot swell. 'One sight of such a coast is enough to make a landsman dream for a week about shipwrecks, peril and death,' Darwin had written.

For the past few nights von Spee's dreams had been filled with death and disaster, but right now, with the Cape bathed in summer sunlight for seventeen hours a day as the December solstice approached, the Horn was an assassin asleep.

'We couldn't hope for better conditions,' Captain Schultz remarked. 'It's hard to imagine her claiming so many.'

'Don't speak too soon,' von Spee said. 'We don't want to wake her up.'

Von Spee knew that the waves could suddenly appear. That a wall of water thirty yards high could form without warning, as if God had slammed his fist into the sea.

And then there were the winds: the Roaring Forties, the Furious Fifties and the Screaming Sixties. Blowing at an already blustery twenty miles an hour, the wind could turn deadly. Called williwaws, the blasts of Antarctic air came at over sixty miles an hour. Like the waves, they struck without warning and brought destruction and death.

There were also icebergs. Gigantic hunks carried by rips and chaotic currents, they moved across the top of the ocean with the speed of a steaming ship. Those that could be seen were dangerous; the unseen ones were deadly.

But for now, the weather was good. The seas were calm.

That soon changed.

Von Spee grabbed at an overcoat as the temperature dropped. He walked over and checked the barometer.

'Air pressure is falling,' von Spee said. 'And fast. Damn you, man, you spoke too soon. She is coming for us.'

'She was always coming,' Schultz replied. 'She doesn't need an invitation. I'll prepare the ship.'

The swell had already risen by the time the order went out. Waves crashed into the side of the ship, water slapped the deck.

The crew worked fast. Ropes were rigged all over the deck for the men to hang onto. Landing boats, ammunition stocks and supply crates were all double-tied to the deck.

The wind now roared. The men held onto the ropes as the ship pitched and crashed. The rigging was the only thing that stopped the waves from washing them into the sea.

Von Spee held onto a metal railing in the bridge and looked towards the smaller ships in the fleet. Binoculars pressed to his eyes, he watched as a collier dumped coal overboard, the shed weight saving her from capsizing.

The fleet marched on.

The storm soon abated, leaving as fast as it had come. Schultz didn't say a word about the fast-improving conditions. Nor did von Spee.

The sun was back, clouds, swell and wind gone. They had survived the squall. But the threat of destruction still loomed large. Von Spee knew he could be sailing straight towards a fleet of British battleships.

'Ship ahead,' said Schultz.

Von Spee froze momentarily before snapping into action and grabbing his binoculars again.

'A barque?' he said, surprised. He checked again to make sure. Yes, four masts. Sails instead of smokestacks A wind ship, not a warship.

'Maintain course,' von Spee ordered. 'Full steam ahead.'

* * *

'It's a gift from God,' von Spee said after *Scharnhorst* had scuttled the ship with the sails.

What he'd first feared to be the tip of the spear at a British fighting force had turned out to be a lonely Canadian merchant ship. And she was carrying coal.

'Yes,' Schultz had confirmed after examining the haul. 'It's 2,500 tons of the good stuff, Cardiff coal.'

The iron barque *Drummuir* had offered no resistance when confronted by the German fleet. The cache of coal was quickly transferred to the German colliers and the small crew of Canadians were taken hostage. The four-masted ship was then sent to the bottom of the sea, another carcass for the Cape.

Von Spee and the German fleet anchored at Picton Island, located in the Tierra del Fuego archipelago on the extreme southern tip of Chile after rounding the Horn. They had stopped hoping to get word from home.

Von Spee had been cut off from all communications since leaving St Quentin's Bay on 26 November. In fact, he had received no word from Berlin since the Battle of Coronel and only titbits of news about the British. The latest suggested the British South Atlantic forces had gone to South Africa.

'Sir,' said a lieutenant. 'The Canadians.'

'What about them?' von Spee queried.

'They have news, sir,' the lieutenant said. 'About the *Emden*.'

Von Spee was then told about the defeat and destruction of *Emden*. That von Müller and his men had been ambushed by an Australian ship called *Sydney* while attempting to destroy a wireless station in the Cocos Islands.

'He fought even though the odds were truly against him,' von Spee told his crew after he'd processed the news. 'A light cruiser armed with only ten 4.1-inch guns, *Emden* showed the damage that can be caused by just a single vessel when a captain is courageous, his crew fearless. We will celebrate these men and their captain for showing skill and courage. They were all to the man willing to give their lives for a cause greater than them. They have shown us all the way. May we be inspired by their example.'

Von Spee did not know if von Müller was dead or alive. He didn't know how many men had survived, if any. He suspected he would not live long enough to find out.

News from the Admiralty finally arrived. 'You are advised to try to break through with all your ships and return home,' the order said. With half the Allied fleet gunning for him and his ammunition half exhausted, von Spee had been ordered to steam back to Berlin.

Inspired by the feats of *Emden* – and saddened by her demise – von Spee gathered his senior officers for a meeting on board *Scharnhorst.* 'We cannot be satisfied with just getting home,' he said. '*Emden* has shown us what a single ship can do, and we are a fleet. A formidable fleet. We cannot be content with just one victory. A war still rages and we must do our bit.'

Von Spee wanted another victory over the British. A final act to cement his legend. Rather than flee the enemy forces, taking the path less travelled and using the cover of night, he wanted to attack.

'I think we should go to the Falkland Islands,' von Spee said.

'Take out the wireless station and leave the British without any way of communicating in the South Atlantic.'

Von Spee also revealed his plan to harass trade, blowing up any merchant ships sailing around the Falklands and the River Plate Estuary in Argentina. The Falkland Islands were home to the sole repair facility for British ships in the southwest Atlantic Ocean. Eliminating the wireless station and destroying the docks would leave them lame.

'This action would also draw the enemy down from Europe,' von Spee said, 'away from the High Seas Fleet. We have an opportunity to land a significant blow.'

'It is risky, sir,' Schultz countered. 'The Falklands will be well protected. It is their main base in the South Atlantic. We will surely face a fight and we will stand little chance with our depleted ammunition stores. We can't trust the reports we've received about the Atlantic fleet steaming to South Africa.'

'Yes, there is a chance that we will encounter the enemy,' von Spee said, 'but I don't believe we will face a superior fleet. They will be preoccupied by the fight for Europe. They will not leave Britain undefended to exact revenge for Coronel.'

Von Spee had no knowledge of the greater war. A lack of intelligence had left him blind. He did not know that there was no significant naval action in Europe. He didn't know the South Africa talk was a ruse.

'So, it is agreed,' von Spee said. 'We go with God.'

Canadians offloaded, fuel replenished, plan in place, the German East Asia Squadron steamed from Picton Island at 12 pm on 6 December, course set for the Falkland Islands.

Falkland Islands, South Atlantic Ocean, 8 December 1914, 2.30 am

Big, brilliant and bright, the moon, falling fast to the southwest, cut a silver path into the sea. A gentle breeze brushed the top of the slight swells as *Scharnhorst*, heading northwest, followed the lunar trail of light laid on top of the water.

'Land ahoy,' Schultz said, spotting a black mass on the horizon.

'Prepare *Gneisenau* and *Nürnberg*,' von Spee said.

The order sparked a flurry of activity on board the two ships that would lead the attack. Small arms and explosives were broken out and given to the men who had been chosen to march onto land. Boarding boats were untied and checked.

The big guns were also readied. They would turn the British defences to rubble and clear the way for the land attack.

The crew also hosed the decks, a layer of water put down to prevent flame turning into fire, sparks from becoming a blaze.

Von Spee ordered the attack shortly after sunrise.

Speed set at fourteen knots, *Gneisenau* and *Nürnberg* steamed towards Cape Pembroke while *Scharnhorst*, *Dresden* and *Leipzig* all remained in the shadows about five miles out to sea.

'*Gneisenau* to *Scharnhorst*,' barked the radio. 'Do you read?'

'Received,' said Schultz, looking down at his watch. It was 8.30 am.

'We have a visual of the wireless masts at Port Stanley,' the radio call continued. 'We also have a visual of several masts belonging to ships. Copy?'

'Copy,' said Schultz. 'Continue.'

'There is a large plume of smoke rising over the harbour,' the operator continued. 'I repeat, a large column of black smoke. What are your orders?'

Schultz conferred with von Spee. 'A warship?' Schultz speculated.

'It could be,' von Spee said. 'But they could also have set fire to their stocks.' Von Spee suspected another Papeete, the British burning their coal before it could be taken. 'Tell them to proceed.'

The order was issued. All was quiet on the bridge of *Scharnhorst* for the next ten minutes.

'*Gneisenau* to *Scharnhorst*,' came the message from the radio. 'We are taking fire. I repeat, we are taking fire. Do you copy?'

'Copy,' said Schultz. 'Can you identify the enemy?'

'Three British warships,' the voice continued. 'The smoke was from warships.'

'What class?' Schultz asked.

'Three British County-class cruisers,' came the reply.

The radio went silent.

'Another two ships sighted,' the radio reported, returning to life after a painful pause. 'Both pre-dreadnought destroyers. And a fifth, a light cruiser.'

The radio went silent again.

'We have been hit,' the operator said.

Von Spee grabbed the radio. 'Do not accept action,' he said. 'I repeat, do not accept action. Proceed at full speed and rejoin the fleet.'

Faced with three cruisers, a light cruiser and two destroyers, von Spee knew this was a battle he could not win. He'd ordered flight, not fight, albeit reluctantly.

* * *

'Prepare the fleet,' von Spee commanded. 'We will make steam for east by north as soon as they return.'

Von Spee might have been outgunned but he would not be outpaced. With even the slowest ship in his fleet boasting a top speed of twenty-two knots, he figured he would have the pace to evade what appeared to be another slapped-together fleet.

The pre-dreadnought ships that had been spotted in the harbour were mighty but slow. Once kings of the sea, they were now ageing battleships with a top speed of just eighteen knots.

'And we will have a six-mile head start,' von Spee said.

Gneisenau and *Nürnberg* steamed into sight at 11 am.

'Let them lead,' von Spee said.

A line of ships soon formed, first *Gneisenau*, then *Nürnberg*, *Scharnhorst* and *Dresden*; last in line was *Leipzig*. They steamed together at a uniform speed of twenty-two knots.

They were home free.

'They are gaining on us, sir,' the navigator said after coming down from his tower.

'Impossible,' von Spee said. 'They were six miles astern and not up to steam. They can't be closing.'

The navigator shrugged. 'Well, they are coming, sir,' he replied. 'And fast. They are five miles and closing.'

Von Spee grabbed his binoculars. 'Not a chance,' he muttered, peering behind. '*Scheisse*,' he cursed. Von Spee was dumbfounded. Up against pre-dreadnoughts, the last incarnation built in 1904, he should have been pulling away. But they were closing. It didn't make sense.

And then it did. He was soon able to make out a silhouette through the smoke: three smokestacks and two masts. 'An Invincible,' he muttered. He studied the next ship in the line: three smokestacks and two masts. 'Two Invincibles,' he said. 'We are doomed.'

Von Spee was being hunted by HMS *Invincible* and HMS *Inflexible*, sister British battleships with a top speed of 25.5 knots. Measuring 567 feet in length, they were metal monsters. The newest, biggest and deadliest ships in the British force, they packed four twin twelve-inch guns, sixteen single four-inch guns and five eighteen-inch torpedo tubes. They were also covered in the thickest armour ever worn at sea.

'We cannot outrun them,' von Spee said, turning to Schultz. 'And we cannot beat them. Order *Nürnberg*, *Dresden* and *Leipzig* to flee. We will sacrifice ourselves in the hope of saving them.'

So that was the plan. *Scharnhorst* and *Gneisenau* would fight so the others could survive. The sisters would become saviours by committing suicide.

Von Spee hoped at least one of his sons would live to return home to his mother.

* * *

'They are firing on *Nürnberg*!' came the cry.

A series of shells had exploded near *Nürnberg*. Von Spee turned and saw waterspouts climbing into the sky. The shells had missed by a sizeable margin.

He drew a deep breath as he thought of his sons, Otto on *Nürnberg* and Heinrich on *Gneisenau*. He had just sentenced the latter to death and given the former a chance in ordering his ship to flee. It was necessary to discriminate as a captain. It was soul-destroying to do so as a father.

'God help me,' he said.

The enemy continued their relentless march, coming at an estimated twenty-six knots. By now HMS *Inflexible* had taken control of the line, the twenty-ton destroyer overtaking her sister ship *Invincible* to lead.

After the warships came three armoured cruisers: HMS *Carnarvon*, HMS *Cornwall* and HMS *Kent*. There were also two light cruisers, HMS *Bristol* and HMS *Glasgow*. And finally, a solitary armed merchant cruiser, HMS *Macedonia*.

He knew his last ships could no longer flee. It would be eight ships against two. Suicide.

Von Spee said a prayer for his sons, and then another for the rest of his fleet. He did not pray for himself.

He watched as *Nürnberg*, *Dresden* and *Leipzig* broke away. He hoped they would survive. He watched on in horror as *Kent*, *Cornwall* and *Glasgow* steamed out of the British line to follow his runaways.

Von Spee turned to Schultz. 'It's time,' he said. 'Are you ready?'

Schultz nodded.

They turned to face what was left of the British line: *Inflexible* and *Invincible*. They would go head first into the uneven fight.

'Let's give him hell,' Schultz said. 'We will go with glory.'

Von Spee would not go down without a fight. He still had a trick or two up his well-worn sleeve. 'Full steam to the northeast,' he ordered.

By 1.25 pm, *Scharnhorst* and *Gneisenau* had outmanoeuvred the cumbersome British fleet to secure the leeward position. With only a slight breeze, firing into the wind would provide an advantage. While the Germans' fire would not be affected by the mild wind, the gun smoke they generated would be quickly swept behind them. The British would have to shoot through their own smoke, which would travel downwind and obscure their sights. They would also have to contend with their own engine smoke.

It was a minor win, he was still doomed, but he might just latch a few to his rope before he was dropped. Von Spee issued his next order. 'Long range battle to port,' he said. 'Fire distribution from the right. Raise the flag.'

With the order issued for *Gneisenau* to fight *Inflexible* and *Scharnhorst* to take on *Invincible*, the signal flag was raised. Von Spee ignored the other three ships.

'Fire!' the artillery sergeant ordered.

The first round of salvos only managed to straddle *Invincible*, and none of the shells came close to hitting *Inflexible*.

The British struggled to fix a target through all the smoke.

'Fire!' the artillery sergeant yelled again.

This time they hit, two shells smashing into *Invincible* at 1.45 pm.

'It's a hit,' came the cry.

Von Spee and Schultz shook hands. The crew could be heard cheering below.

'We may do this yet,' von Spee said.

The joy was short-lived.

'They are pulling away,' the navigator yelled. 'They are moving out of range.'

The British ships' superior firing range meant they could move away and hit the German fleet from a distance, where the fire could not be returned.

'Shall we chase?' Schultz asked. 'Close the gap?'

Von Spee pondered. 'No,' he said. 'This could be our chance. Full about.'

With the enemy retreating and expecting them to chase, and a cloud of gunsmoke keeping them hidden, von Spee thought he could flee.

'Full steam ahead,' he ordered when *Scharnhorst* had turned away from the fight.

The engines had just been rung to full when the radio cracked.

'We've been hit,' came the call from *Gneisenau*. 'Two shots to the rear.'

The first shot had exploded against the aft funnel, the force of the fire smashing through the deck. An officer had both arms ripped off in the explosion and a stoker was killed in the corridor.

The second shot had landed in the middle of the deck. Another ten men were wounded. The decks were stained with blood.

'Are you compromised?' von Spee asked.

'No,' came the reply. 'All systems working.'

Von Spee ordered them to continue the set course away from the British. Full steam ahead.

For a moment, von Spee thought he would get away. Looking back through the smoke that blinded the British, he saw the squadron continue to retreat. 'This might just work,' he said.

But just minutes later he saw *Carnarvon* turn. She pointed her bow towards *Scharnhorst* and started the chase.

'Damn it,' von Spee grunted as the Invincibles followed.

There would be no escape.

* * *

Water rushed into the air as a twelve-inch shell exploded a hundred yards away. The British were back in range. Again, von Spee looked to his captain.

'Ready?' he asked.

And again Schultz nodded. 'Didn't think we would get this far,' he said.

Von Spee smiled. 'Well, give the damn order,' he said. 'Let's get wherever it is that we are going. If death awaits, then let us go proudly.'

Von Spee ended the chase at 2.53 pm. In a move that surprised no one, the admiral of the fleet, a man as brave as any who had steered a ship, ordered *Scharnhorst* and *Gneisenau* to turn and once again face the British fleet.

Smoke cleared by a stiffening wind, British gunfire incessant, von Spee steamed towards his death.

Scharnhorst was hit relentlessly, shell after shell crashing into her body. So was *Gneisenau*. The second funnel of *Scharnhorst* was the first to be wiped out. The third funnel was next.

'Fire,' von Spee ordered in defiance.

His men sent off a fresh round. Another shell struck the casemate armour near the number two port and water began to flood the ship. The wireless room was hit, a blast wiping out all the communications equipment and killing three men.

And then the fires broke out. Small and scattered at first, the flames quickly caught, ammunition fuelling them. Up on the bridge, von Spee could feel the rising heat. The ship was covered in a red glow.

The fire spread to the engine room and the ship slowed.

'More power,' Schultz ordered.

Then the ship began to tip-starboard.

Von Spee watched Schultz attempt to redress the ship. 'This is a fight to the death,' he shouted. 'There will be no surrender.' He ordered fresh fire, shouting for whatever guns he had left to spit their shells.

'A hit,' came the cry. 'We landed a blow.'

'Never say die,' von Spee said.

The British fleet made another sudden turn, this time to port. Again, they were attempting to clear both gun smoke and range.

'Turn to starboard,' von Spee shouted. 'We don't want to get into a circular fight. Nor do we want to surrender the leeward position.'

Schultz ordered the ship to turn to the southwest; SMS *Scharnhorst* could barely respond. She now dipped a yard to the draught and listed as much to the port. Water was rushing into the ship, after two shells had ripped through the hull.

'Why is the admiral's flag at half-mast?' came the radio call from *Gneisenau*. 'Is he dead?'

The reply was prompt.

'I am still going well,' von Spee said. 'Have you landed any hits?'

'Owing to the smoke I have been unable to observe,' the captain replied.

'Keep up the fight,' von Spee said. 'We are still here.'

Scharnhorst continued to list and dip, water still rushing into the hull. The fires raged but still she shot. She would keep on going until her ammunition was spent.

'All we can do is try to save *Gneisenau*,' von Spee said. 'We will make a charge. Maybe she can find a way.'

At 4 pm the order was issued.

'If your engines are intact, attempt to escape,' von Spee commanded. 'Save yourself.'

Von Spee thought of his son. Maybe he had just given Heinrich a chance.

'Turn eight points towards the enemy,' von Spee ordered, 'and ring the engines to full. Tell them to give us whatever she has left.

'And prepare to fire the torpedoes. We will attempt to get them into range.'

Schultz passed on the order.

It was an ambitious order. The burning engines now screamed. They would soon blow. Steam and smoke were coming from the bridge. The aft was completely engulfed in flame. The bow of the ship was only six feet above the water line.

Von Spee's final charge lasted just seventeen minutes. 'We now go proudly to God,' he said as the ship began to roll.

Scharnhorst capsized and sank at 4.17 pm. With her battle flag still flying and her propellers turning, she went down like a brick.

The battle had been lost after two hours and thirty-four minutes. None of the 860 souls on board survived.

* * *

One kill was not enough for the British fleet. With death delivered to *Scharnhorst*, the German flagship already on the ocean floor, *Invincible* and *Inflexible* turned their attention – and their guns – to *Gneisenau*. HMS *Carnarvon* also decided to join in, making it a three-on-one fight.

Gneisenau was already bruised and battered. The starboard engine had suffered a direct hit, cutting her power in half. Her two remaining engines could only deliver a top speed of fourteen knots. She could not run.

Another direct hit had toppled the forward funnel and the boiler room was on fire. The starboard side of the bridge had been wiped out by a further blow.

At 4.15 pm, just two minutes before *Scharnhorst* sank, a shell ripped through the portside hull of her sister ship. Another tore through the starboard and exploded, killing all the injured men and medical staff in the dressing room.

Still *Gneisenau* did not quit. Circled by the trio of British ships, she ducked, weaved and fired. Occasionally she landed a blow, but mostly she took them, and they came in rapid succession.

Boom! An underwater hit further shredded the hull.

Boom! Another hit to the hull, the explosion shaking metal from the ship.

'All men on deck,' the order finally came at 5.35 pm. 'Clear the ship for sinking.'

Like wounded ants, blackened and beaten, they crawled from their nests and limped onto the deck. They were forced to cover their ears as a rogue gunner ignored the order to surrender and delivered a parting shot, the forward turret throwing its last punch.

When the survivors had gathered, Captain Maerker issued his final order. 'Scuttle the ship,' he said. He would deny the British the knockout blow.

A series of self-inflicted detonations rocked *Gneisenau*. Red, orange and yellow fireworks leaped into the pink sky.

Maerker thought he could hear the British cheer as *Gneisenau* rolled.

Four men stood arm in arm singing on the torpedo tube, the tune suddenly ceasing when they were dunked to their death. Others dived from the deck, attempting to find a section of water not covered in burning oil. Some attempted to run along the hull as it rolled, forming a life-or-death treadmill.

Otto von Spee was not one of the 187 who were saved, the 22-year-old among the 598 killed in the four-hour fight. He joined his father at the bottom of the sea.

* * *

Nürnberg had bolted when von Spee issued the order to split.

'*Kent* is giving chase,' Captain von Schönberg yelled. 'Full speed ahead.'

Von Schönberg was confident of outrunning *Kent*. Smaller than *Scharnhorst*, SMS *Nürnberg* was nimble and fast.

'Twenty-five knots, sir,' the engine room informed. 'We have reached full power.'

Nürnberg was steaming for survival. And there was a chance she might just make it.

'What's going on?' von Schönberg asked when the speed of the ship suddenly dropped. 'Why have we slowed?'

The answer signalled his end. 'Broken boiler tubes, sir,' came the reply. 'They pushed too hard.'

Nürnberg now had a top speed of just eighteen knots.

'Prepare the guns,' von Schönberg ordered. 'She will soon be in range.'

The fight began at 5 pm.

'Fire,' von Schönberg ordered.

The two 4.1-inch SKL/40 rapid-fire guns on the back of the ship were unleashed, a volley of shells flying into the sky.

The other eight guns – three on either side and two on the forecastle – were loaded and waiting. They would get their chance.

The gunnery lieutenant reported the shots had fallen short.

'Turn two points to port,' von Schönberg ordered. 'Let's bring some more into play.'

The three guns on the port side were soon firing. New guns, same result.

Unhurt by the early barrage, *Kent* began its own thirty minutes after *Nürnberg* opened fire. The two twin turrets, one on the fore, one on the aft, were finally ordered to return serve, fire spitting from barrels as the six-inch Mark VII guns tossed hundred-pound shells into the sky.

'We are hit,' came the cry aboard *Nürnberg*.

A shell had taken off the aft funnel. Von Schönberg watched as his men rushed to extinguish the flames with water and blankets. Another explosion rocked the ship just minutes later, this time as a shell crashed onto the middle deck. The shrapnel flew, killing men and taking out the number-three gun.

'Eight points to port,' von Schönberg ordered as *Kent* continued to close in and fire.

The captain was attempting to bring all of his portside guns into play. Some swift steering soon had five guns pointing at the British blaster.

'Another hit,' came the cry.

They now had only four guns pointing at *Kent*, the latest shell wiping out another SKL/40 and eight men.

'Another hit,' came the cry again.

Three guns left. *Nürnberg* attempted to stop *Kent* from making a move across her bow, firing shot after shot. She was now close enough to use her smaller guns, so the SKL/35s joined in. But both the big guns and small failed to deliver a significant blow.

And then the hits came. In a brutal rapid-fire barrage, *Kent* unleashed. *Nürnberg*'s rudder room was hit first, steel bent and twisted, bodies ripped apart. The boilers and engines were destroyed next.

Nürnberg was now unmanoeuvrable, a sitting duck. Von Schönberg issued the dreaded order at 6.30 pm.

'All men on deck!' he commanded. 'Clear the ship for sinking.'

The surviving men went overboard. Like soot-covered lemmings, mindless and mangled, they formed a line and dropped into the sea.

Otto von Spee gasped as he broke through the surface. He had avoided the shredded steel and flames and made it into the sea. He grabbed onto a piece of flotsam; another three sailors soon joined him on the make-do life raft and desperately kicked away from the hellish scene.

As Otto watched *Nürnberg* sink, the British warship approached. 'They're coming to save us,' he said, pointing.

They waved their hands in the air. 'Over here,' they shouted.

And with that *Kent* opened fire with machine guns and shells. They slaughtered the survivors. All of them. Otto was reunited with his father and his brother.

* * *

Leipzig's last-ditch, all-or-nothing play had failed. All three torpedoes, fired in a desperate final act, had missed.

'Sink the ship,' came the order from the bridge of the burning and beaten ship. 'All men on deck!'

The sea valves were opened and the vessel was flooded. Men poured onto the deck, climbing from doors and blast holes. Only those covered by the armour of the deck during the battle had survived; all the gunners, navigators and riggers were dead. The survivors jumped into the sea as *Leipzig* rolled, grabbing onto whatever wreckage they could and waiting for help.

HMS *Glasgow* flashed at the sinking ship. 'Do you surrender?' the message, delivered in morse code, came.

Already sinking, *Leipzig* could not respond.

The survivors watched as *Glasgow* and *Cornwall* steamed towards the carnage, the sea a mess of twisted metal and men.

The men thought they were about to be saved. They were wrong. *Glasgow* and *Cornwall* opened fire at 8.30 pm.

'This is sheer murder,' shouted a gunner aboard *Glasgow*, refusing the captain's directive and instead giving his own order to the crew: 'She is a sinking ship. Cease fire!'

But the damage had been done. Only eighteen men from *Leipzig* survived the bloodbath.

Chapter 17

SOUVENIRS AND SEND-OFFS

Falkland Islands, South Atlantic Ocean, 1 January 1915

Patey put down his binoculars. 'Stop the ship,' he said.

The order was issued and the engines were killed. HMAS *Australia* slowed, stalled and then stopped.

The warship was floating in a sea of debris.

'Send out a launch and see what you can find,' Patey said.

The party reported back an hour later. 'Sir,' the sailor said. 'We thought you may want this.' He handed Patey a lifebuoy, red and white except for the black print, the name of a ship.

'SMS *Scharnhorst*,' he read. 'Well, I'll be damned.'

Patey and HMAS *Australia* had stumbled over the wreckage belonging to *Scharnhorst* twenty-four days after von Spee and another 1,870 German sailors had died in the Battle of the Falklands. Only ten British sailors had perished in the fight.

Heading to the Falkland Islands to repair a rudder damaged

while sailing through the Strait of Magellan, *Australia* had steamed into a graveyard.

'I might have to keep this,' Patey said. 'I did get a piece of *Scharnhorst* after all.'

In what was a bittersweet moment for Patey and his men, *Australia* had been informed of the destruction of the German East Asia Squadron on 10 December. The Australian flagship had been stalking the coast just outside the Gulf of Panama when Patey learned he would not be the man to bring down von Spee.

'German East Asia Squadron destroyed off Falkland Islands,' the cable had said. 'Stand by for new orders.'

Patey had done his best to remain upbeat. He'd told his men it was a great victory. A day to be celebrated. That there would be more battles to fight. That glory would be had.

But deep down he knew *Australia* could have had this victory if not for the Admiralty and their incompetency.

His crew had felt the same. 'The worst piece of really good news we have yet had,' an officer wrote soon after Patey broke the news. 'We are, of course, very glad it has been done; but that we should be disappointed after four months' expectations, in the most trying climate and after all these long trips, is very hard. It makes one feel everyone is alike, that we have been through a war which is now over, and that peace has been declared without our even seeing our much-respected enemy. We are now, as it were, on leave, about to see the Panama Canal and go through it, and when our next opponent is named or we are actually ordered home again, it will be like starting again – beginning a fresh war – and we shall try to forget our bad luck.'

HMAS *Australia* was ordered to sail to Jamaica via the Panama Canal shortly after the message came through that the enemy had been vanquished. But it had been forced to sail down the coast of South America and pass through the Strait of Magellan after learning that the Panama Canal had been closed to heavy shipping.

Australia had become the first Royal Australian Navy ship to successfully pass through the strait when she'd completed the journey on 31 December. But it had come at a cost when a rudder had been damaged on a shallow reef.

Patey had been forced to make an unplanned trip to the Falkland Islands for repairs. They'd been limping their way across the South Atlantic to the islands when they'd stumbled on the debris.

'Those poor souls,' Patey said after taking his souvenir. 'We mightn't have achieved glory but we also avoided the guilt. Perhaps it all worked out for the best.'

Melbourne, 10 January 1915

Wheatley walked into Captain Thring's office for the last time.

'Frederick,' Thring said, arm outstretched as soon as he walked in the door. 'I'm going to miss you, old boy. It won't be the same without you here.' The captain shook the code breaker's hand.

'I'll only be a phone call away,' Wheatley said. 'I'm sure you haven't seen the last of me.'

Code cracked, German squadron destroyed, Wheatley's job was done. Section E had been disbanded. The Admiralty was now in possession of all Wheatley's codes and keys. They also had his method. Room 40 at Whitehall had taken over, Churchill insisting on complete control.

Frederick William Wheatley would be an intelligence officer for the Royal Australian Navy no more. He had just finished his last shift as Australia's chief cryptographer. After 152 days at the Navy Office in Melbourne, he was going back to his chalk and his students.

Wheatley had earlier held back tears as he'd said goodbye to the women of Section E. Hugs and kisses were not appropriate, so he shook hands instead.

'I couldn't have done this on my own,' he'd said in his farewell speech.

'You have done both me and your country a service. I will forever remember your contribution and the world should too.'

Wheatley now stood before Thring, his time as a code cracker about to end.

'And I hear further congratulations are in order,' Thring continued.

For a moment Wheatley looked like a student puzzling at one of his incomprehensible blackboards.

'Oh, you haven't been told?' Thring asked. 'Seems I get to break the good news.'

A knighthood? The Victoria Cross?

'You won't be returning to the naval college as an instructor,' Thring said. 'You will be going back as the chief instructor, second-in-command of the brand-new facility at Jervis Bay when it opens next month. Congratulations. I couldn't think of a better man.'

Wheatley shook Thring's outstretched hand again, slightly dazed. He would be paid a salary of £550 and live rent-free with his family in a brand-new residence at the college on the South Coast of New South Wales.

'Thank you, sir,' he said through gritted teeth. 'My family will be thrilled. This is a great honour. I shall continue to serve to the best of my ability.'

'Remember our first meeting?' Thring smiled. 'When you told me about your trip to Germany and travelling with the prince, the general and the admiral in the Black Forest?'

Wheatley nodded as he took a sip of freshly delivered tea.

'Well, I thought it was codswallop,' Thring said. 'It sounded so fanciful. But after what you have achieved here, well, I have no doubt now that it was all true.'

Wheatley raised his eyebrows before putting his cup back on its saucer. 'Of course it was true.' Wheatley grinned. He sat silent for a moment. 'If that story was hard to believe then how are people going to react when I tell them about all this?'

'Well, you won't have to worry about that for a while,' Thring said. 'You will need to sign a secrecy agreement before you leave. The code is still in use and it has to remain hush-hush. This is also a very sensitive issue for the Admiralty, given what happened at Coronel. But don't worry, it will all come out in the wash. You will get your dues when this whole business is done. History will give you the recognition you deserve.'

At that moment, Wheatley believed that might be true.

Epilogue

Potts Point, Sydney, 5 August 1934

Wheatley picked up the phone and dialled. By now he had memorised the numbers.

'Mr Hadfield, please,' Wheatley asked. 'Dr Wheatley. Yes, again.'

Wheatley had spent the last five weeks telling the editor of *Reveille* his remarkable tale. He'd told him of the spies and the secrets, of the code he'd cracked and of the battle called Coronel. Of his role in bringing down a German fleet. Of how Australia helped win the war.

'So why are you coming forward with this now?' Hadfield had asked. 'Why haven't you told your story before?'

Wheatley had tried to. When Arthur W. Jose's history of the Royal Australian Navy was published in 1928, he'd asked the former intelligence officer cum navy historian why his contribution had not been included in the 649-page account, part of Charles Bean's ninth volume of *The Official History of Australia in the War of 1914–1918*.

'Mr Jose told me that it was too sensitive,' Wheatley had related. 'He said what had happened was a source of embarrassment for the Admiralty and they would never allow the full story to come out.'

'Because they didn't listen?' Hadfield had asked.

'Because they could have stopped it,' Wheatley had said. 'And because they needed to take credit for what happened in the Falklands to regain some face.'

Wheatley told Hadfield that Jose had agreed to acknowledge his contribution in the first revision of the book.

'And he did,' Wheatley continued. 'But it was just a mention.'

Hadfield obtained a copy of the revised history. 'The steamer *Hobart*, caught as she entered Port Phillip, contained valuable beauty,' Jose had written on page forty-six. 'In her we found not only the semi-official "Instructions to Shipping as to their Conduct in a Naval War" with their Secret Appendix, but also a key to the code cipher used by German warships in communicating with German merchant vessels.

'This proved of great importance. Messages intercepted by African and South American stations, as well as by British warships, were for some time transmitted to the Navy Office to be deciphered; and when early in November the German authorities apparently discovered that their cipher was known, and substituted another, this also (as well as a third introduced about the middle of November) was deciphered by the strenuous and excellent work of Dr F.W. Wheatley.'

There was also an appendix entry at the bottom of the page. 'Among these were several [messages] stating that the German Pacific Squadron proposed to proceed to the Atlantic,' the entry said, 'and had arranged a rendezvous with the *Eleonore Woermann* near Abrolhos Rocks off Brazil and was then going to South Africa. The information possibly assisted the Admiralty in its task of deciding where to direct reinforcements after Coronel.'

Hadfield still had his questions. 'But why now?' he asked again. 'Why wait until 1934?'

Wheatley explained. 'I did not want to jeopardise my job. I couldn't speak out whilst I was still employed by the navy. It's only now that I am retired that I can tell the truth.'

Wheatley had gone on to tell him that he had retired in 1931 after serving sixteen years at the Royal Australian Naval College at Jervis Bay. 'Even then I was going to let it lie,' he had said, 'be content with what was written in the official history, even though nobody had noticed it. My son, Ross, is now an officer in the Royal Australian Navy. He started as a midshipman and has worked his way through the ranks. He has done it all on his own. I thought speaking out might hurt him.'

'So why did you change your mind?' Hadfield had asked.

Wheatley had a long list. First, he told him about the war gratuity, how he'd had to fight to receive what was his right.

'I had to fill out form after form,' Wheatley said. 'I had to go to interviews just to prove I was involved in the war. And then when they finally acknowledged my service, they wrote me a cheque for £9. That is all the extra I got for 152 days of service.

For working eighteen hours a day and sleeping on the floor. For helping stop the German fleet.'

He then told Hadfield about his arthritis. How all the scribbling, the filled-up foolscap folders and blackboards had taken their toll. And how, despite providing pages of reports from doctors, they had even knocked back his medical claim for his bad back and repetitive-strain injuries.

He also told him of the credit wrongly given to Jens Lyng. That navy draughtsman of Danish descent had been praised in both the official history and in the press for playing a vital role in cracking the code, when in fact he had merely served as a translator.

'But ultimately, I changed my mind because of my son,' Wheatley had said. 'Ross urged me to speak. He does not care for the consequences. He wants the story to be told.'

What Wheatley had not told Hadfield was that he felt this was his legacy, the mark he would leave on the world. Now sixty-three, Wheatley could see the end. He knew he would not live forever. He also now knew that what he had done in 1914 was his best work. He'd always believed he would have another moment of greatness, another chance to prove his genius and produce a great work that would not be subject to secrecy and a cover-up. But that moment had never come. His only chance to be remembered, for his name to live longer than him, was to have his code-cracking history credited.

Wheatley had spent five weeks telling Hadfield every detail. But he still got the feeling the editor thought the story was more fiction than fact.

'Frederick,' Hadfield said when he finally came on the line. 'Good news. I managed to get through to Captain Thring. Did you know he is now living in Britain? No wonder he was hard to find. Anyway, he confirmed your story. All of it and down to the smallest detail. So we will publish your article in our next edition. Thanks for being patient, but I had to dot my I's and cross my T's. This is one hell of a story and I had to be sure.'

Potts Point, 1 September 1934

The September issue of *Reveille* was delivered to Wheatley's door.

'It's arrived,' said Wheatley as he hurried into the kitchen. He was suddenly moving like he was thirty again. He placed the magazine on the table and began flicking through the pages. 'Here it is,' he said, pointing to the first page.

'Don't you look handsome,' said his wife, smiling at the picture he had given the magazine.

Side by side, they read the article from beginning to end. From his adventures in the Black Forest that eventually led him to be recruited as an intelligence officer, to the heroics of Captain Richardson in gaining possession of the precious codebook. From his initial efforts decoding messages of little strategic use to the war effort, to the major breakthrough of unravelling the superenciphered second key after his epiphany at the Melbourne Cup. And from the messages that could have saved thousands of British lives at the Battle of Coronel, to the information that cost so many lives in the Falkland Islands when the German squadron was finally hunted down and sunk. It was all there.

Wheatley smiled after reading the last sentence. 'They didn't change a thing, just as Hadfield promised,' he said, looking up at Alice.

'It's wonderful, darling,' said Alice. 'Surely now you will finally get the recognition you deserve.'

Potts Point, 7 September 1934

'Righto, I'm coming,' Wheatley yelled as he hobbled towards the ringing phone. 'Yes, yes, I'm moving as fast as I can. I can hear you.'

He picked up the receiver halfway through the eighth ring.

'Fred, it's Hadfield,' the caller said. 'Hello?'

'Mr Hadfield,' Wheatley said. 'How are you?'

'Bloody busy, mate,' Hadfield said. 'Thanks to you, my phone hasn't stopped since the magazine came out. The calls have been coming from everywhere. I've even had reporters from Fleet Street wanting to know more about you. Have you seen any of the press?'

He hadn't. 'I'd best get the papers then,' Wheatley said.

Wheatley was soon back at home with a copy of the *Sydney Morning Herald* sitting next to the still-open *Reveille* on the kitchen table. The article read:

CREDIT TO AUSTRALIA

London, 4 September

The Daily Telegraph*'s naval correspondent Mr Hector Bywater quotes extensively from the disclosures made by Mr Frederick*

Wheatley in an article published in the Australian Reveille *and says:*

'If they be verified, it must lead to a complete revision of all the existing versions of the Battle of the Falklands. Such well-documented evidence is difficult to resist. It is a very important contribution to the history of the naval operations in 1914, putting an entirely new complexion on Admiral Lord Fisher's pact, contriving at the destruction of the German Pacific Squadron, which now appears, instead of a stroke of genius, as merely a routine order based on advanced information.

'If, as Mr Wheatley's revelation suggests, the credit for ending Admiral von Spee's career rests mainly with the Australian navy's intelligence service, then it seems high time that the fact was made known and misleading versions corrected.'

Mr Wheatley was senior naval instructor (1914–19) and headmaster (1920–31) in the Royal Australian Naval College, Jervis Bay. In 1914–15 he was seconded to the Intelligence Branch of the War Staff at Navy Office, Melbourne, and was in charge of intercepted wireless messages, and he discovered the key to the code that the German Pacific Squadron was using at the outbreak of the war. The decoded messages were of international importance, and also gave the itinerary of von Spee and the German squadron.

Wheatley once again smiled. 'Well how about that?' he said. 'They are talking about me in London.'

Alice, who had come up behind him to read, gave her husband a kiss on the cheek. 'And so they should be,' she said.

Wheatley was not going to be caught out by the phone today. There would be no yelling as he hobbled his way to catch the caller before they hung up. He planted his bum in the sofa next to the black rotary phone and settled in. And there he sat all day.

But no one called.

The smile was long gone when he tucked himself into bed.

'No one cares,' Wheatley said to Alice. 'It's ancient news. No one gives a damn about what happened in 1914. The war is long forgotten. No one wants to remember all the horror. The heartbreak.'

Ring! Ring!

Wheatley threw off the sheets and sprang from the bed, this time moving like he was a teenager. He picked up the receiver after just five rings.

'Who was that, Fred?' Alice asked when he returned a few minutes later. 'Who's calling at this hour?'

'That was the Navy Office, dear,' he said. 'You won't believe it but they just received a cable from London. From Whitehall.' Wheatley paused and stood silent.

'Well, spit it out,' Alice said. 'What did they say?'

'I'm getting an official honour,' Wheatley said. 'They are going to make me a CBE – a Commander of the Most Excellent Order of the British Empire.'

And with that Dr Frederick William Wheatley, BSc, BA, DSc, and soon to be CBE, tucked himself back into bed.

He went to sleep with a smile and woke with one too.

Norfolk, United Kingdom, 4 October 1936

The morning fog was suffocating, greens gone, no blue, everything winter white. Sitting outside on mornings like this, ghosts dancing on his sun-starved lawn, Thring missed Australia. The sun. The surf. The colour.

He heard the engine before he saw the car.

'Are you expecting anyone?' Thring shouted towards the house.

He didn't get a response.

He stared at the wall of fog in front of him until a sporty MG that had no right to be in the countryside emerged from it and came to a stop in the drive.

A well-dressed man in jacket, dress hat and shiny shoes climbed out. 'Walter,' he smiled as he approached. 'It has been a while.'

Thring had to focus. 'Hector,' he said after a moment. 'What the hell are you doing here?'

As naval correspondent for the *Daily Telegraph* in London, Hector Bywater had contacted Thring in 1934 to ask if he knew an Australian called Wheatley. If he knew anything about cracked codes and the end of von Spee.

'I'm here on a bit of business,' Bywater said. 'It's going to be the twenty-second anniversary of that business at Coronel in a month and I am hoping you are finally ready to talk.'

Thring had thought he would never talk about Coronel. For a while he just didn't care. His world had come crashing down in 1922 when his wife – his Lydia – had died of a sudden illness. She had held his hand as he'd walked into Buckingham Palace to receive his CBE just a year earlier. He was shattered.

A heartbroken Thring had resigned from the Royal Australian Navy after his wife's death to become the full-time carer for his three children, aged just five, seven and nine at the time. Already posted to the United Kingdom as Australian advisor to the Admiralty, he had stayed in Britain, moving to a farm in Gloucestershire to rebuild his broken life, and remarried. He had given little thought to his former life as a navy captain in Australia until 1934, when Bywater had called to ask him about an alleged code cracker named Wheatley.

'I recently picked up a story from Australia about a fellow called Wheatley,' Bywater had said. 'He wrote an article claiming to have broken a German cipher that directed the Royal Navy to von Spee. His evidence was quite compelling, but I have since had a number of letters and calls from the Admiralty telling me it is the stuff of fancy. They are quite intent on cutting him down. Do you care to vouch for him or has he misplaced the truth?'

Thring's former life had come rushing back. He was compelled to act. 'I'll send you a statement,' Thring had said. Then he'd gone straight to his typewriter and drafted a three-page letter.

'The *Daily Telegraph* has opened the inner history of the operations against the German squadron,' Thring wrote. And then he told the whole story, from the seizing of the codebook to Wheatley's recruitment and the frustration of HMAS *Australia* being restrained from acting against the German fleet in the Pacific. He detailed how a second key had to be uncovered by Wheatley and the important information about the likely position of von Spee's fleet on the west coast of South America that resulted. And how once again *Australia* was cheated out of her role in the downfall of the German East Asia Squadron.

Now Thring looked at the well-dressed reporter and his city car, who had braved the fog to visit him.

'You hinted at Coronel in that last letter,' Bywater said. 'But I didn't press you because the story was about Wheatley and his code. But what do you say? Let's tell the world the whole story.'

Now sixty-three, forever heartbroken, Thring had nothing to lose. 'I'll put the kettle on,' he said. 'You get your notepad and pen.'

Thring returned with two steaming cups of tea his wife had prepared. 'You ready?' he asked.

The correspondent was already clutching his pen.

'I'll start with how they first took us off the hunt,' Thring said.

Bywater nodded. 'Go ahead,' he said. 'You're on the record.'

Thring unleashed.

* * *

The first story was published on 1 November 1936, exactly twenty-two years after 1,660 British sailors were sent to the bottom of the sea.

'Disaster of Coronel could have been averted', the headline screamed. 'New revelation from Captain Thring.'

Another paper picked up the story.

'Secret history of Coronel', the headline said. 'Australia could have averted disaster.'

Others in Fleet Street were more brutal. 'War disaster Coronel bungle by Admiralty', another headline read. 'Revealed after 22 years.'

One was even more succinct. 'Coronel disaster', it said. 'Australian advice ignored.'

His conscience clear and Australia's extraordinary effort finally revealed, Thring realised his heart was now a little less broken.

Appendix

ORIGINAL DOCUMENTS

SECRET
CONFIDENTIAL FILE

Not to go out of Central Office.

COMMONWEALTH NAVAL BOARD.

Year 1914

No. 0351

24/6/15

INDEXED.

SUBJECT—

Codes found on board German Merchant Ships on Outbreak of War, 1914

Translation and Distribution of H.V.B. Code taken from S.S "Hobart".

File Indexed CKh 18.7.19

W.R. Nos Located. RON 21/7/19.

REFERENCES.

FILE.	SUBJECT
14/0444	Documents found on board German Merchant Ships
14/0444	Code to be used in event of Ships of N.D.L. Co. being requisitioned by the Imperial German Admiralty
21/0328.	German Merchant Ship Code - Captured 1914 - Proposal to transfer to Austn. War Museum
	Note: Two Copies of "Bord-Code" are in Pigeon-hole 76

Year 1914

No. 0351

A Navy document recording the seizure of the *Handelsverkehrsbuch*, or German naval codebook, from SS *Hobart*

BORD-CODE

des

Norddeutschen Lloyd

Gültig ab 1. Mai 1913

Für den Telegrammverkehr der Verwaltung, der Agenturen und Inspektionen mit den Schiffen des Norddeutschen Lloyd

---

Dieser Code ist Eigentum des Norddeutschen Lloyd; für sichere Aufbewahrung ist Sorge zu tragen, damit einer mißbräuchlichen Benutzung vorgebeugt wird

BREMEN, Januar 1913

The title page of the German *HVB* naval code book

Gebrauchsanweisung.

Dieser Code dient dem Telegrammverkehr

a) der Dampfer des Norddeutschen Lloyd untereinander,

b) der Verwaltung, Hafenagenturen, Inspektionen und Gepäckbureaus (Verzeichnis s. S. 5—7) mit den Dampfern des Norddeutschen Lloyd auf drahtlosem und auf dem Drahtwege.

Benutzung.

Spalte 1 enthält die **Codeworte** von je 5 Buchstaben,
Spalte 2 die fünfstelligen **Codeziffern,**
Spalte 3 den Text nach dem Alphabet geordnet.

Die **Codeworte** sind für die Übertragung des Textes zu benutzen:

1. bei **allen** Telegrammen **im drahtlosen Verkehr,**
2. bei Telegrammen im **Draht**verkehr **nur** bis zur Fertigstellung des voraussichtlich 1914 erscheinenden Einheitscodes.

Die **Codeworte** sind zu je zweien zusammenzuziehen, bleibt am Schlusse eines übrig, so ist das Wort „abaca", das keine Bedeutung besitzt, anzuhängen, z. B.:

evegi = 1 großer Eisberg wurde passiert auf . . . . . am . . . . .
dakud = 39°
disut = 03 ′ N
damus = 47°
efafa = 18 ′ W
rurar = Montag 1 Uhr nachmittags
gamis = Höhe war 150 Fuß
gozub = Länge betrug 1000 Fuß
foder = Dampfer „George Washington"

zusammenzuziehen in:

evegidakud disutdamus efafarurar gamisgozub foderabaca.

Ein weiteres Beispiel:

gefog = Kaiser Wilhelm II.
ixiru = passierte Dover
sasum = Mittwoch 10 Uhr vorm.
agusu = voraussichtliche Ankunft Southampton-Pier erfolgt
saxad = Mittwoch 4 Uhr nachm.
geral = brauchen keine Kohlen

zusammenzuziehen in:

gefogixiru sasumagusu saxadgeral

Die **Codezahlen** sind nach Inkrafttreten des 1914 erscheinenden Einheitscodes für alle **nur auf dem Drahtwege** (nicht drahtlos) beförderten Telegramme zu benutzen. Sie sind nach dem dort angegebenen System in Codeworte zu übersetzen.

3

An introductory page explaining how the code book worked, annotated with Frederick Wheatley's handwriting

Codewort	Code-zahl	Text
aroto	00219	**beantworten**
arubi	00220	Anfrage wird mit „ja" beantwortet
aruco	00221	Anfrage wird mit „nein" beantwortet
arudu	00222	Beantworten Sie keine Anfrage in bezug auf
asata	00223	Anfrage wurde nicht beantwortet
asaxi	00224	Anfrage kann nicht beantwortet werden
aseca	00225	Wie sollen wir die Anfrage beantworten?
		s. a. Antwort
asede	00226	**beauftragen**
asefi	00227	Wer ist mit . . . . . . beauftragt?
asego	00228	Wir beauftragen Sie hiermit . . . . . .
asika	00229	Wir haben . . . . . . beauftragt
asele	00230	Wir haben . . . . . . nicht beauftragt
asimi	00231	Beauftragen Sie . . . . . . mit
asino	00232	Haben Sie . . . . . . beauftragt?
asipu	00233	**Bedenken**
asora	00234	Unsererseits bestehen keine Bedenken
asoti	00235	Wenn schiffsseitig keine Bedenken bestehen
asudo	00236	Wenn schiffsseitig keine Bedenken bestehen, sind wir einverstanden
asufu	00237	Gegen Weiterreise bestehen keine Bedenken
atabo	00238	Besichtiger haben gegen Weiterreise Bedenken
atacu	00239	Gegen Weiterreise bestehen Bedenken
		s. a. fortsetzen
—	—	**Bedingungen** *s. u. Abschluß, einverstanden, Erlaubnis*
atava	00240	**beendigen**
ateda	00241	Wann wird das Laden beendigt sein?
atefe	00242	Wann wird die Entlöschung beendigt sein?
ategi	00243	Wann wird die Reparatur beendigt sein?
atejo	00244	Entlöschung wird (am . . . . . .) beendigt sein
ateku	00245	Beladung wird . . . . . . beendigt sein
atila	00246	Reparatur wird . . . . . . beendigt sein
		s. a. Vorbereitungen
atime	00247	**befinden (Ort)**
atini	00248	befinden uns . . . . . .
atipo	00249	befinden uns querab
		s. a. Bord, Nachlaß
atiru	00250	**Befinden** zufriedenstellend
atosa	00251	Befinden ernst, aber nicht hoffnungslos
atote	00252	Befinden hoffnungslos
atoxo	00253	Befinden unverändert
		s. a. Geburt, Krankheit
atuba	00254	**Befördern**
atudi	00255	Wohin sollen wir Passagiere befördern?
atufo	00256	Passagiere sind nach . . . . . . zu befördern
atugu	00257	Passagiere sind nach . . . . . . befördert
avaxa	00258	Passagiere werden nach . . . . . . befördert
avefa	00259	**Beladung**
aveko	00260	Mit Beladung kann . . . . . . begonnen werden
avelu	00261	Wann kann mit Beladung begonnen werden?
avima	00262	Beladung wird fortgesetzt
avipi	00263	Beladung kann nicht fortgesetzt werden, da
		s. a. beendigen, Beschleunigung
aviro	00264	**Belgien, belgisch (e, er, es)**
avisu	00265	**bemühen, Bemühungen**
avobu	00266	Setzen Sie Ihre Bemühungen fort
avota	00267	Bemühungen sind erfolglos geblieben
avuca	00268	Bemühungen sind bis jetzt erfolglos geblieben
avude	00269	**benachrichtigen, Benachrichtigung**
avugo	00270	Benachrichtigen Sie . . . . . .
avuju	00271	Benachrichtigen Sie Direktion
axado	00272	Benachrichtigen Sie Agentur Bremerhaven
axafu	00273	Benachrichtigen Sie Agentur

12

Here and opposite, pages from the code book showing how seemingly nonsensical groups of letters corresponded with real words and phrases

Code-wort	Code-zahl	Text	Code-wort	Code-zahl	Text	Code-wort	Code-zahl	Text	Code-wort	Code-zahl	Text	Code-wort	Code-zahl	Text
peguz	03851	264	pigux	03913	326	pojax	03975	388	pugut	04037	450	rajig	04099	512
pejab	03852	265	pijaz	03914	327	pojib	03976	389	pujex	04038	451	rajuk	04100	513
pejid	03853	266	pijeb	03915	328	pojud	03977	390	pujob	04039	452	rakal	04101	514
pejof	03854	267	pijod	03916	329	pokaf	03978	391	pukad	04040	453	rakem	04102	515
pejug	03855	268	pijuf	03917	330	pokok	03979	392	pukef	04041	454	rakin	04103	516
pekek	03856	269	pikag	03918	331	pokul	03980	393	pukuk	04042	455	rakop	04104	517
pekil	03857	270	pikik	03919	332	polam	03981	394	pulal	04043	456	rakur	04105	518
pekom	03858	271	pikol	03920	333	polen	03982	395	pulem	04044	457	ralas	04106	519
pekun	03859	272	pikum	03921	334	polip	03983	396	pulin	04045	458	ralet	04107	520
pelap	03860	273	pilan	03922	335	polor	03984	397	pulop	04046	459	ralox	04108	521
peler	03861	274	pilep	03923	336	polus	03985	398	pulur	04047	460	ramab	04109	522
pelis	03862	275	pilir	03924	337	pomat	03986	399	pumas	04048	461	ramid	04110	523
pelot	03863	276	pilos	03925	338	pomix	03987	400	pumet	04049	462	ramof	04111	524
pemax	03864	277	pilut	03926	339	poned	03988	401	pumox	04050	463	ramug	04112	525
pemib	03865	278	pimex	03927	340	ponif	03989	402	punab	04051	464	ranek	04113	526
pemud	03866	279	pimob	03928	341	ponog	03990	403	punid	04052	465	ranil	04114	527
penaf	03867	280	pinad	03929	342	popak	03991	404	punof	04053	466	ranom	04115	528
peneg	03868	281	pinef	03930	343	popel	03992	405	punug	04054	467	ranun	04116	529
penok	03869	282	pinig	03931	344	popim	03993	406	pupek	04055	468	rapap	04117	530
penul	03870	283	pinuk	03932	345	popon	03994	407	pupil	04056	469	raper	04118	531
pepam	03871	284	pipal	03933	346	popup	03995	408	pupom	04057	470	rapis	04119	532
pepen	03872	285	pipem	03934	347	porar	03996	409	pupun	04058	471	rapot	04120	533
pepip	03873	286	pipin	03935	348	pores	03997	410	purap	04059	472	rarax	04121	534
pepor	03874	287	pipop	03936	349	porit	03998	411	purer	04060	473	rarib	04122	535
pepus	03875	288	pipur	03937	350	porux	03999	412	puris	04061	474	rarud	04123	536
perat	03876	289	piras	03938	351	poseb	04000	413	purot	04062	475	rasaf	04124	537
perix	03877	290	piret	03939	352	posod	04001	414	pusax	04063	476	rasok	04125	538
peroz	03878	291	pirox	03940	353	posuf	04002	415	pusib	04064	477	rasul	04126	539
perub	03879	292	pisab	03941	354	potag	04003	416	pusud	04065	478	ratam	04127	540
pesed	03880	293	pisid	03942	355	potik	04004	417	putaf	04066	479	raten	04128	541
pesif	03881	294	pisof	03943	356	potol	04005	418	puteg	04067	480	ratip	04129	542
pesog	03882	295	pisug	03944	357	potum	04006	419	putok	04068	481	rator	04130	543
petak	03883	296	pitek	03945	358	povan	04007	420	putul	04069	482	ratus	04131	544
petel	03884	297	pitil	03946	359	povep	04008	421	puvam	04070	483	ravat	04132	545
petim	03885	298	pitom	03947	360	povir	04009	422	puven	04071	484	raxed	04133	546
peton	03886	299	pitun	03948	361	povos	04010	423	puvip	04072	485	raxif	04134	547
petup	03887	300	piver	03949	362	povut	04011	424	puvor	04073	486	razak	04135	548
pevar	03888	301	pivis	03950	363	poxob	04012	425	puvus	04074	487	razel	04136	549
peves	03889	302	pivot	03951	364	pozad	04013	426	puxat	04075	488	razim	04137	550
pevux	03890	303	pixud	03952	365	pozef	04014	427	puxub	04076	489	razon	04138	551
pexod	03891	304	pizaf	03953	366	pozig	04015	428	puzed	04077	490	razup	04139	552
pexuf	03892	305	pizeg	03954	367	pozuk	04016	429	puzif	04078	491	rebap	04140	553
pezik	03893	306	pizok	03955	368	pubak	04017	430	puzog	04079	492	reber	04141	554
pezol	03894	307	pizul	03956	369	pubel	04018	431	rabar	04080	493	rebis	04142	555
pezum	03895	308	pobal	03957	370	pubim	04019	432	rabes	04081	494	rebot	04143	556
pibam	03896	309	pobem	03958	371	pubon	04020	433	rabit	04082	495	redaf	04144	557
piben	03897	310	pobin	03959	372	pubup	04021	434	rabux	04083	496	redeg	04145	558
pibip	03898	311	pobur	03960	373	pucar	04022	435	raceb	04084	497	redok	04146	559
pibor	03899	312	pocas	03961	374	puces	04023	436	racod	04085	498	redul	04147	560
pibus	03900	313	pocet	03962	375	pucit	04024	437	racuf	04086	499	refam	04148	561
picat	03901	314	podab	03963	376	pudaz	04025	438	radag	04087	500	refen	04149	562
picub	03902	315	podid	03964	377	pudeb	04026	439	radik	04088	501	refip	04150	563
pided	03903	316	podof	03965	378	pudod	04027	440	radol	04089	502	refor	04151	564
pidif	03904	317	podug	03966	379	puduf	04028	441	radum	04090	503	refus	04152	565
pidog	03905	318	pofek	03967	380	pufag	04029	442	rafan	04091	504	regat	04153	566
pifak	03906	319	pofil	03968	381	pufik	04030	443	rafep	04092	505	regix	04154	567
pifel	03907	320	pofom	03969	382	pufol	04031	444	rafir	04093	506	regub	04155	568
pifon	03908	321	pofun	03970	383	pufum	04032	445	rafos	04094	507	rejed	04156	569
pifup	03909	322	pogap	03971	384	pugan	04033	446	rafut	04095	508	rejif	04157	570
pigar	03910	323	poger	03972	385	pugep	04034	447	ragob	04096	509	rejog	04158	571
piges	03911	324	pogis	03973	386	pugir	04035	448	rajad	04097	510	rekak	04159	572
pigit	03912	325	pogot	03974	387	pugos	04036	449	rajef	04098	511	rekel	04160	573

Navy Office, Melbourne,

9th September. 1914.

I hereby solemnly swear that I will at no time during the course of the present war divulge the nature of the work upon which I am engaged in the Navy Office or discuss outside the office any of the ~~details~~ connected with the work.

Witness to Signatures.

Frederick W. Wheatley

The non-disclosure document signed by Wheatley's first group of assistants

GERMAN CODE BOOK - DISTRIBUTION LIST OF COPIES

MADE AT NAVY OFFICE, MELBOURNE.

ADMIRALTY, LONDON	25 copies, Nos. 1 to 25.
COMMANDER IN CHIEF, EAST INDIES	5 copies, Nos. 31 to 35.
COMMANDER IN CHIEF, MEDITERRANEAN........... (Senior Naval Officer, Malta).	5 copies, Nos. 26 to 30.
COMMANDER IN CHIEF, CAPE......................	5 copies, Nos. 36 to 40.
COMMANDER IN CHIEF, CHINA.....................	5 copies, Nos. 41 to 45.
VICE ADMIRAL COMMANDING H.M. AUST'N FLEET....	5 copies, Nos 46 to 50.
THE SENIOR NAVAL OFFICER, HONG KONG..........	3 copies, Nos. 51 to 53.
THE SENIOR NAVAL OFFICER, NEW ZEALAND........	2 copies, Nos. 55 & 56.
H.M.S. "PYRAMUS".............................	1 copy, No. 54.
THE COMMANDING OFFICER, H.M.A.S. "MELBOURNE"............	1 copy, No. 57.
THE CAPTAIN IN CHARGE, NAVAL ESTABLISHMENTS, SYDNEY.....	1 copy, No. 58.
THE INTELLIGENCE OFFICER, WELLINGTON, N.Z....	1 copy, No. 59.
H.M.S. "MINOTAUR"............................	1 copy No.60.
ADMIRALTY....................................	25 copies Nos. 61 to 85.

A report detailing how many copies of Wheatley's translated codebooks were made and where they were sent

To · Admiralty.

We have a ~~and~~ German code book and key "Handelsschiffs Verkehrsbuch" for intercourse ~~of~~ between German merchant ships ~~with~~ and war ships ~~and with one another~~ or between merchant ships. It is issued to all German warships, Admiralty, Marine Stations, and leading merchantmen.

Messages are sent in four letter groups, or in ten letter groups. In the latter the first or last group of five letters often recurs.

Messages for the Admiral begin OCRP or HANIB UNYRU

Messages by open cypher begin HAVAUBE.

Messages to be decoded by the cipher key (only to be used in war time) begin PCZA or KISAHACIBA

The general war call signs for German warships is DK and for merchantmen DH

The ten letter groups all begin with a consonant and run alternately consonant and vowel.

In this code the four letter war call signs for all German warships begin with D and for merchantmen with G.

We have decoded many intercepted messages and could decode any in this code ~~[illegible]~~ if you cable them to naval secretary.

[illegible signature]
7-9-14

A page from Wheatley's initial notes on the code

W R A26

SECRET

14/W.50 November 1914.

The Captain-in-Charge,

Naval Establishments, Sydney.

German Ships on South American Coast have altered the cipher key to the H.V.B. Code, copy No.58 of which was supplied to you.

The new key has been discovered and is as follows:-

Of the following 48 letters the odd ones arranged alphabetically, omitting J and Q, represent the letters in the message, and the even ones the corresponding letters for decoding, viz:-

A I B L C K D W E O F T G R H F I E K B L C M D N S O A

P X R P S Z T V U Y V M W N X H Y U Z G

By direction of the Naval Board.

Naval Secretary.

Mr Holmes

CL

The letter sent to the Admiralty after Wheatley cracked the first code

Secret

~~South American Squadron~~ Movements and destruction of German Pacific Squadron. (1)

by F. W. Wheatley

For a long time the whereabouts of the Scharnhorst and Gneisenau was in doubt until they suddenly appeared at Apia on Sept. 14th. That they were in Australian waters was evident from wireless calls that emanated from them, and that they were kept informed of the movements of the Australian fleet by the Planet & Komet was also evident.

They passed very close to the Melbourne while she was proceeding from Suva to Samoa during the first week of September. This may be seen from the track chart drawn of their movements and it is confirmed by the opinion of the Wireless Officer of the Melbourne who heard their signals very distinctly on the nights of Sept 7th and 8th.

The appearance of these war ships at Apia, and the fear that they might return to Australia to interfere with the transports caused the New Zealand & Commonwealth Governments to make strong representations to the Secretary of State for the Colonies to delay the departure of the troops until a strong escort could be provided.

The Admiralty was evidently of the opinion that the Scharnhorst & Gneisenau had left these shores permanently as on Sept. 24th the Secretary of State for the Colonies cabled as follows "Admiralty adhere to opinion despatch of transports from New Zealand and Australian ports to point of concentration at Fremantle is an operation free from undue risk, but in view of anxiety felt by your ministers & Government of Australian Commonwealth they propose to send "Minotaur" and "Ibuki" to Wellington to fetch New Zealand convoy & escort it westward along the Australian coast picking up Australian transports on the way & bringing the whole to their destination. This will involve about three weeks delay."

The first page of Wheatley's full report on the code

Copy No. 1.

S E C R E T

MOVEMENTS AND DESTRUCTION
OF GERMAN PACIFIC SQUADRON.

For a long time the whereabouts of the "SCHARNHORST" and "GNEISENAU" was in doubt until they suddenly appeared at Apia on September 14th. That they were in Australian waters was evident from wireless calls that emanated from them, and that they were kept informed of the movements of the Australian Fleet by the "PLANET" and "KOMET" was also evident.

They passed very close to the "MELBOURNE" while she was proceeding from Suva to Nauru during the first week of September. This may be seen from the track chart drawn of their movements and it is confirmed by the opinion of the Wireless Officer of the "MELBOURNE" who heard their signals very distinctly on the nights of September 7th and 8th.

The appearance of these warships at Apia, and the fear that they might return to Australia to interfere with the transports caused the New Zealand and Commonwealth Governments to make strong representations to the Secretary of State for the Colonies to delay the departure of the troops until a strong escort could be provided.

The Admiralty was evidently of the opinion that the "SCHARNHORST" and "GNEISENAU" had left these shores permanently as on September 24th the ~~Admiralty~~ Secretary of State for the Colonies cabled as follows "Admiralty adhere to opinion despatch of transports from New Zealand and Australian ports to point of concentration at Fremantle is an operation free from undue risk, but in view of anxiety felt by your Ministers and Government of Australian Commonwealth they propose to send "MINOTAUR" and "IBUKI" to Wellington to fetch New Zealand convoy and escort it Westward along the Australian coast picking up Australian transports on the way and bringing the whole to their destination. This will involve about three weeks delay".

The same page after it was edited and typed up by Wheatley's staff

15

They were.

1. VGX to VYC } unintelligible
2. VYC to VGX } Chilian Transport steamer has left. May 1 ran out of the harbour with one mast and one funnel black with southerly course
3. VSF to VGX }
4. VGX to VFS } unintelligible.
5. VGX to VFS }
6. VGX to VSF Did you get into ~~wireless~~ communication with the Sacramento by wireless last night.

(12)

7. WCV - WLK War code
8. DK - GCSK Rendezvous is Mas a fuera Island.
9. DAFO - GCSK On the order of the Commander in Chief of the Squadron the San Sacramento is not to go to Valparaiso but to Mas a fuera Island. The Commander in Chief has sent the Dresden to meet the San Sacramento ~~in order~~ and transmit this order."

From these and ~~the~~ the previous messages it is clear that VGX, VCX ~~or~~ GXV ~~is~~ the call signs of the "Scharnhorst" and VSF or VFS the call sign of the "Dresden". Then VYC, WCV & WLK will remain for the "Gneisenau", "Nurnberg" and "Leipzig".

DK is the secret call sign of all German men of war, DAFO the secret call sign of the Dresden and GCSK the secret call sign of the San Sacramento.

These messages prove conclusively that Germany was violating Chilian neutrality by using Mas a fuera Island as a base, and also that the statement of the Captain of the Sacramento on arrival at Valparaiso was not true. ~~He~~ said that he had been seized by a German warship & taken to Juan Fernandez Island where he was obliged to transfer the steamer's cargo and six thousand tons of coal to the warship ~~According to the above message everything had~~ According to the above messages everything had been arranged before the Sacramento left San Francisco.

Another page from Wheatley's handwritten report

15
021
(Not to go out of Central Office.)
SECRET
SECRET

COMMONWEALTH NAVAL BOARD.

BY WHOM		DATE
Dr. F.W. WHEATLEY,	15/021	5th January 1915

REFERRED TO	SUBJECT
1st N.M. 2nd N.M. 3rd N.M. Minister No 4 copy sent to Mr Trumble	Movements and destruction of German Pacific Squadron.

FORMER
RETAIN
Schedule No 47

MEMORANDUM AND MINUTE.

Recommend that a copy of this report should be sent to the Minister for Defence.

I do not think copies should be sent out of Australia until they can be sent by Man-of-War.

Copies should be numbered and registered.

W.H.C.S. Thring

7. 1. 15

Concur
W.R.C. 7.1.15

Concur [initials]
JAN 7 - 1915

[initials] 8/1/15 I consider that, as the most secret documents have been entrusted to Captains of mail steamers before & that no man of war seems to be available, ~~the~~ a copy should be sent to admiralty for information by the hand of master of next mail steamer going to England

AGB 14.1.15

N 15
021
C.13955.

A covering note signed by Captain Thring recommending that Wheatley's report be sent to the Australian Minister of Defence

DEPARTMENT OF DEFENCE.
MINUTE PAPER.

SUBJECT: GERMAN CODE BOOK FOR USE OF MERCHANT CRAFT IN WAR

On 12th August, 1914, Admiralty were informed by cable that one copy of above had been captured at Melbourne (from "Hobart"), and another at Fremantle (from "Friefswald").

2. Other copies were obtained from "Prinz Sigismund" and "Wildenfels".

3. On 7th ~~August~~ September, 1914, Admiralty were informed by cable that Naval Board had a secret German Code Book and key for intercourse between German ships and Warships or between Merchant ships - brief details of working were sent. The Admiralty were informed that Naval Board had decoded many intercepted messages by wireless and could do the same for Admiralty intercepted messages if sent by cable.

4. On 8th ~~November~~ September, 1914, Admiralty cabled asking that a copy be made of the Code and key and sent to them by first opportunity. They said they would cable messages pending receipt of the copy.

5. On 21st September, 1914, Admiralty cabled two intercepted messages for translation. Decode was sent on 22nd September.

6. On 22nd September, 1914, Captain Irving, R.M.S. "Maloja" took copies of the translation of the code to C-in-C, East Indies; S.N.O., Malta; and Admiralty. Copies were sent to other Stations by Navy Office. 50 copies were sent to Admiralty, and 35 other copies to different officials on various Stations.

7. On 3rd November, 1914, a cable was sent to Admiralty and Vice Admiral Commanding Australian Squadron saying German Ships on South American Coast had altered the cypher key to Code Book, and that the new key had been discovered. The new key was then given.

8. On 6th November, 1914,a cable was received "Admiralty compliment Naval Board on their success in discovering the trans~~lation~~position of H.V.B. Code".

9. On 16th October, 1918, Dr. Wheatley wrote to the Naval Board thro' the C.O., College, drawing attention to his work in discovering the key of the Code, pointing out that since then many had been promoted in rank and honoured in other ways, and submitting that the Board give his case their consideration.

10. The Naval Board had, on 17th June, 1916, issued a minute deprecating letters of this nature, and in forwarding Dr. Wheatley's letter the C.O. College said he had pointed out to the Officer that the procedure was irregular.

11. In March, 1919, the Naval Board approved of accelerated promotion for Dr. Wheatley. The recommendation read:-

"SENIOR MASTER
WHEATLEY - Frederick William, B.Sc (Oxon), B.A.
Date of Birth 7/6/71. Seniority 6/2/14
In view of this gentleman's position at the Head of the Senior Masters - his good service in tuition at

A Department of Defence summary outlining Wheatley's involvement in breaking the code, the initial lack of recognition of his achievements, and his subsequent 'accelerated promotion' in 1919

<u>**UNRAVELLING OF A GERMAN CODE.**</u>

by
F.W. WHEATLEY.C.B.E.

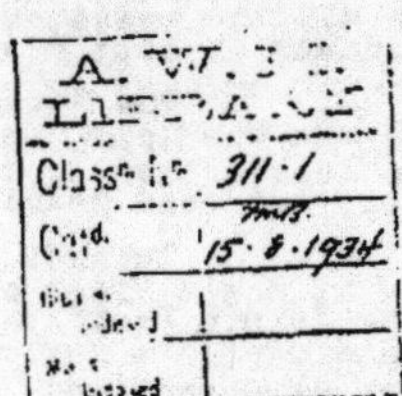

The following pages present Wheatley's explanation of how he broke the code, written in 1934 when he was seeking further recognition for his contribution.

Unravelling of a German Code.

by Frederick William Wheatley, C.B.E., B.Sc.(Oxon.), B.A., D.Sc.(Adel.) A.S.A.S.M

late Head Master, Royal Australian Naval College, Jervis Bay.

In January 1914 I was appointed Senior Naval Instructor at the Royal Australian Naval College, Geelong, having just returned from two years' Research Work in Physics at Oxford.

Towards the end of 1913 I had been invited to Germany to confer with a professor of the University of Freiburg about the work on which I had been engaged. Whilst a guest at his house, he was called up to attend the manoeuvres of the German Army in the Black Forest and he asked me if I would care to go with him. He obtained the consent of the Kaiser, a personal friend of his, and for a month I travelled with the army as an honoured guest. During this time I had several lengthy conversations with the Crown Prince, Admiral von Tirpitz and General von Hindenburg.

This enabled me to perfect my knowledge of German, and when war broke out I was immediately seconded from the Naval College and attached to the War Staff at Navy Office, and put in charge of all intercepted wireless messages.

All the wireless stations in Australia were taken over by the Navy and placed under the control of Mr.Balsillie, a wireless expert. He sent me every wireless message that was intercepted, but as most of them were in an unknown code, nothing could be done but file them for future reference.

On August 4th, the Nord Deutsche Lloyd steamer "Seydlitz" left Sydney hurriedly without her clearance papers, and when news of the Declaration of War came we were convinced that she would endeavour to warn German vessels on their way to Australia. The "Hobart" had left Fremantle, her next port of call being Melbourne, and in order to prevent her receiving messages from the "Seydlitz" every wireless station from Sydney to Fremantle sent out messages continuously day and night.

We were successful and the "Hobart" steamed into Port Phillip. She was boarded by the pilot at the Heads, and with him was Capt.Richardson R.A.N. who placed the Captain under arrest, informing him that we were at war with Germany. The "Hobart" was taken up the harbour and CaptainRichardson slept that night in the Captain's cabin. The Captain was given one of the Officers' cabins and allowed his liberty. During the night he came quietly into his own cabin and went to a secret cupboard in the wall. Richardson was ready with his torch and revolver and found the Captain trying to get possession of a code book.

This was the Code Book H.V.B. (Handels Verkehr Buch) which was issued to all important merchant ships. With it was a sealed envelope, only to be opened on the outbreak of war, and this gave a cypher key to be used for communication with war ships.

This book, with the key, was sent to me, and I went through all the messages that had been intercepted, but the information received was of little value.

The German Pacific Squadron had come down from Wai Hai Wee and was being searched for by the Australian Squadron. We were able to locate them occasionally by the sound of their telefunken wireless, but were unable to decode any of the messages intercepted.

Towards the end of October the Naval Intelligence Officer at Monte Video began to send us messages which evidently came from the German Pacific Squadron. Admiral Cradock of the "Good Hope" also intercepted a number of messages a few days before Coronel. These we also received. Although they would not decode with the key to H.V.B. it was evident that this book was still in use, but that the key had been altered. My duty was to find the new key.

The messages were in ten letter groups made up of two separate five letter combinations. The similarity of the groups in different messages was noted and compared with words in the Code Book. After working day and night for three days and two nights and filling thousands of sheets of foolscap with letters, I discovered the key.

(2)

<u>Method of attack</u>.

It was impossible to try all the changes that could be made, because any letter could be altered to any other letter and there are 52 million, million, million, million different ways of doing this. At the rate of one a second it would take two million, million, million years to try them all.

The system adopted therefore was as follows:-

One group from the messages was taken viz. LIKIS IMOFI.

It will be noticed that the 2nd, 4th, 6th, & 10th letters are all alike viz. I.

It was therefore necessary to find all the combinations in the code book with the 2nd, 4th, 6th & 10th letters alike.

On searching through the book hundreds of groups with this similarity were found and each one was tested. Here are some of them.

(1) BABAC ACIBA	(2) BABAC ANOHA	(3) BABAC AZYPA
(4) BEKEL ECEFE	(5) BEKEL EGYVE	(6) BEKEL EHIGE
(7) BEKEL ENUME	(8) BEKEL ETONE	(9) BISIT ICIFI
(10) BISIT IHULI	(11) BISIT INOMI	(12) BISIT ITASI
(13) BISIT IVADI	(14) CEBEF ECEFE	(15) CEBEF EGYVE
(16) CEBEF ENUME	(17) CEBEF EHIGE	(18) CEBEF ETONE
(19) Cebef EZATE	(20) CANAT ACIBA	etc.

Some of these could be struck out at once, because in LIKIS IMOFI there were no other duplicated letters except these four.

(1) was discarded because letters 1 3 & 9 were similar
(2) " " " " 1 3 " "
(3) " " " " 1 3 " "
(4) " " " " 2 4 6 8 10 " "

Nos. (5) (6) (7) (8) were retained

(9) was discarded because letters 2 4 6 8 10 were similar

Nos. (10) (11) were retained.

(12) was discarded because letters 5 7 were similar.
(14) " " " " 2 4 6 8 10 " "
(20) " " " " 1 7 " "

(13) (15) (16) (17) (18) (19) were retained.

Then a table was made of the possible changes of the 10 letter These were as follows if the selected group was the correct one.

	(5)	(6)	(7)	(8)	(10)	(11)	(13)	(15)	(16)	(17)	(18)	(19)
L	B	B	B	B	B	B	B	C	C	C	C	C
I	E	E	E	E	I	I	I	E	E	E	E	E
K	K	K	K	K	S	S	S	B	B	B	B	B
I	E	E	E	E	I	I	I	E	E	E	E	E
S	L	L	L	L	T	T	T	F	F	F	F	F
I	E	E	E	E	I	I	I	E	E	E	E	E
M	G	H	N	T	H	N	V	G	N	H	T	Z
O	Y	I	U	O	U	O	A	Y	U	I	O	A
F	V	G	M	N	L	M	D	V	M	G	N	T
I	E	E	E	E	I	I	I	E	E	E	E	E

The next thing was to take these groups and see what their meaning was in the code book. Some meanings were so utterly absurd that they could be discarded at once. In this way further groups were eliminated.

Then group (5) say was taken and where ever the letters LIKSMOF occurred in the messages BEKLGYV were substituted. If nothing like the groups in the code book came out (5) was discarded and (6) was tried and so on.

Then when it was certain that these seven letters were right 18 more letters had still to be discovered.

On the third day, which happened to be Melbourne Cup Day, I was so wearied and fuddled that at 2.30 I made up my mind to go and see the Cup run. I was back at the Office at 4.30 and at 6 o'clock was satisfied that I had solved the problem.

All that night had to be spent in decoding and translating the messages, which, of course, were all in German.

These messages, which cannot be made public, were all from the German Pacific Squadron, and gave their itinerary through the Magellan Straits, up to the Abrolhos Islands off Brazil to meet the Elinor Wöhrman (afterwards sunk by the Australia) and then to West Africa.

That night the Admiralty was informed by cable and Lord Fisher immediately ordered the Invincible and Inflexible to refit hurriedly and proceed to the Falkland Islands. They reached there a few hours before the German Squadron and the Scharnhorst, Gneisenau, Nurnberg and Leipsig were sunk.

The Admiralty cabled out congratulations on the discovery of the code and instructed the Navy Office to send a copy of the code book and key to every ship in the British Fleet.

The Naval Board instructed me to take the matter in hand and find out the best way to do this. I first interviewed the Government Printer, but he hadn't enough type-setters familiar with the German script and could not promise it under six weeks.

The next idea was to have the pages photographed, but that proved unsatisfactory.

It was then decided to type-write on wax sheets and reproduce the requisite number of copies. Twenty girls from one of the typewriting agencies were engaged, sworn to secrecy and installed in a room at Navy Office. Their qualifications were to be able to read the German letters and type accurately.

The book of 300 pages was cut up and distributed. Each printed page required three typewritten pages.

Four men with knowledge of German were engaged to read the proofs and then two men with Roneo Duplicators printed two hundred copies of each page. The number of pages printed was therefore 300 x 3 x 200 i.e, 180,000.

These 180,000 sheets had to be collected, arranged in proper order and bound in book form.

Shelves were hurriedly built along one wall and my daughter and a trusted small boy arranged the sheets on the shelves, and when the first fifty pages were printed they were collected and pinned together with staples.

The 200 books were finished in 10 days; 100 were sent to the Admiralty, 50 to the Commander in Chief of the American Station, and the others sent to the different ships of the China Squadron and the Australian Navy. Every one reached its destination safely.

There were many messages of international importance decyphered including one which exonerated the "Kent" from the charge of offending against Chilian neutrality when she destroyed the "Dresden" in the harbour of Mas-e-fuera.

The cypher was changed twice before the German squadron was destroyed, but it was a comparatively easy matter to find the key in both cases.

The same cypher was used by the German troops in West Africa.

(1) was discarded because letters 1 3 & 9 were similar

(2) " " " " 1 3 " "

(3) " " " " 1 3 " "

(4) " " " " 2 4 6 8 10 " "

Nos. (5) (6) (7) (8) were retained.

(9) was discarded because letters 2 4 6 8 10 were similar.

Nos. (10) (11) were retained.

(12) was discarded because letters 5 7 were similar

(14) " " " " 2 4 6 8 10 " "

(20) " " " " 1 7 " "

(13) (15) (16) (17) (18) (19) were retained.

Then a table was made of the possible changes of the 10 letter. These were as follows if the selected group was the correct one.

	(5)	(6)	(7)	(8)	(10)	(11)	(13)	(15)	(16)	(17)	(18)	(19)
L	B	B	B	B	B	B	B	C	C	C	C	C
L	E	E	E	E	I	I	I	E	E	E	E	E
K	K	K	K	K	S	S	S	B	B	B	B	B
I	E	E	E	E	I	I	I	E	E	E	E	E
S	L	L	L	L	T	T	T	F	F	F	F	F
I	E	E	E	E	I	I	I	E	E	E	E	E
M	G	H	N	T	H	N	V	G	N	H	T	Z
O	Y	I	U	O	U	O	A	Y	U	I	O	A
F	V	G	M	N	L	M	D	V	M	G	N	T
I	E	E	E	E	I	I	I	E	E	E	E	E

The next thing was to take these groups and see what their meaning was in the code book. Some meanings were so utterly absurd that they could be discarded at once. In this way further groups were eliminated.

The group (5) say was taken and wherever the letters LIKSMOF occurred in the messages BEKLGYV were substituted. If nothing like the groups in the code book came out (5) was discarded and (6) was tried and so on.

Then when it was certain that these seven letters were right 18 more letters had still to be discovered.

On the third day, which happened to be

Melbourne Cup Day, I was so wearied and fuddled that at 2.30 I made up my mind to go and see the Cup run. I was back at the Office at 4.30 and at 6 o'clock was satisfied that I had solved the problem.

All that night had to be spent in decoding and translating the messages, which, of course, were all in German.

These messages, which cannot be made public, were all from the German Pacific Squadron, and gave their itinerary through the Magellan Straits, up to the Abrolhos Islands off Brazil to meet the Elinor Wohrman (afterwards sunk by the Australia) and then to West Africa.

That night the Admiralty was informed by cable and Lord Fisher immediately ordered the Invincible and Inflexible to refit hurriedly and proceed to the Falkland Islands. They reached there a few hours before the German Squadron and the Scharnhorst, Gneisenau, Nurnberg and Leipzig were sunk.

The Admiralty cabled out congratulations on the discovery of the code and instructed the Navy Office to send a copy of the code book and key to every ship in the British Fleet.

The Naval Board instructed me to take the matter in hand and find out the best way to do this. I first interviewed the Government Printer, but he hadn't enough type-setters familiar with the German script and could not promise it under six weeks.

The next idea was to have the pages photographed, but that proved unsatisfactory.

It was then decided to type-write on wax sheets and reproduce the requisite number of copies. Twenty girls from one of the typewriting agencies were engaged, sworn to secrecy and installed in a room at Navy Office. Their qualifications were to be able to read the German letters and type accurately.

The book of 300 pages was cut up and distributed. Each printed page required three type-written pages.

Four men with knowledge of German were engaged to read the proofs and then two men with Roneo Duplicators printed two hundred copies of each page. The number of pages printed was therefore 300 x 3 x 200 i.e. 180,000.

These 180,000 sheets had to be collected, arranged in proper order and bound in book form.

Shelves were hurriedly built along one wall and my daughter and a trusted small boy arranged the sheets on the shelves, and when the first fifty pages were printed they were collected and pinned together with staples.

The 200 books were finished in ten days; 100 were sent to the Admiralty; 50 to the Commander in Chief of the American Station, and the others sent to the different ships of the China Squadron and the Australian Navy. Every one reached its destination safely.

There were many messages of international importance decyphered including one which exonerated the "Kent" from the charge of offending against Chilian neutrality when she destroyed the "Dresden" in the harbour of Mas-a-fuera.

The cypher was changed twice before the German squadron was destroyed, but it was a comparatively easy matter to find the key in both cases.

The same cypher was used by the German troops in West Africa.

DECODING.

1. Look up every letter of the code word or group which has been sent, (translated by the cipher key), in column 1 of the accompanying decoding table and place opposite them the letters standing in column 2.

2. The code words or groups thus obtained are looked up in the H.V.B.

Decoding Table

	1	2	
E	a	e	I
T	b	k	L
D	c	m	K
V	d	o	W
U	e	y	O
H	f	t	T
W	g	p	R
Z	h	z	F
O	i	a	E
r	k	w	B
M	l	b	C
G	m	f	D
G	n	l	S
Y	o	i	A
K	p	v	X
L	r	x	P
C	s	d	Z
X	t	r	V
I	u	e	Y
P	v	n	M
N	w	e	N
S	x	g	H
A	y	u	U
R	z	h	G

EXAMPLE.

The following message has been received:-

Dampfer Neckar Singapore

havaube kisahaciba

zosuwazeti xexofipewy zapozifyvi

sunywirefa zivolecaki

DECODING.

1.	Group		Key word.	
2.	Group	....	kisahaciba	the following is ciphered with the Cipher Key to H.V.B.
3.	Group	zosuwazeti	hidosehyra	Shorten your stay
4.	Group	xexofipewy	gygitavysu	Take the negative form of the following message
5.	Group	zapozifyvi	hevihatuna	run up to
6.	Group	sunywirefa	dolusaxyte	Hongkong
7.	Group	zivolecaki	hanibymewa	Admiralty.

--------ooOoo--------

kocitileca mywasapumi
Drohend Kriegsgefahr

melden, sobald vereinigt.
intsarage krsakaciba vynavamomy wakim anfpu
alrdexepy nulenefifu sewafelavo

Gottingen setze eine punkt standort angeben
lymaxadifo xexofiakto lozugixyma
bufehbcalzi gygitaffri rakopaguf

ukisaheci krnahaciba vyavaromoh wuimantpu
wadezyma nuenalifix

es wird sein 155° E. Long.
ludusadus tipolafyratt vinucowuoe
bocomecod ravelbe tunez nalom isoxy

ozacibylgeltapt
ihema kubpm

A — I
B — L
C — K
D — W
E — O
F — T
G — R
H — F
I — E
K — B
L — C
M — D
N — S
O — A
P — X
R — P
S — Z
T — V
U — Y
V — M
W — N
X — H
Y — U
Z — G

24

P

KERUG UXATA

A......I
B.....L
C.....K
D ....W
E ....O
F ....T
G ....R
H ....F
I ....E
K ....B
L C
M ....D
N ....S
O ....A
P X
R ....P
S ....Z
T V
U ....Y
V ....M
W ....N
X ....H
Y ....U
Z ....G

PCWT

KERUG UZEFA

A......E
B..... T
C..... D
D V
E .... U
F .... H
G .... W
H .... Z
I .... O
K .... F
L .... M
M .... G
N .... B
O .... Y
P .... K
R L
S C
T X
U. I
V .... P
W .... N
X .... S
Y .... A
Z .... R

KERUG UXATA   KERUG UZEFA

A	E
B	T
C	D
D	V
E	U
F	H
G	W
H	Z
I	O
K	F
L	M
M	G
N	B
O	Y
P	K
R	L
S	C
T	X
U	I
V	P
W	N
X	S
Y	A
Z	R

SELECT BIBLIOGRAPHY

Archives

'Crews of captured enemy ships', NAA: MP16/1, Y1920/108.

'De Haaz – Alleged German spy', NAA MP84/1 1877/4/7.

'Detention of German steamers *Pfalz* and *Hobart* at Williamstown', NAA: MP1049/14, 1919/468.

'Documents found on board German merchant ship on outbreak of war 1914', NAA: MP1049/1 1914/0444.

'Establishment of Commonwealth Naval Intelligence Service', NAA: A6661, 1357.

'Examination of wireless telegraphy intercepted messages – war period 1914/1918', NAA: MP1049/1, 1916/0235.

'Formation of Australian Intelligence Corps', NAA: MP84/1, 1849/2/13.

'Movement & destruction of the German Pacific Squadron', NAA: MP 1049/1, 1915/021.

'Outbreak of war, Aug 1914, placing of HMA ships at disposal of Admiralty,' NAA: MP1049/1, 1914/0276.

'Report of Intelligence Branch, Navy Office, Melbourne, on wireless messages of German origins intercepted by Australian shore stations during the week preceding the outbreak of war, May 1916', NAA: MP1049, 16/0235.

W.H. Thring, 'Naval operations in the Pacific in 1914: An Australian point of view', 28 April 1922, Naval Historical Section, Canberra.

'Transmission of secret and confidential correspondence between Australia and England,' NAA: MP1049/1 1914/033.

Stanley Veale, 'Autobiographical recollections of a Naval Reserve officer', 1997, State Library of New South Wales.

Stanley Veale, interview, Sea Power Centre, Royal Australian Navy Museum, Canberra.

Frederick Wheatley, 'All wireless messages intercepted during the week before the outbreak of war', Navy Office, Commonwealth of Australia, 1916, NAA: MP1049/1, 1916/0235.

Frederick Wheatley, 'Notes, digests and decodes of German wireless messages', Navy Office, Commonwealth of Australia, 1915, NAA: MP1049/1, 1916/0235.

Frederick Wheatley, personal letters to R.D. Hadfield, 1934, Australian War Memorial, AWM36 BUNDLE 22/13.

Frederick Wheatley, 'Statement of war service and application for war gratuity', 1920, NAA: A6769, WHEATLEY, FW.

Frederick Wheatley, 'Unravelling of a German code', 1926, Australian War Memorial, AWM252 A229.

Published sources

Argus, Melbourne, 'Australia's flagship, Rear Admiral Patey interviewed', 6 October 1913.

Argus, Melbourne, 'Australia's flagship, Sydney's stirring welcome', 6 October 1913.

Richard Arundel, 'Communications at the outbreak of World War I and their evolution: the war at sea, 1914–1918', *Proceedings of the King-Hall Naval History Conference*, Sea Power Centre, Canberra, 2013.

John Beaumont, *Broken Nation: Australians in the Great War*, Allen & Unwin, Crows Nest, 2013.

Patrick Beesley, *Room 40: British Naval Intelligence 1914–1918*, Hamish Hamilton Ltd, London, 1982.

Geoffrey Bennett, *The Battles of Coronel and the Falklands 1914*, Pen & Sword Military, Yorkshire, 1962.

Geoffrey Bennett, *Naval Battles of the First World War*, B.T. Batsford, London, 1968.

John Connor, Peter Stanley, Peter Yule, *The War at Home*, Oxford University Press, Melbourne, 2015.

John F. Dooley, *Codes, Ciphers, and Spies: Tales of Military Intelligence in World War I*, Copernicus Books, Illinois, 2016.

Sir Robert Randolph Garran, *Prosper the Commonwealth*, Angus and Robertson, Sydney, 1958.

Bruce Gaunson, *Fighting the Kaiser Reich: Australia's Epic within the Great War*, Hybrid Publishers, Melbourne, 2018.

Wayne Gobert, 'The evolution of the RAN Intelligence Service, part one, 1907–1918', *Journal of the Australian Naval Institute*, November 1989.

Richard Guilliatt and Peter Hohnen, *The Wolf: How One German Raider Terrorised Australia and the Southern Oceans in the first World War*, Random House, North Sydney, 2010.

Herald, Melbourne, 'How Australia warned the Empire', 27 May 1926.

David Horner, *The Spy Catchers: The Official History of ASIO, 1949–1963*, Allen & Unwin, Crows Nest, 2014.

Peter Jones, *Australia's Argonauts: The Remarkable Story of the First Class to Enter the Australian Naval College*, Echo Books, West Geelong, 2016.

A.W. Jose, *The Official History of Australia in the War of 1914–1918, Volume IX: The Royal Australian Navy*, Australian War Memorial, Canberra, 1928.

George Lasry, 'Deciphering German diplomatic and naval messages from 1914–1915', *Proceedings of the First Conference on Historical Cryptology*, Uppsala, Sweden, 2018.

Military History and Heritage, 'The first fateful shot: Port Phillip Bay, August 1914', *Proceedings of the Conference Held at the Queenscliff/Point Lonsdale RSS*, Victoria, 2 August 2014.

The Navy List, 1 July 1914, Commonwealth of Australia, Albert J. Mullet, Government Printer, Melbourne, 1914.

Peter Overlack, *German Cruiser Warfare in Australian Waters*, 2009, unpublished, 2009.

Peter Overlack, 'German interest in Australian defence, 1901–1914: new insights into a precarious position on the eve of war', *Australian Journal of Politics and History*, 1994, issue 40, pp.36–51.

Peter Overlack, 'The personal experience of naval warfare:

Graf Spee and the German East Asian Cruiser Squadron in 1914', *Proceedings of the King-Hall Naval History Conference*, Sea Power Centre, Canberra, 2013.

A.M. Robertson, *War in Port Phillip*, Nepean Historical Society, Melbourne, 1968.

Royal Australian Navy, *Instructions for Naval Intelligence Service*, Albert J. Mullet, Government Printer, Melbourne, 1915.

Gary Staff, *Battle on the Seven Seas: German Cruiser Battles 1914–1918*, Pen & Sword Maritime, Yorkshire, 2011.

Jozef H. Straczek, 'The origins and development of Royal Australian Naval Signals Intelligence in an era of imperial defence 1914–1945', thesis, University of New South Wales, 2008.

Jozef H. Straczek, 'The other Room 40: the Royal Australian Navy and Signals Intelligence 1914–18, the war at sea, 1914–1918', *Proceedings of the King-Hall Naval History Conference*, Sea Power Centre, Canberra, 2013.

Desmond Woods, 'Invidious choices: the German East Asia Squadron and the RAN in the Pacific 1914', *Naval Historical Review*, Australian Naval Institute, 2014.

Acknowledgements

My first and biggest thanks go to my publisher. Helen Littleton signed me to HarperCollins, offering a two-book deal. Showing remarkable faith in someone who had written only true-crime books, she simply gave me delivery dates and a non-fiction mandate and told me to write something good. Her guidance and support helped secure my future as a writer and have allowed me to move across genres, from true crime to historical non-fiction and, soon, fiction. Thanks, Helen.

Before getting to the other remarkable individuals at HarperCollins, I'd like to thank a couple of Navy historians who helped me bring a 105-year-old untold story to life.

Following a cold call and a very vague description of what would become this book, Petar Djokovic, Navy History Officer at the Sea Power Centre, Canberra, welcomed me to the centre – essentially, the Australian Navy archive – and allowed me unrestricted access to all unclassified files. A font of knowledge, Petar sent me information, ideas and contacts, and even conducted his own unpaid research.

Dave Jones, Lieutenant Commander, RANR, proved instrumental in helping me uncover details about the life of Frederick Wheatley. The Historical Collections Officer for

HMAS Creswell, Wheatley's former college, Dave gave me a full tour, allowed me to dig through the college's historical files, and put me onto a number of publications that provided me with details I needed for this book.

Rather than offering 'thanks', I feel I should be issuing an apology to a true gentleman named Scott Forbes. Surely left more frustrated than Admiral Patey during his hunt for von Spee, Scott was the editor who was forced to become a cryptologist when my writing read more like code. Eliminating confusion and correcting flaws in timing, grammar and fact, Scott was utterly diligent – and absurdly patient – as he fixed my mistakes. So, sorry, Scott, and thanks. Not just for this one, but also for *Australian Heist*.

I'd also like to thank copy editor Simone Ford, another *Heist* veteran, for ensuring that no stone was left unturned in making sure this story was accurate and every detail correct. Her general knowledge is remarkable; so is her attention to detail. Thanks also to proofreader Pam Dunne, who gave my once-dirty copy a final polish.

I can't write an acknowledgement without thanking my boss, Mick Carroll, the *Sunday Telegraph*'s fearless editor. Mick was the first to validate me as a writer by telling me my copy was good, and he has since defended and encouraged me and helped me craft my sometimes unique style of writing. Thanks, Mick, for having my back. Same goes for my sports editors, Tim Morrissey and James Silver.

Finally, a huge thanks to everyone at HarperCollins and particularly CEO James Kellow for bringing both *Australian*

Heist and *Australian Code Breakers* to life. James is truly a visionary publishing boss and I greatly appreciate the backing and encouragement he has offered me, as well as his high hopes for my writing career – which I will do my utmost to fulfil.